Henry V

'This is a vivid reaffirmation of the traditional view of Henry V. Perhaps the fact that after reading it I felt even greater distaste than before for the man and all his works is testimony to the book's quality.'

A.J. Pollard, *Teesside University, UK*

Henry V of England, the princely hero of Shakespeare's play, who successfully defeated the French at the battle of Agincourt and came close to becoming crowned king of France, is one of the best known and most compelling monarchs in English history. This new biography takes a fresh look at his entire life and nine-year reign, and gives a balanced view of Henry, who is traditionally seen as a great hero but has been more recently depicted as an obsessive egotist, or worse, a ruthless warlord.

The book locates Henry's style of kingship in the context of the time, and looks at often neglected figures who influenced and helped him, such as his father and his uncles, Henry and Thomas Beaufort. John Matusiak shows that the situation confronting Henry at the outset of his reign was far more favourable than is often supposed but that he was nonetheless a man of prodigious gifts whose extraordinary achievements both in battle and in government left the deepest possible impression upon his contemporaries.

John Matus   ment at
Colchester R

Routledge Historical Biographies

Series Editor: Robert Pearce

Routledge Historical Biographies provide engaging, readable and academically credible biographies written from an explicitly historical perspective. These concise and accessible accounts will bring important historical figures to life for students and general readers alike.

Henry V

John Matusiak

Routledge
Taylor & Francis Group

LONDON AND NEW YORK

First published 2013
by Routledge
2 Park Square, Milton Park, Abingdon, Oxon OX14 4RN

Simultaneously published in the USA and Canada
by Routledge
711 Third Avenue, New York, NY 10017

Routledge is an imprint of the Taylor & Francis Group, an informa business

British Library Cataloguing in Publication Data
A catalogue record for this book is available from the British Library

Library of Congress Cataloging in Publication Data
Matusiak, John.
Henry V / John Matusiak.
p. cm. – (Routledge historical biographies)
Includes bibliographical references and index.
1. Henry V, King of England, 1386-1422. 2. Great Britain–Kings and rulers–Biography.
3. Great Britain–History–Henry V, 1413-1422. I. Title. II. Title: Henry the Fifth.
DA256.M37 2012
942.04'2092–dc23
[B]
2012021528

ISBN: 978-0-415-620260 (hbk)
ISBN: 978-0-415-620277 (pbk)
ISBN: 978-0-203-079829 (ebk)

Typeset in Garamond
by Saxon Graphics Ltd, Derby

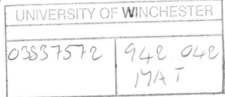

MIX
Paper from
responsible sources
FSC
www.fsc.org   FSC® C004839

Printed and bound in Great Britain by
TJ International Ltd, Padstow, Cornwall

Contents

List of plates

Plates (between pages 180 and 181)

Acknowledgements

Six centuries after his accession to the English throne, Henry V is still apt to excite the emotions, while books about him are no less likely than ever to ruffle feathers and rattle cages. This one, however unintentionally, is no exception. Indeed, it has already left its own particular imprint upon the small community of academics, friends and former colleagues who have been kind enough to read it in manuscript form. Yet marked differences of perspective, ardent debate and the occasional biting comment have never detracted from the overall generosity of all those who have helped to make the book what it is. To Tony Pollard, I deliver my sincere thanks, and the same is true for the long list of scholars and writers, past and present, upon whose work I have drawn in varying degrees. They include Gerald Harriss, Christopher Allmand, Maurice Keen, Anne Curry, Edward Powell, T. B. Pugh, E. F. Jacob, Ian Mortimer, Keith Dockray, Juliet Barker, Michael Jones, Desmond Seward, Margaret Wade Labarge and Harold Hutchison. Special mention must be made, too, of the series editor, Bob Pearce, whose insight, energy and encouragement were unstinting. Were it not for Bob, this book would almost certainly have remained confined to my study forever. Another mainstay was my very good friend and former colleague, Jerry Hadcock, whose considerable wisdom was matched only by his generosity at every stage of the writing process. Nor, of course, should the valuable assistance of Vicky Peters, Michael Strang, Laura Mothersole, Emma Hudson and the rest of the team at Routledge go unmarked either. Their efficiency and friendly guidance, like that of Rob Brown at Saxon Graphics , were all a writer could hope for.

Yet most books are firmly founded upon other kinds of support as well. What, therefore, of those who know me best of all? To Barbara, whose confidence always exceeded my own, and the rest of my family, this work is dedicated.

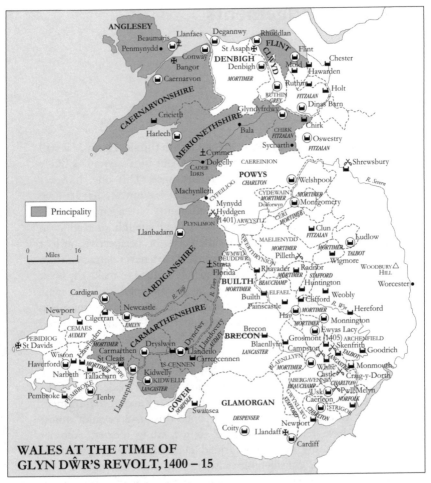

WALES AT THE TIME OF GLYN DŴR'S REVOLT, 1400 – 15

Wales at the time of Glyn Dŵr's revolt, 1400–15

France, 1413–22

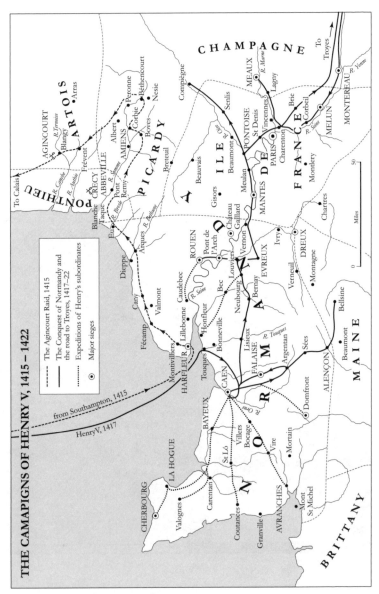

The campaigns of Henry V, 1415–22

Introduction

Exploring the evidence

In the early dawn of Friday 25 October 1415, a member of Henry V's royal chapel was nearby as the French army, 'with its forest of spears' and 'great number of helmets gleaming in between them', deployed for battle. The priest concerned had been present throughout the campaign of recent months, witnessing the gruelling siege of Harfleur and enduring all the hardship of the nerve-wracking march to Calais that followed. As tension, disease and exhaustion took their toll along the way, he had 'looked up in bitterness to heaven', praying to St George and the Virgin Mary that the English king and his men might be 'delivered from the swords of the French'. And once the long-anticipated battle was finally underway, he would watch from the rear 'in fear and trembling' as the 'perilous events' unfolded, praying all the while that 'God would have compassion upon us and upon the crown of England'. When the fighting was done, moreover, he walked among 'the masses, the mounds, and the heaps of the slain', reflecting ruefully upon the carnage. 'And as I truly believe', he later wrote, 'there is not a man with heart of flesh or even of stone who, had he seen and pondered on the horrible deaths and bitter wounds of so many Christian men, would not have dissolved into tears, time and again, for grief.'[1]

Perhaps it should come as little surprise that this particular account eventually went on to assume such prominence across the centuries. For as a detailed and sober description of the Agincourt campaign and the celebrations and negotiations that ensued, the so-called *Gesta Henrici Quinti* or 'Deeds of Henry V' is unrivalled. Yet for all its undoubted merits, the *Gesta*, like so much contemporary and near-contemporary evidence for the reign of Henry V, is by no means the open window on the past it might at first seem. Most obviously, we do not know the author's name. Even his role as royal chaplain, for that matter, is ultimately based upon surmise. Nor, by any means, is his account impartial, for if he laments the enemy dead on the field of Agincourt, he is no less inclined elsewhere to condemn their 'adamantine obduracy'.[2] And while the French, 'double-dealers that they are', stand roundly condemned, the King of England emerges, by complete contrast, as the very embodiment of piety and humanity whose 'most devout intention', we are told, was 'to extend the Church and encompass the peace of kingdoms' – his victories the surest possible proof of divine approval of his cause.[3]

The author did not mince his words either when it came to Lollard heretics and in particular their leader, Sir John Oldcastle – 'that follower of Satan', 'sly deceiver' and 'man of bloody and unheard-of treachery'.[4] This, too, is unsurprising. For while there is no direct evidence that he commissioned it, Henry V was nevertheless hotly pursuing international approval for the renewal of war when the *Gesta* was written at some time between November 1416 and July 1417. Indeed, its main unifying themes – the justice of the king's conflict with France and his unflinching defence of religious orthodoxy – are confidently interpreted today as propaganda. Earlier in 1415, after all, Henry had ordered that a dossier of previous pacts and conventions with France be sent to both the Holy Roman Emperor and the ecclesiastical council then in progress at Constance, so that 'all Christendom might know what great acts of injustice the French in their duplicity had inflicted upon him'.[5] And the fact that only two medieval texts of the *Gesta* exist, one of which is a copy, further suggests that the work was devised with a very specific purpose in mind.

Nor may other contemporary and near-contemporary accounts be approached without due caution. For not only do they, too, project a glorified one-dimensional image of the king, they freely borrow from each other and, on occasion, casually embroider the truth to heighten dramatic tension. The influence of classical authors like Vergil, Lucan, Suetonius and Caesar is also clearly detectable at times, along with a variety of chivalric archetypes which serve to create further unease about the authenticity of the narrative. Invented direct speech is not uncommon either. Indeed, the fiercely eulogistic style of many sources, along with their over-emphasis upon military exploits and unquestioning acceptance of any excesses entailed by them, not to mention their tendency to explain the historical process almost exclusively in terms of providence, moral imperatives and heroic individuals, makes them all too easy to doubt.

Thomas Elmham's *Liber Metricus de Henrico Quinto,* written a year or so after the *Gesta,* is a case in point. Originally a monk of St Albans and from 1415 vicar-general of the Cluniacs of England and Wales, Elmham aimed his curiously enigmatic history of the first five years of Henry V's reign very specifically at a learned clerical audience, and for this reason employed an abstruse verse style, incorporating various types of complex word play and hidden meaning. He did so, he tells us, in order to restrict his readership, since the king's pious humility was such that he did not like his victories widely praised.[6] But obscurity is by no means the only problem, since Elmham also incorporated the *Gesta* into his own account – so extensively, in fact, that he was once wrongly considered to have been its author. And though the *Liber Metricus* corrected and amplified its source in places, it also added a variety of errors and misconceptions. The resulting account was therefore not only partially unreliable, but, like the *Gesta*, very much indicative of the government's chosen historical slant.

By the time that the earliest posthumous biography of Henry V was produced, a new factor had emerged to complicate the task of interpretation. For the *Vita Henrici Quinti*, written by the Italian humanist, Tito Livio, fifteen years after Henry's death, encapsulated not only the 'official' image of the former king but also the priorities of his youngest brother, Humphrey, Duke of Gloucester. Livio had, in fact, joined Gloucester's household in 1436 and it was in his capacity as the duke's 'poet and orator' that he was subsequently encouraged to stir up support for a renewal of war while glorifying, in the process, his patron's exploits in the previous reign.[7] In addressing the work to Henry VI, Livio gave clear notice of his intentions by urging the sixteen-year-old ruler 'to imitate that divine king your father in all things, seeking peace and quiet for your realm by using the same methods and martial valour as he used to subdue your common enemies'.[8] And while Gloucester was not himself the central hero of the work, it is no coincidence that Livio began with a panegyric dedicated to his 'most noble' patron, or that the sieges and battles in which he took part featured so prominently in what followed.[9]

Around ten years later, the *Vita et Gesta Henrici Quinti* was also written at the behest of a former member of Henry V's circle.[10] Once thought by its eighteenth-century editor, Thomas Hearne, to have been another work by Elmham, the author is likely to have been an anonymous Italian humanist, which would help to explain the work's particularly florid style. But 'Pseudo-Elmham', as it is now known, was certainly inspired by Walter Lord Hungerford, steward of the royal household between 1415 and 1421, and a man who had not only fought in the king's campaigns but also acted as one of the executors of his will. Through his own personal connection to Humphrey of Gloucester, moreover, Hungerford may well have given his author direct access to Livio's manuscript, upon which the *Vita et Gesta* is clearly modelled. The result, predictably enough, was another work with many propagandist features, closely duplicating Gloucester's original anti-French stance.

By the middle of the fifteenth century, therefore, the perspective that would later be so keenly gilded by Tudor apologists was already firmly in place. It had originated with authors closely connected to the government and royal court, all of whom were writing for the purpose of promoting war with France. And by the time that the anonymous *First English Life of King Henry V* was produced between June 1513 and the autumn of 1514, an identical need had emerged once more. Mainly based upon a translation of Livio's work and, to a lesser extent, the French chronicle of Enguerrand de Monstrelet, this new account also seems to have employed additional information from some unidentified book of personal reminiscences by James Butler, fourth Earl of Ormonde, who was present at both Agincourt and the siege of Rouen in 1418. Yet the author's underlying aim remained the time-honoured one: to encourage the king – in this case Henry VIII – to emulate his illustrious predecessor's exploits across the Channel, as well as 'his great wisdom and discretion in all his acts'.[11] And the *First English Life* became, in consequence, merely one more monument to the conventional image of a virtuous, wise and all-conquering ruler.

Some evidence, it is true, was less overtly linked to the patronage of the political elite, though it, too, showed no sign of deviating significantly from what was, in effect, the standard template. Monastic sources, for instance, are certainly not in short supply, and some of the chroniclers concerned were well placed to glean their information. John Strecche, canon of the Augustinian priory of St Mary's at Kenilworth where Henry frequently stayed with his court, is a case in point. But Strecche's high-blown praise for the king – who, it seems, had the character of Augustus, the wisdom of Solomon, the strength of Achilles, not to mention the good looks of Paris and the loving heart of Troilus – closely resembles Elmham.[12] And the *Liber de Illustribus Henricis*, written in 1446 or 1447 by John Capgrave, Augustinian prior of Lynn, is another entirely panegyric work, also employing Elmham's *Liber Metricus* as its main source, with the specific intention of winning favour from the former king's son for both the author and his friary.[13]

At St Albans, meanwhile, Thomas Walsingham had been compiling from 1376 onwards a full-scale history of the reigns of Richard II, Henry IV and Henry V, which restored his monastery to its rightful place as the most important centre of historiography in England. Appearing down the years in various recensions and, somewhat confusingly, under a range of titles, Walsingham's *Chronica Maiora* remains, in spite of its frequently homiletic tone and heavy reliance upon the operation of the divine will, a work of primary interest.[14] For not only was the monk a perceptive judge of events who recorded his observations in impressive detail relatively soon after they happened, he was also exceptionally well informed – not least of all, because his monastery lay on a major royal route within twenty miles of London.

Yet Walsingham, too, did not write in a vacuum, and his pro-Lancastrian and anti-French sentiments frequently surface. His account of Richard II's deposition, for instance, is derived largely from the new regime's official account, the so-called 'Record and Process', and those other passages dealing with the political crisis of 1397 to 1399 are plainly too melodramatic to be wholly convincing. Henry V, on the other hand, once again has the chronicler's unwavering support. 'He did not leave his like upon earth among Christian kings or princes', wrote Walsingham when the king died, while in the dedication of another work, the so-called *Ypodigma*

Neustriae ('Image of Normandy'), Walsingham describes his sovereign unequivocally as 'the most magnificent and illustrious Henry, king of the French and the English, conqueror of Normandy, most serene prince of Wales and lord of Ireland and Aquitaine, by the grace of God, everywhere and always victorious'.[15] The French, for their part, are 'grave robbers' – cowardly and cruel oppressors of their own people.[16]

Nor, sadly, do the writings of Adam Usk provide us with anything like clear-cut evidence.[17] Born about 1352 at Usk in Monmouthshire, this particular chronicler was a colourful, learned and acute observer of affairs who had travelled widely after fleeing from England in 1402 – in response, it seems, to a spurious charge of horse theft – to end up as an ecclesiastical lawyer attached to the Archbishop of Canterbury. But although Usk undoubtedly lived through the key events of Henry V's life, he was by that time elderly and no longer close to the heart of politics in the way that he had been in the previous reign when he had been one of the scholars appointed to establish legal grounds for the deposition of Richard II. In consequence, his coverage of the reign is both unsystematic and prone to omissions. And while Usk was at least prepared ultimately to criticise the expense of Henry V's wars, he, too, had earlier taken the same unquestioning line adopted by other writers of the time, commending Henry's many gifts and delighting in his military success.

Further relevant sources for the reign include the brief chronicle of Thomas Otterbourne, derived mainly from Thomas Walsingham, and the *Versus Rhythmici*, a contemporary panegyric in Latin verse by an anonymous Benedictine monk of Westminster, which emphasises above all the king's piety at the time of his accession.[18] There are also popular ballads and poems, such as the so-called 'Agincourt Carol' and the detailed verse account of the siege of Rouen by the soldier John Page, as well as the further verse chronicle produced in 1451 by John Hardyng, who claimed, apparently falsely, to have been a member of Sir Robert Umfraville's retinue on the Agincourt campaign.[19] Nor should we overlook the historical significance of courtly poets like John Lydgate whose *Troy Book* was commissioned by Henry in 1412 to extol the virtues of martial glory, and Thomas Hoccleve who specifically dedicated to him his *Regement of Princes*, a manual of advice on statecraft and the conduct of war. Both provide important insights into Henry's personal priorities, as well as the ethos and expectations that shaped them.

And then there is the vernacular chronicle known as the *Brut* – so-called because its historical narrative begins with Brutus, legendary founder of the ancient British kingdom. Produced in the capital by a series of anonymous authors, who drew upon contemporary ballads, government newsletters, eyewitnesses and what may broadly be termed 'popular tradition', it was certainly well informed, and widely read too – particularly among the mercantile classes who largely favoured the business opportunities afforded by foreign war. Indeed, with up to 172 manuscripts and transcripts still extant, it may well have been, with the sole exception of the Wycliffite bible, the most popular written work in English prior to 1500. But in catering for its intended audience, the *Brut*, too, was very much immersed in the euphoria of the day, and its stridently patriotic tone and graphic descriptions of warfare were matched only by the usual ringing endorsements of the king as 'a gracious man and a great conqueror' whose 'true title of conquest and right heritage in France' was beyond all shadow of doubt.[20]

For reasons that are all too apparent, then, it would seem that no wholly satisfactory understanding of Henry V can be derived purely from the narrative sources available in English. Crucially, however, a mass of material relating to the operation of central government still survives, which not only throws much light on the fine detail of Henry's rule, but broadly accords with the image of his kingship encapsulated in the sources already mentioned. The Chancery rolls, for instance, have thrown considerable light upon the king's skilful exercise of patronage, while the records of the royal Exchequer have revealed a wealth of information about the intricacies of military finance and organisation. Of great value, too, are the various records relating to law, order and justice – especially those produced by the Court of King's Bench. And though parliamentary records are comparatively scanty, the transcriptions of speeches delivered by Henry's chancellors upon the opening of sessions are of particular value in demonstrating the finesse with which the government projected its policies and curtailed potential opposition. More personal glimpses of the king's thinking, on the other hand, can be found in his letters, written increasingly in English rather than French or Latin as the reign progressed.

Perhaps even more significant from some perspectives are the observations of Henry's enemies. Naturally enough, French chroniclers were less concerned with the King of England personally than with his impact upon their country and the internal repercussions of faction-fighting between Armagnacs and Burgundians which assisted his cause so greatly. Nor, of course, is it at all surprising that when they do mention him, they are sometimes scathing. To the Burgundian chronicler Georges Chastellain, for instance, Henry was 'a cruel man', 'a tyrant and a persecutor', while to the Norman Robert Blondel he was 'prince of all the sacrilegious'.[21] Similarly, in the *Quadrilogus Invectif* of Alain Chartrier, who was secretary to both Charles VI and the Dauphin in succession, he is described as 'this flail of persecution', inflicted on France by the hand of God.[22]

But the overall picture is much less clear-cut, and nowhere more so than in what is arguably the most discerning French source of all – the *Histoire de Charles VI*, produced by the so-called 'Religieux de Saint-Denys'. Although this particular account is anonymous, the monk responsible may well have been the abbey's *chanteur*, Michel Pintoin, who died in 1421. If so, Pintoin was responsible for a work that is not only well informed and perceptive, but also remarkably objective under the circumstances. Making his judgement partly on the basis of what he had heard from French prisoners and envoys, he did not minimise Henry's ruthlessness, freely admitting that the king 'worried little about divine wrath'.[23] But he was also prepared to concede ultimately that his countrymen were largely responsible for their own downfall and that Henry may actually have been the lesser of evils. 'No prince of his time', the monk concluded, 'appeared more capable than he to subdue and conquer a country, by the wisdom of his government, by his prudence and by the other qualities with which he was endowed.'[24]

While not quite so explicit, perhaps, the *Journal d'un bourgeois de Paris 1405–99* also reaches a comparatively favourable conclusion. More probably the work of an anonymous cleric than a member of the bourgeoisie in the way that the title suggests, the journal was in fact erroneously named by a seventeenth-century editor. But if the origin of the work remains in doubt and its Burgundian sympathies sometimes make it less reliable on the larger scale, its importance as a remarkable social and economic commentary revealing mentalities in the French capital is still beyond dispute. Certainly, in describing the traumas and privations of his fellow-Parisians, the 'Bourgeois' pulls no punches. The pillaging, killing, rampant inflation and hunger which the author witnessed are all recorded in depressing detail. He leaves us in no doubt either about the excesses of 'those cruel tyrants the English'.[25] Yet even this first-hand observer is once again surprisingly muted on the King of England's personal responsibility, blaming the dissent between his own countrymen for encouraging him to invade in the first place.

The same is no less true, ultimately, for the *Chroniques* of Enguerrand de Monstrelet, a Picard of noble stock, probably born between 1390 and 1395. From 1444 to 1446, Monstrelet was *prévôt* of Cambrai in the service of Philip the Good, Duke of Burgundy, to whom he presented his work in 1447. For his trouble, the chronicler received the comparatively meagre award of 50 *écus*, and there is no denying that the work has its shortcomings. But in spite of its lack of literary polish and occasional susceptibility to both chronological lapses and errors of naming, the depth and range of Monstrelet's account remain undeniable. And if Monstrelet makes no pretence about his Burgundian sympathies, he, too, shows little overall antipathy to the King of England personally. On the contrary, he considered Henry V 'wise and able in every business he undertook'. Moreover, Monstrelet's verdict that Henry ruled by fear carries little hint of overall condemnation. For though he punished 'without mercy', he also did so, we are told, 'without favour.[26]

Indeed, even the much more overtly hostile *Histoire de Charles VI, roy de France*, written by Jean Juvénal des Ursins, is not without praise for the leader of the English enemy.[27] A Parisian advocate who entered the service of the Dauphin Charles at Poitiers after his expulsion from Paris, des Ursins became Bishop of Beauvais from 1433 to 1444 and eventually Archbishop of Reims. But while the date of his chronicle is unknown and the work itself is tainted by rabidly anti-Burgundian sentiments, des Ursins was nevertheless a prolific researcher and political writer with a great interest in documentary sources. And in compiling his bitterly anti-English account in which the King of England's soldiers roast recalcitrant clergy and 'tear out the teeth of others', the author remained fully prepared to recognise Henry's own courage and skill as a warrior, as well as his personal reputation for justice.[28]

Perhaps the most curious common feature of the main French sources is, then, their surprising readiness to concede Henry V's virtues. While the English as a whole were dismissed as a people who, 'like birds of prey ... live by robbery at the expense of their simple and well-disposed neighbours', Henry himself was frequently presented as an honourable, prudent, courageous and just man.[29] At the end of 1417, the humanist Nicolas de Clamanges, declared him 'the person by whom the house of France shall be revived, rebuilt and recalled to its former greatness'.[30] And even Georges Chastellain accepted that Henry was a king 'in whom valour and courage shone forth as befitted a mighty conqueror'.[31] Partly, of course, such views may well have been influenced by Henry's own very self-conscious image-building across the Channel. Nor is there any doubt that French chroniclers were able to explain their kingdom's defeats rather more palatably when they were inflicted by so imposing a figure. But the match between English and French accounts on a number of essentials remains striking, and raises the intriguing possibility that behind the stylised presentations and undoubted propaganda there is still a core of hard historical reality upon which the myth of Henry V's kingship is actually founded.

The fact that Henry was the object of so much panegyric literature in England does not, after all, automatically imply that his admirers were consciously pedalling falsehoods any more than their less rational excursions confirm that they were entirely incapable of objective judgement. Fifteenth-century chroniclers were undoubtedly highly selective in their choice of material and clearly prepared to exaggerate, in order to provide a consistently and compellingly flattering picture of their subject. But their hero did unquestionably win a succession of unprecedented victories in France, and his piety and commitment to justice, law and order are equally demonstrable. For in each of the relevant sources – and particularly in government records – a kernel of fact does indeed stand out over and beyond the distortions and rhetorical embellishments, which were equally characteristic, it must be said, of earlier royal biographers, such as William of Poitiers and Robert of Avebury.

Nor should it be assumed too readily that the bulk of the material shared by the narrative sources was somehow derived from a single corpus – especially one devised and manipulated from above. The process by which a fifteenth-century government might exercise such extensive intellectual control is, on the one hand, far from clear. Certainly, a chronicler like Adam Usk cannot be straightforwardly regarded as a Lancastrian apologist, since his natural loyalties lay at one time with the House of Mortimer. Yet Usk did not hesitate to sing Henry V's praises until just before the end of the reign. And although the description of the Agincourt campaign in the *Vita Henrici Quinti* may, for instance, closely resemble that of the *Gesta*, there is still no direct evidence that the author derived his account from this work. Indeed, such similarities may well suggest that Livius, like other writers, was drawing upon a generally accepted oral tradition, which closely conformed to public opinion as a whole.

Propaganda – or at least successful propaganda – must, in any case, convince in order to be worthwhile. And it can do this only if it accords, at least partially, with the preconceptions of those to whom it is addressed. There is a crucial difference, too, between bias on the one hand and objective preference on the other, just as there is an important distinction between dependence and subservience. It is worth remembering, for instance, that the pro-Lancastrian Walsingham had been an outspoken critic of Richard II before he became an ardent advocate of Henry V. And the occurrence of such a transformation does not necessarily imply the existence of a sustained and more effective programme of literary or cultural control by the Lancastrian monarchy. Equally significantly, the *Brut* would not spare Henry V's successor from criticism, even though it had previously been so unstinting in its praise of the father. In this and other cases, therefore, there seems no compelling reason to suggest biased motives, hidden agendas or outright duress merely on the basis of a particular 'reading' of the text concerned.

If so, then the task of writing Henry V's biography may not be quite the historiographical minefield it first appears. The evidence, as we have seen, is plentiful and most of it, though coloured in some cases by the literary conventions and prejudices of the day, is not without considerable value. If, moreover, individual sources may seem problematic under close inspection, their collective message remains persuasive. For though many of Henry V's predecessors had been found wanting by their contemporaries, he most certainly was not. On the contrary, the second Lancastrian was consistently lauded in his own kingdom and, much more significantly, recognised for his merits even in the realm where his impact was harshest. He had clearly captured not only the respect but also the imagination of his contemporaries. And he had done so on a scale not seen before, leaving behind him a reputation which, until comparatively recently, had stood unchallenged for centuries. Indeed, the very depth of support he engendered among his contemporaries and the renown that survived him may partly explain the intensity of the counter-reaction in certain quarters today.

Debates and perspectives

If contemporary and near-contemporary English commentators were united in their adulation, then time has only served to sow deep misgivings and stubborn controversy about a ruler once generally hailed as the 'perfect pattern of the medieval hero'.[32] Where, in 1901, Henry V was eulogised by Charles Lethbridge Kingsford, as 'the champion of unity against disintegration' – 'a ruler who, through the splendour of his achievements, illumined with the rays of his glory the decline of the medieval world' – he is now described by Ian Mortimer as 'a deeply flawed individual', 'undermined by his own pride and overwhelmed by his own authority', who 'set himself on the path to his own destruction'.[33] Indeed, for Mortimer, writing in 2010, Henry was a 'wanton destroyer of lives' who serves as conclusive proof that 'a man may be a hero and yet a monster'.[34] Clearly, the contrast could not be starker. And though the victor of Agincourt still has more than his fair share of advocates among a distinguished array of scholars, there is now an increased need not only to justify the kind of claim that might once have been made routinely, but also to defend the very methodology upon which such judgements are founded.

Perhaps the classic case for Henry V's pre-eminence among English kings remains that reprised by K. B. McFarlane in a brief essay of 1972. By the time of his death, in McFarlane's view, Henry 'had transformed the spirit of his own people' and become the 'arbiter of Christian Europe, dwarfing Emperor and Pope'. He was, it seems, 'superlatively gifted' and 'born to rule and conquer' – 'the greatest man', claimed McFarlane, 'that ever ruled England'. And his faults, such as they were, arose mainly 'from the excess of his qualities'. True, he could be 'imperious and harsh', but he should not, McFarlane suggested, be indicted upon 'standards inapplicable to his time', since contemporaries 'expected no less in time of war' and his justice, 'however roughly applied', was 'fairly and indifferently at the disposal of the conquered'. If, moreover, his achievements were to be 'completely destroyed' within thirty years, it was nevertheless 'nonsense', said McFarlane, to suggest that he could not have changed the course of history permanently. On the contrary, 'his military genius and diplomatic resource made a forceful combination, which it would have been difficult for his opponents to withstand'.[35]

Echoes of this same broad line can also be found in the work of Maurice Keen amongst others. For Keen, 'Henry possessed in a remarkable degree those qualities that contemporaries looked for in a monarch: piety, chivalrous courage and devotion to justice'. And while he was not in Keen's view an innovator in government, his reign was nevertheless 'the record of a tremendous English achievement', which 'triumphantly demonstrated that the English administrative machine was up to any task that could be imposed upon it'. What made the reign of Henry V so distinctive, in fact, was 'the directing mind of the ruler and his personality', even though reactions to some of his defining characteristics have altered so considerably over time. 'With his reserve, his enormous ambition, and his conviction of his right to have things his own way, his is not a character that can command wide sympathy with the present generation', Keen acknowledged in 2003. But it is precisely for this reason that we need to remember 'how deeply he was admired, even venerated, by contemporaries who knew and served him'. Indeed, 'the unity of purpose and the unprecedented effort that Henry was able to evoke in England make it possible to argue', in Keen's view, 'that, had he lived, he might have completed the conquest that he began'.[36]

For Gerald Harriss, writing two years later, Henry is also 'the model king' – a ruler of 'high intelligence and disciplined vigour' who exhibited 'dignity, reserve and inner confidence', and commanded 'respect, fidelity and devotion'.[37] 'Brisk, decisive and indefatigable, demanding of others and not sparing himself', Henry saw warfare as 'an instrument not an end', serving 'a political vision as radical and far-reaching as his military strategy'. His wars were also, we are told, 'interwoven with diplomacy and underpinned by government, in both of which he displayed an originality and fixity of purpose transforming the assumptions of his followers and confounding those of his opponents'.[38] Nor was Henry's ultimate objective of ruling both England and France utterly implausible, for 'multiple kingdoms of this kind were both conceivable and feasible in this and the following century'. 'Had Henry V lived to establish this new order and embody it in his kingship, it might', Harriss concludes, 'have acquired political legitimacy.'[39]

The same claim is firmly endorsed, too, by Anne Curry. In her opinion, Henry was 'strong, decisive, athletic, energetic, pious and above all successful' – the 'golden boy' of fifteenth-century history. But this is not all. For though 'in customary fashion, academics have whittled away at the king's reputation', accusing him of 'sowing the seeds of defeat overseas and civil war at home', Curry remains convinced that 'for every bad thing one can say about Henry V, there are dozens of good things to say in his defence'. From her perspective, 'Henry met all the characteristics of a medieval king' – actively pious, renowned for justice and impartiality, and a military hero in his own lifetime. 'All kings were feared', she claims, 'but Henry was admired and appreciated by his people.' Equally importantly, 'it took the French twenty-seven years to recover what Henry had taken in less than seven'. 'With Henry at the helm for longer', therefore, 'the course of English and French history might have been quite different.'[40]

Other modern scholars have placed particular emphasis upon Henry V's domestic achievements, especially in the area of law and order. According to Edward Powell, for instance, 'Henry V demonstrated that England was not ungovernable in the fifteenth century.' He did this, we are told, by 'fulfilling contemporary expectations of justice through a more effective use of the existing machinery, and in adapting his judicial policy so successfully to the demands of his military campaigns'. No ruler, in Powell's view, 'came closer to embodying the contemporary ideal of the just king than Henry V', in whose eyes domestic peace and foreign conquest were inextricably linked. 'But', Powell adds, 'it took a king of extraordinary ability to combine the two so effectively, and, working within the limitations of his slender resources, to make each serve the interests of the other.'[41]

French historians, meanwhile, have been much more inclined to deal with their own country's internal disunities rather than to dwell upon Henry V specifically. But where he is mentioned, the views expressed, not altogether surprisingly, are mainly negative. Writing during the Second World War, while a fugitive from the occupying German forces, Edouard Perroy accepted that Henry was 'a good soldier' and 'sound administrator', but emphasised his 'hypocritical devoutness', 'the duplicity of his conduct', 'the cruelty of his revenge' and 'his pretence of defending rights, and redressing wrongs when he sought solely to satisfy his ambition'.[42] He also, claimed Lannoy, 'behaved brutally' in France, initiating 'a reign of terror' which 'injured every interest without compunction'.[43]

For Françoise Autrand, by contrast, Henry was 'a great statesman' whose retribution was sometimes minimal – 'a rare thing for the era'.[44] Furthermore, the King of England's diplomacy 'looked to the future' at a time when the French government had 'no real policy' beyond 'old reflexes'.[45] But, in spite of his 'fine promises and excellent administration', Autrand contended that Henry nevertheless remained 'a stranger' in France, dismissing French manners and customs, and failing to treat his would-be subjects as he should have done – 'in the French manner'.[46] Likewise, for Philippe Contamine, Henry's attempt to secure the throne of France by the Treaty of Troyes was, in effect, a political non-starter, since the mental instability of the French king, Charles VI, 'removed all value' from the arrangement, and because it entailed a further war against a fully-functional rival government, headed by the Dauphin, 'with its own resources, its own army, its own external alliances, its own judicial and administrative machinery and its own functionaries'.[47]

The most virulent criticism, however, has still tended to come from English commentators. To Richard Vaughan, for instance, 'the perfidious Henry V' was one of the 'champion double-crossers of the age', while for David Douglas he was 'calculating', 'superstitious' and 'revoltingly cruel', creating an image of himself 'very different from the private reality it masked'.[48] Desmond Seward, in his turn, suggested in 1987 that there was something 'a little inhuman' about Henry and that, ultimately, 'the man always gave way to the warlord'.[49] The charge of recklessness has also been levelled at him repeatedly. 'In the last analysis', wrote E. F. Jacob, 'he was an adventurer, not a statesman: the risk he took in the creation of a double monarchy was too great, depended on too many uncertainties, and fundamentally misread the nature of France.'[50]

But perhaps the most comprehensive attempt at revisionism was produced in 1988 by T. B. Pugh who argued that 'although he was more talented than any of his predecessors on the English throne since Henry II', Henry V was nevertheless 'a man of limited vision and outlook'.[51] 'Cold and singularly lacking in generosity', 'hard, grasping and unscrupulous', he died, in Pugh's opinion, 'almost as insolvent as his father had been'.[52] And while Parliament obediently voted the taxes required of them, there was otherwise little important legislation to speak of during his reign. Similarly, when it came to developing new sources of revenue, Henry was, according to Pugh, 'even less enterprising than his father had been', and he failed into the bargain to make satisfactory provision in his will for the prolonged minority that followed his death.[53] Most damningly of all, however, 'he won unity for his realm and glory for himself at the price of immediate misery for France and eventual confusion for England'. In fact, his 'great adventure' could 'easily have been avoided' and ultimately proved 'a fatal error ... inevitably bound to end in failure and disillusionment', because, Pugh contended, 'an imperialist war on French soil' and 'obsolete schemes of conquest' were 'not in England's real interests'. By dying when his fortunes were at their zenith, therefore, Henry V avoided 'the inevitable harvest of defeat', only to leave it as part of his legacy to his son.[54]

More recently, in a work attempting to integrate techniques of literary and historical analysis, Paul Strohm has suggested that 'texts' like the *Gesta* and Walsingham's *Chronica Maiora*, which have been so important in underpinning Henry's reputation, were 'effectively invented within large and commonly held interpretative structures' and, as such, are historical 'only in the sense of providing information about time-bound patterns of perception and belief'.[55] From this perspective, the available evidence is of value purely because it tells us what contemporaries were prepared or enabled to believe rather than as objective evidence of those events they purport to describe. Furthermore, the chroniclers who have shaped so many of our assumptions about the period were, in effect, serving as propagandists, forming part – either consciously or unconsciously – of what Strohm describes as 'the circle of complicit Lancastrian commentators'.[56] In the process, Strohm claims, key events of Henry's reign, such as the Lollard rising of 1414 and Southampton Plot, were nothing more than 'fabrications', exploited by the king and his government as part of a deliberate programme of 'self-legitimisation'.[57]

Far from moderating, then, the debate has actually broadened over the last decade or so, and the inherent tension at the core of Henry V's reputation has been reflected, to some extent, in the work of his main biographer. Certainly, Christopher Allmand does not deny the king's merits. In his view, Henry was 'much more complex than may at first appear, driven less by personal ambition than by what he saw as right'. His reign, moreover, was characterised by 'a marked sense of harmony among the English people which was deliberately fostered by the king'. Although he left large debts, he was an advocate of forward financial planning and worked with Parliament 'in a cordial atmosphere'. He was also 'a natural commander of men' and 'a fine, indeed, a remarkable soldier' whose war with France was 'certainly not that of a lone megalomaniac'. On the contrary, Allmand argues, 'the reasons which made Henry invade France were too intricate, too much rooted in the ideas and assumptions of Englishmen of the time, to be dismissed so easily'. On the basis of 'a careful consideration of his whole achievement', therefore, Henry 'emerges as a ruler whose already high reputation is not only maintained but enhanced'.[58]

This, however, is not where things end. For Professor Allmand bases his final evaluation on the principle that 'Henry is best estimated by separating his foreign from his domestic achievements', mainly, it seems, because he was ultimately responsible for a 'serious error of judgement' in attempting to alter the succession to the French crown. Nor are the scale or consequences of this error minimised. Henry failed to see, for instance, that in France there existed 'a rapidly growing sense of national spirit and awareness, centred upon the monarch, and inspired by war' – a spirit, ironically, which was not so very different from that which he himself was trying to encourage in England. And while Allmand's overall verdict remains favourable, he nevertheless acknowledges that in France the king passed on to his son an inheritance 'which may justly be termed "damnosa hereditas"', because 'his appeal was essentially to the past'.[59]

'Good governance', 'just rights' and the logic of conquest

So where, then, on the eve of the six hundredth anniversary of Henry V's accession to the English throne, does the balance of probability reside? Is it indeed the case that once 'the propaganda-oriented chronicles' have been placed to one side and his 'pseudo-achievements' laid bare, 'there are a number of areas where Henry's record falls well short of the glorious unblemished career we have been led to believe in by traditional historians'?[60] Or was he, after all, 'every inch a king' – a ruler who brought about a 'dramatic transformation in the conduct of government and in the minds of the governed' and who became, during his short reign, 'the symbol of national identity'?[61] Is there, for that matter, also scope for fresh perspectives or, better still, some kind of synthesis, which allows us to relate the second Lancastrian king of England to the modern world without de-historicising either the man or his legacy?

Plainly, the issue of time and 'the times' is a crucial one – and not only in terms of the brevity of Henry's life or the considerable cultural and moral divide between his era and our own. For the period in which he ruled was an exceptionally turbulent one. Nor was it so entirely by his making. Upon his accession, the formidable sequence of social, political and religious crises, which had characterised much of the recent past was far from forgotten. The scandals and military defeats of Edward III's last years, the Great Uprising of 1381, the spread of Lollardy, the divisions among the nobility which had led to Richard II's deposition, the outbreak of rebellion in Wales, the spread of lawlessness, the growing burden of insolvency and the spectre of French aggression had all led to a desperate call for moral regeneration and 'good governance' based upon honesty, stability and financial accountability.

In such circumstances all hopes of salvation and reinvigoration rested squarely on the ruler's shoulders. 'Where a virtuous king does not rule', wrote the poet John Gower, 'the people are unsound and lack good morals.'[62] Obedience to God, zeal for true religion, justice, wisdom, benevolence, magnificence and freedom from vice

– especially greed – were all hallmarks of the well-governed and well-governing monarch. And perfect kingship went hand-in-hand with perfect knighthood, too. For in a social setting where war between kingdoms was the norm and a king's subjects knew all too well that peace either sprang from or entailed weakness, there was little scope for moderation. Even poets like John Lydgate and Gower, who were acutely aware of the costs and follies of war, knew also that if a cause was just and all other avenues had been exhausted, then war must surely follow and be fought to the limit.

It was with all this in mind, therefore, that Henry V ascended the throne with that profound sense of mission that lay at the root of so much that followed. Still shadowed by the illegitimacy of his dynasty and his own failures as Prince of Wales, he remained, at one and the same time, utterly persuaded of his potential, wholly convinced of the righteousness of his cause, and perhaps most important of all, fully aware that both God and circumstance could not have been more firmly on his side. As such, there was never any likelihood of restraint or half-measures. Once good government had been swiftly restored in England, the pursuit of his just rights across the Channel must follow automatically. Henry would conquer, moreover, not simply for ambition's sake – though he had this in abundance – but because, with a prostrate enemy and a kingdom raring for action, he had little, if any, choice. And once committed, the logic of conquest would swiftly develop a further momentum all of its own.

The result was a reign of spectacular success or unbridled folly according to chosen perspective. Ultimately, in fact, there were elements of both as events unfolded. But if the success seems to have sprung in no small measure from the stature of the man himself, the folly belongs rather more, perhaps, to the age that produced him. For it is easy to forget that Henry V still merits his status as a 'typical medieval hero', precisely because he was so entirely willing to smite his foes and raze their towns in pursuit of his cause.[63] In this regard, of course, there is something deeply perplexing, indeed chilling, about the victor of Agincourt at the start of the twenty-first century. At a time when triumph in war – and perhaps, too, the relentless pursuit of honour in politics – is no longer the norm, such misgivings require little explanation. But there remains nevertheless something uncomfortably impressive, even awesome, about the story of the man's life and ambitions. It is a tale that continues to resonate today with all its old significance, and it is also one, as Henry's chroniclers were fully aware, that stretches imagination to the limit.

1 The making of a Lancastrian prince

Family and prospects

When England's very own 'celestial knight' and 'princely hero' slipped into the world largely unnoticed in the late summer of 1386, there was little to suggest the enduring fame that lay ahead. According to astrological evidence contained in a treatise on his birth written after he had become king, Henry V was born on 16 September at 11.22 a.m. But no fanfares greeted him, no exultant crowds thronged the streets in his honour and no chronicler even troubled to report the event for posterity. Nor, it seems, was the place of his birth any more auspicious, for he drew his first breath within the cheerless stone walls of Monmouth Castle's gatehouse tower, as far away from London and the centre of political gravity as he was from the thoughts of his future subjects.

Yet if young 'Henry of Monmouth' was widely ignored as a possible successor to the reigning monarch, Richard II, his pedigree was not without serious potential. John of Gaunt, his grandfather, was, after all, the senior surviving son of Edward III and eldest uncle to the king – a quasi-regal figure in his own right whose marriage to Blanche of Lancaster had underlined his status as by far the most powerful magnate in the land. Not only was Blanche descended from Edmund Crouchback, the second son of Henry III, she was also heiress to the mighty earls whose title she bore. And when she died from bubonic plague in 1369, her husband soon turned personal tragedy to good advantage by marrying the seventeen-year-old Infanta Constanza and staking his own audacious claim to the crown of Castile and Leon.

By any standards, then, John of Gaunt was a force to be reckoned with and this was something that none of his successors would ever forget. As Duke of Lancaster he came, in effect, to rule a semi-autonomous state, encompassing the ancient earldoms of Leicester, Derby, Lincoln and Salisbury, and extending into all but seven of England's counties. Equipped with its own elaborate bureaucracy, Gaunt's duchy also boasted massive financial resources. For at a time when only a tiny handful of England's nobles possessed an annual income of more than £4,000, his was already fast approaching £13,000 – at least a quarter as much again as that once enjoyed by his dead brother, the Black Prince.

And with unrivalled wealth came military muscle to match. Some thirty castles in all were under his direct control, spread mostly throughout Yorkshire, the Midlands and South Wales – with the pick of them, Kenilworth, boasting a great banqueting hall to rival the king's own at Westminster. Gaunt's knights, meanwhile, were no longer feudal tenants in the traditional sense, performing military service only in time of war, but men bound by indenture to serve him in peace as well. In 1385, he had been able to raise a force of 3,000 for the campaign against the Scots, including 2,000 archers – a fifth as many men again as the king's own contingent and almost four times more than the retinue of the next most powerful nobleman, Henry Percy, Earl of Northumberland.

The immediate heir to all this – and the man who was to become Henry V's father – was another imposing character. Still only nineteen at the time of his first and most famous son's birth, Henry Bolingbroke was from all accounts a fearless, forceful and restless young man whose marriage to Mary de Bohun had added significantly to his already considerable status as first cousin to the king. When the couple were betrothed in 1380, Mary was still no more than ten years old and intended for a nunnery. But as one of two immensely rich heiresses to the last Bohun Earl of Hereford, she was, in contemporary terms, far too valuable a resource to be lost forever to a life of prayer and contemplation, and John of Gaunt had accordingly purchased her hand for his son at a cost of 5,000 marks (£3,333 13s 4d).[1]

Nor would Mary de Bohun fail to provide good value in perhaps the most crucial respect of all – her fertility. Since fourteen was considered to be the minimum permissible age for cohabitation, the young bride had at first continued to live apart from her husband, but from the time that the couple established their own household in 1385, she was more or less continually pregnant. By the summer of 1392, indeed, Mary had already borne no fewer than five children, and would give birth to six in all over a total of eight years: four sons (Henry, Thomas, John and Humphrey) and two daughters (Blanche and Philippa). Equally significant in the longer term was her husband's fidelity, since this ensured that there would be no awkward string of royal bastards on hand to complicate matters at some future date. All later accounts suggest, in fact, that the marriage was a model of love and devotion, though it was not to prove long-lasting, since Mary died prematurely in June 1394 from the birth of her final daughter.

Predictably, the husband who survived her had few doubts about his rightful place within the social order. As Earl of Derby and Duke of Hereford, Henry Bolingbroke thought and behaved much more like a prince of the realm than the son of a great noble – and not without good reason. It was widely rumoured, for instance, that John of Gaunt had commissioned a forged chronicle purporting to establish his son's claim to the throne through Edmund Crouchback. Much more significantly, however, Gaunt had managed in 1376 to persuade Edward III to settle the throne of England upon his male descendants only, which had the immediate effect of nullifying the rights of the rival Mortimer family and placing Bolingbroke third in line to the throne after his own father and the Black Prince's son, Richard. Whether the heir to the House of Lancaster actually believed that he would also one day inherit the crown is altogether another matter, but there can be no doubt that his already ample sense of self-worth was much boosted by this turn of events, just as his son's would be in years to come.

There is no denying either that Bolingbroke was reared for power from his earliest days. Related to the Visconti dukes of Milan as well as the rulers of England, he had been admitted into the Order of the Garter at the same time as his royal cousin, Richard, on St George's Day in 1377, and less than three months later, he featured prominently at Richard's coronation, bearing the so-called 'sword of mercy' at the conclusion of High Mass. Soon after, while John of Gaunt was overseas, he was also given his first limited role in controlling his father's estates and household, and by December

1384 he had gained outright control of the numerous lands and titles that came with his wife's hand. More strikingly still, from his fifteenth birthday onwards the heir to the Duchy of Lancaster had even begun to perform the ceremony of the *pedilavium* – the washing of paupers' feet on Maundy Thursday – which was a ritual typically associated with the king himself.

Everything, then, seemed to affirm Henry Bolingbroke's brimming self-confidence and suggested, too, that he was sure to have a broad and potent influence on his eldest son – not least of all when it came to the nature and depth of his religious faith. For though Bolingbroke generally preferred converting heretics to burning them, his zeal for orthodox religion still went well beyond the usual parameters of conventional piety. He attended mass scrupulously, supported the Church with his offerings, and was a keen purchaser of ornate prayer books and crucifixes. He also exhibited a particular devotion to the Holy Trinity and became a zealous founder of chantries. Nor was Bolingbroke's religious fervour any empty token as the references in his will to his sinful soul and 'mispended' life clearly show.[2] Indeed, this acute awareness of his own shortcomings may well explain his readiness to undertake several unusually arduous pilgrimages, including one to Jerusalem. It may also explain why – like his son after him – he would dream of uniting Christendom under his leadership as a first step in the quest to recover the Holy Land.

Above all, however, it was his yearning for recognition as a knight and warrior that Henry Bolingbroke would pass on most unmistakably to each of his sons. He had, in fact, been distinguishing himself as a jouster since at least 1381 when he had taken part in his first tournament. But it was in 1385 that he gained his first actual experience on campaign – at John of Gaunt's side in Scotland – and from this point onwards there was no looking back. During the winter of 1386–7, for instance, he contracted to defend his country against the threat of a French invasion with some 2,000 men of his own retinue. Then, in the autumn of 1387, he seems to have been away on his travels once more – this time on the marches of Wales, eagerly anticipating the first hint of trouble. Such, indeed, was Bolingbroke's insatiable appetite for adventure that he would soon be widely recognised as an almost archetypal fork-bearded late medieval man of action. And it was in this capacity, more than any other that he would prove so decisive in shaping the mental world of his four sons. Each, in fact, was born and bred for combat, and as the eldest grew to maturity, he especially would come to exhibit that same blend of tact, energy, caution, guile and ruthlessness that had once made his father such a formidable foe.

The Beaufort connection

When the time came for Henry of Monmouth to become Henry V in 1413, he would inherit a number of distinct advantages over his predecessors, some of which are still by no means fully appreciated. Not least of all, he was to enjoy the invaluable assistance of a large and loyal family circle which shared his goals and pursued them with a tenacity that closely matched his own. On the one hand, Henry's three brothers – Thomas, Duke of Clarence, John, Duke of Bedford, and Humphrey, Duke of Gloucester – all provided him with invaluable military, political and administrative service, and though they were not all equally talented or, for that matter, equally enamoured of their eldest brother, they would all work tirelessly on his behalf. From some perspectives, indeed, their collective impact upon the shape of Henry's reign would prove almost comparable to his own.

But if three dependable brothers were a rare enough luxury for any late medieval ruler, Henry V would also be able to call upon the unwavering assistance of his two uncles, Henry and Thomas Beaufort. The marriage of John of Gaunt to his Spanish wife in 1371 had, in fact, been purely a matter of cold-blooded policy, and at about the same time that the match occurred, he began an illicit affair with Katherine Swynford, sister-in-law of Geoffrey Chaucer. A quarter of a century later, the two would be married. In the meantime, however, Katherine bore her 'husband' four children – three sons and a daughter – all of whom were exceptional in their own distinctive ways. Joan, for instance, would go on to make her mark in history by becoming the grandmother of both Edward IV and Richard III, while the eldest son John, who was born in 1375, would eventually become Earl of Somerset and serve with distinction as Captain of Calais, Lieutenant of South Wales and Deputy Constable of England before his death in 1410.

It was, however, the second and third sons, and in particular the former, who later assumed such importance in assisting and supporting King Henry V. After acting as his nephew's tutor long before he came to the throne, Henry Beaufort would eventually serve him as Lord Chancellor and go on to become one of the most brilliant ecclesiastics of the age. High-handed, hot-tempered and the father of an illegitimate daughter into the bargain, he had been appointed Bishop of Lincoln in 1398 at the age of twenty-one before acquiring Winchester, the richest of all bishoprics, six years later. On the wider international front, moreover, he would eventually play a significant role in the reunification of the papacy under Martin V.

Henry Beaufort's main value, however, lay ultimately in the field of secular politics. As a brilliant orator and ardent advocate of his nephew's aggressive ventures against the French, he was, for instance, instrumental in justifying royal policy to Parliament and frequently acted as a royal propagandist in the country at large. Predictably, it would be his task to announce the news of Agincourt at St Paul's Cathedral on 29 October 1415, and in a letter of congratulation to the king, he also became the first to propound the myth of English invincibility under God's guidance and protection, comparing his sovereign to the heroes of biblical antiquity. In similar vein, it was he who later drew a parallel between Henry's achievements during the course of his six parliaments and the creation of the world in six days. And when the Bishop of Winchester was not serving as the king's mythmaker-in-chief, he was always ready to use his immense wealth – derived, in part, from the export of wool – to provide the Crown with huge loans at critical moments.

Thomas Beaufort, in his turn, would also uphold the Lancastrian cause with utter devotion, albeit in slightly less conspicuous ways. It was in 1410 that he reached the pinnacle of his career, becoming, first, Lord Chancellor and then Captain of Calais. Thereafter, in 1412, he was created Earl of Dorset before his appointment as the King's Lieutenant in Aquitaine, which, with typical magnanimity, he chose to defend at his own cost. A first-rate administrator, he could fight as well as govern and when the time came, he was with the vanguard of the victorious English army at Agincourt. Likewise, upon the fall of Harfleur in 1415, he served as its captain before being appointed Lieutenant of Normandy and Duke of Exeter in 1416. Impervious to corruption of any kind, the youngest of the Beaufort brothers therefore came to epitomise the kind of selfless service that Henry V, unlike so many of his predecessors and successors, was always able to count upon.

There was good reason, too, for the unerring loyalty of the Beaufort family. As a result of pressure from John of Gaunt himself, each of his bastard offspring was declared legitimate by an initial Act of Parliament in 1397, which was confirmed by a further statute in 1407. This second measure, however, came with a sensible precaution, debarring all four from any possibility of succession to the throne. Consequently, the Beauforts became a highly prestigious noble house, freed at a stroke from any taint of birth and fully at liberty to utilise their blood ties to the crown. Yet their fortunes would always be inextricably linked to the House of Lancaster, since they could now never aim for the throne in their own right. Henceforward, they would come to assume a unique role – one characterised by both immense power and guaranteed commitment to the Lancastrian cause.

The domestic and international background

Though he was not without certain admirable qualities, the king who ruled England at the time of Henry V's birth was never a man to inspire confidence. On the contrary, the damage done by Richard II's numerous flaws and miscalculations would help dictate the outlook of his successors for at least the next two reigns. In some respects, his wish to exalt the independent power of the monarchy was a worthy response to the cruder, more brutal drives of the nobility, and one that anticipated the practice of his Yorkist and early Tudor successors. But he was stricken by a series of crippling defects that became more and more debilitating as his reign progressed. Arrogant, profligate and easily moved to anger, he was sometimes energetic, sometimes lethargic, and generally displayed little grasp of either people or political realities. Worst of all, he became obsessed with the exercise of his royal prerogative and behaved too frequently as though the law was 'in his mouth' alone.[3]

Before very long, Richard had come to rely almost entirely for counsel and protection upon a private coterie of favourites who progressively alienated the traditional political elite. In 1383, for instance, Michael de la Pole, the base-born son of a Hull wool merchant, was made Chancellor, and two years later the king once more flew in the face of all good sense by creating him Earl of Suffolk. Robert de Vere, Earl of Oxford, was another dubious character who thrived under the king's patronage. Suspected by the chronicler Thomas Walsingham of cultivating an 'obscene familiarity' with his royal master, de Vere became Duke of Ireland in 1386.[4] And when in the same year Parliament sought the dismissal of de la Pole as Chancellor, the king responded with typical intransigence. He would not, he told MPs, dismiss 'even the least boy in his kitchen' on their account.[5]

As events unfolded, the principal target of this troublesome crew became none other than John of Gaunt who had long been wrongly suspected of angling for the throne in his own right. Even before his father's death, Gaunt had been the dominant force in politics and from the moment that Richard mounted the throne as a minor in 1377, there were widespread whispers that the head of the House of Lancaster would waste no time in pressing home his advantage. In the first Parliament of the new reign, Gaunt had even felt it necessary to seek public vindication of his loyalty.[6] And for many observers, the 'continual council' appointed to govern in young Richard's name served only to mask Gaunt's controlling presence. Indeed, there were also those who harboured darker fears about the new monarch's very survival.

But while Gaunt remained pre-eminent over the winter of 1381–2, the ground was already shifting beneath his feet as the king began to disdain the advice of those best suited to help him. In 1380, at the age of fourteen, he had finally reached majority and the successful suppression of the following year's Great Uprising seems to have transformed his adolescent egotism into a much more dangerous fixation with his own personal sanctity and regal status. Almost inevitably, therefore, both the size and influence of the royal household became an increasing cause for concern as Richard wilfully threw in his lot with the clique surrounding him.

From now onwards, in fact, the main concern of John of Gaunt was simply to save his royal nephew from himself. But it was precisely this that almost became his undoing. In a sensational episode at the Salisbury Parliament of 1384 Gaunt found himself facing a potentially deadly accusation that he had been plotting to murder the king and usurp the crown. A Carmelite friar had, it seems, denounced him while saying Mass before Richard in Robert de Vere's apartments. Nor was the danger over once the charge had been refuted. Next year Gaunt was forced to enter Richard's presence with a breastplate concealed beneath his gown, for fear of assassination. And by 1386, during a temporary lull in his stormy relationship with the king, the embattled duke was left with little other choice than to cut his losses and head to Spain in a vain attempt to win the crown of Castile.

Meanwhile, as Richard grew more and more unapproachable, so his name became synonymous with mismanagement and failure. Though he was prepared to fight in Scotland his military expedition of 1385 failed to result in any decisive engagement. On the other hand, demands for an investigation into the expenses of the royal household had been raised in 1381, 1382 and 1385, and rejected on all three occasions. Even the king's choice of wives left much to be desired. His first marriage to Anne of Bohemia produced neither heir nor dowry, and as the Holy Roman Emperor's daughter, she also failed to bring with her any useful alliance against France. Worse still, when Anne died, Richard made the costly error of marrying none other than the French king's six-year-old daughter, Isabella – though not before he had struck the Earl of Arundel full in the face at his first wife's funeral.

The marriage to Isabella of Valois was, moreover, just one element of an ongoing quest for peace with France, which was wholly at odds with the deep-seated prejudices of virtually all Englishmen. During the first century and a half after the Norman Conquest, France had aroused mixed emotions in the minds of England's ruling elite. Though a fundamental conflict of interest existed over the issue of overlordship in Normandy itself, a feudal baronage with branches on both sides of the Channel had remained something of a unifying influence. English nobles, after all, commonly spoke French, and French, in the Anglo-Norman form, remained, among other things, the language of the law courts. At the same time, a steady stream of higher clergymen had also come to England from across the Channel as a result of the conquest, and English culture had been affected by a whole host of other French influences. The knightly code of chivalry which became so influential was, for example, largely French in conception, while at the other end of the spectrum, the great schools of Chartres, Orléans and Paris continued to attract many of England's aspiring scholars.

The English loss of Normandy to the French monarchy in 1204, however, brought about a fundamental shift in the relationship. With the accession of Henry II in 1154, England and Normandy had both become part of a great continental empire whose centre was, in effect, the Loire valley rather than Westminster. Two years earlier, Henry had already inherited the Duchy of Normandy from his mother Matilda, and after he succeeded his father as Count of Anjou in 1151 he came to control not only Anjou itself, but also the territories of Maine and Touraine. More important acquisitions were still to come, however, when in 1152, his marriage to Eleanor of Aquitaine brought him Gascony, Poitou and Auvergne, along with Aquitaine itself, which was also known, mainly among the French, as Guienne. Eventually, in 1171, Brittany, too, was incorporated into Henry's domains by the marriage of his son Geoffrey to the heiress of Duke Conan IV.

During the second half of the twelfth century, therefore, the whole relationship between the kings of England and their French counterparts took on a new and ominous significance, for although Henry II's continental lands were technically fiefs, held from the King of France as their feudal overlord, the new King of England's French possessions constituted, to all intents and purposes, an independent state. The concentration of so much territory in the hands of one man was thus a serious threat to the French monarchy, which, paradoxically, exercised effective control of a much smaller area of land. Faced with this intolerable situation, the Capetian kings of France, from the time of Philip Augustus (1180–1240), had steadily detached territories from English control by an opportunistic policy that achieved its most impressive success with the capture of Normandy as England descended into impotency during the reign of King John.

Nor were subsequent efforts to heal the Anglo-French rift successful. The Treaty of Paris, which was agreed in 1259 between Henry III and Louis IX, would become the reference point for all diplomacy between the two countries over the next eighty years. By it, Henry accepted the break-up of the old Angevin empire by renouncing all right to Normandy, Anjou, Touraine and Poitou. For his part, meanwhile, Louis granted Henry a number of fiefs and territories in, or on the borders of, Aquitaine on condition that the King of England promised to hold these lands, as well as his existing duchies of Gascony and Aquitaine, as a vassal of the French monarchy.

In retrospect, however, such an arrangement was hardly likely to stand the test of time, for although England now held a southern French feudal kingdom from the King of France, many of her newly acquired territories, such as those in Quercy, Limoges, Cahors and Perigeux, were not actually the French king's to give. There followed interminable wrangling over the resulting territorial muddle, and acts of pillage and piracy on both sides were the subject of continual claim and counter-claim. French royal officials, meanwhile, continued to exert steady pressure in Gascony and gave every encouragement to the southern French feudatories of the English king to act in the interest of their overlord in Paris. When, on the other hand, Henry III's successor, Edward I, tried to rectify the position by staging a comprehensive inquiry into his feudal rights, as well as by creating a series of defensive posts or *bastides* at various points along his borders, the result was further sniping and border warfare, which only increased in Edward II's reign.

It was therefore almost inevitable that outright war would follow as soon as any clear-cut opportunity arose, and eventually it was King Richard's own grandfather who launched the conflict that would become known to posterity as the Hundred Years War. By virtue of his maternal grandfather, Philip IV, Edward III had inherited a claim to the French throne, and after France had pre-empted matters by renewing its claim to outright control in Aquitaine, he finally launched an outstandingly successfully military campaign of his own against the French 'aggressors'. The English victories at the battles of Crécy (1346) and Poitiers (1356), and the resulting Treaty of Brétigny (1360) seemed, on the surface at least, to avenge all previous wrongs. In return for the release of their king, John II, who had been captured at Poitiers, the French were now made to pay the huge ransom of 3 million gold crowns over six years. On the other hand, the territorial losses imposed on France seemed to be equally punishing. The whole Duchy of Aquitaine, including Poitou in the north, was handed over to England, together with Calais and the surrounding territory of Ponthieu. Calais in particular would prove of immense economic and strategic importance, controlling as it did the narrow sea separating England from the continent.

Yet the outcomes of the Treaty of Brétigny were neither unalloyed nor long lasting. Edward had not, for instance, actually succeeded in regaining all the lands formerly ruled by Henry II. Normandy, above all, still remained in French hands. Similarly, the clause formally renouncing French suzerainty over Aquitaine was never actually implemented, and when war broke out once more in 1369, France was soon in the ascendant. The shrewdness of Charles V and his gifted general Bertrand du Guesclin, who systematically avoided pitched battles or large engagements out of a healthy respect for English archers, brought about a revival of French military power, while her naval success at La Rochelle in 1372 helped ensure that France would swiftly win back the territories lost just over a decade earlier.

In the aftermath of these setbacks, then, Richard II now sought in vain to break the vicious circle that continued to bedevil Anglo-French relations. He realised quite correctly, of course, that the expense of war had seriously undermined the strength of monarchical authority that he was so committed to defending. On several occasions during the 1380s, in fact, Parliament had already signalled its desire for more control of central government by resisting royal requests for taxation. To his credit, Richard was also right in recognising that England remained an economically fragile and thinly-populated land, ill-suited to the pursuit of permanent gains overseas. Only two generations before his accession, the population of England probably stood at close to 6 million, but the Black Death had reduced it to no more than 2 or 3 million. France, by contrast, could still boast a population around double that figure. Edward III's war needs had, moreover, damaged the English wool trade, and although the late fourteenth and early fifteenth centuries witnessed a modest recovery from the general trade depression which had been besetting Europe in the aftermath of the Black Death, further conflict still carried with it serious risks.

The king therefore fully appreciated the dangers involved in military adventure. But he was also largely blind to the substantial political cost entailed by too much play at peace. Geoffrey Chaucer's verse, which was extremely popular in court circles, provided ample proof that while French might still be used for formal or official purposes, it was now no longer the living language of the ruling class. Much more importantly still, Englishmen, high and low alike, refused to forget the victories of Crécy and Poitiers. Indeed, the English remained belchingly contemptuous of their French counterparts, whose peasants, it was said, walked unshod and drank only water. Above all, however, they coveted the loot and ransom that had once flooded back across the Channel so freely. And if a fresh spate of conquest was not quite yet an option, the current limp-wristed attempts at conciliation with the French enemy were more intolerable still.

By the time that Henry V was born, therefore, a menacing tide of opposition was mounting against the reigning king, which included key members of the nobility, such as Thomas of Woodstock, the Earl of Arundel, and indeed Henry's own father who found during the Parliament of 1386 that Richard was keen to exclude both him and his heirs from the succession in favour of Roger Mortimer, the current Earl of March. In fact, Richard's pro-French leanings, not to mention the arbitrary taxation, which had provoked the Great Revolt of 1381, were already combining all classes against him, and his personal extravagance and reliance upon favourites only served to compound his problems. His high-handed treatment of the City of London, meanwhile, had made him other influential opponents and even the clergy were objecting more and more to his stubborn pacifism. When, therefore, a 'great and continual council', consisting of Woodstock and Arundel among others, was imposed upon him in November 1386 to oversee his activities, it came as no surprise.

Nor was the king's reaction to this personal humiliation any less predictable. The flashpoint duly came in November 1387 when Richard collected an army in the royal earldom of Cheshire with the express intention of crushing his enemies. In the meantime, however, Thomas of Woodstock and the earls of Arundel and Warwick had also assembled retinues near London to defend themselves and in a position of clear advantage, they met the king in Westminster Hall to demand the impeachment of his cronies. Faced with a fait accompli, Richard bowed uncharacteristically to the inevitable, only to find that de Vere, his favourite, had elected to pre-empt matters by raising an army in the north and was marching towards London.

On this occasion, however, the gambler's throw was both desperate and doomed to failure, since de Vere was intercepted by the rebel lords and roundly defeated in battle at Radcot Bridge in Oxfordshire, after which the victors then returned to London and demanded satisfaction from the king. Frightened by threats of deposition and with no further help at hand, Richard was accordingly forced to imprison or banish a number of his most undesirable courtiers and replace them with officials appointed by his opponents. When the 'Merciless' Parliament met in February 1388, therefore, the victors were able to proceed unimpeded to their main purpose.

This time they avoided the usual method of impeachment and employed the more direct procedure of accusing, or 'appealing', their victims in person before Parliament. The five so-called 'Lords Appellant' were Thomas of Woodstock, Arundel, Warwick, Nottingham and, significantly, Henry Bolingbroke. The accused, on the other hand, included de la Pole and de Vere, along with the Archbishop of York, several of the king's justices, a leading London merchant by the name of Nicholas Brembre and the king's old tutor, Simon Burley. Brembre and Burley were executed, while de la Pole and de Vere would die in exile.

At a single stroke, then, the king's clinging circle of friends was uncompromisingly routed, leaving him with no other choice than to follow the path of passive compliance as dutifully as he might. In consequence, Bolingbroke soon appeared fully reconciled to his sovereign, while John of Gaunt's return from Spain in 1389 restored a stabilising influence, which would help secure some nine years of comparative political peace. And there, for the moment, the matter rested – like a heavy boulder perching delicately on a fragile mountain ledge.

Boyhood

While the tumultuous events of 1388 were duly unfolding around him and in the lull that followed, young Henry of Monmouth proceeded to live out his early years both securely and inconspicuously. According to the household accounts of the Duchy of Lancaster, he spent a good deal of his childhood in the company of his mother at Peterborough. From time to time he also visited his maternal grandmother, Joan, Countess of Hereford, whose earnest household of pious elderly ladies probably played no small part in stoking the boy's growing spiritual zeal. Certainly, he seems to have developed an especial fondness for the ageing countess over the years that followed. Indeed, even though he saw significantly more of his grandfather, John of Gaunt, he would still make two references to her in the will he made in July 1415 before leaving for France, calling her 'our dearest grandmother' and bequeathing her a cup and ewer of gold worth 100 marks.[7]

The same accounts also provide us with a number of other trivial yet tantalising details about Henry's everyday life at this time. We know, for instance, that he at first shared a bedchamber with his brothers and a governess named Mary Hervy, and we know, too, that his nurse was a certain Joan Waring, who was paid forty shillings a year to look after him. Elsewhere, we learn of the clothes he wore – cloaks, mantles, scarlet caps, green russet gowns, broad black hats made of straw – and find references to items like an iron chain that was purchased for one of his greyhounds. We even discover that surprisingly large amounts were spent on soap and shoes for the future King of England and his brother Thomas.[8]

More significantly, there are glimpses of detail concerning Henry's education. For example, several books of grammar contained in one volume were bought for him in London at a cost of four shillings, while the sum of eight pence was paid to a certain Adam Gastron for harp strings for 'the young Lord Henry' when he was about ten years old.[9] On the other hand, the same accounts also confirm that Henry was being schooled in the use of arms from an early age. An individual by the name of Stephen Furbour, for instance, received one shilling for a new scabbard, while three-quarters of an ounce of tissue of black silk were purchased in London from a certain Margaret Stranson for another of Henry's swords. Both of these payments happen to coincide neatly with Henry's attendance at his first tournament just before the age of ten at Pleshey Castle in Essex.

As well as the random glimpses of Henry's everyday existence provided by the Lancaster accounts, there is also the evidence of the *Versus Rhythmici*, written by a Benedictine monk of Westminster who seems to have had some kind of first-hand acquaintance with him. Here, too, Henry is shown to have enjoyed a contented and wholly conventional childhood. Like all noblemen's sons, he devoted much of his time to falconry, fishing, riding and walking, and, in the process, he seems to have developed an enduring enthusiasm for hunting of all kinds. Indeed, when he was Prince of Wales, his cousin, Edward, Duke of York, dedicated to him an English translation of the best-known contemporary hunting manual, the *Livre de Chasse* by Gaston Phebus, Count of Foix. And less than a year before his death, Henry would have a total of twelve books on the same subject specially written for him by a London scrivener at a cost of £12 8s 6d.[10]

But in spite of his enthusiasm for sport, Henry did not, according to the *Versus Rhythmici*, neglect the 'learned counsels of his elders'.[11] Furthermore, the tuition he received under the personal supervision of his uncle, Henry Beaufort, is likely to have been second to none. Beaufort, who was only a dozen years older than his pupil, had been educated at Peterhouse, Cambridge, before migrating to Oxford and briefly becoming that university's chancellor during 1397–8 at the remarkably young age of around twenty. Not altogether surprisingly, therefore, a legend arose that Henry had actually gone on to study under Beaufort at Queen's College, though the claim is now rejected on the grounds that the boy was too young to gain much benefit from the university's curriculum. More conclusively still, his father's accounts for 1397–8 refer only to stays for him at London, Hertford, Pontefract and Kenilworth, with no mention whatsoever of Oxford.[12]

Nevertheless, Henry's educational accomplishments are apparent from the state papers he eventually left as king. Although he could read, write and speak both French and Latin, he later insisted upon the use of English in all official documents and the personal letters that he produced, especially when he wished to maintain secrecy, are well formed, if characteristically terse. Moreover, Henry's education under Beaufort's wing helped fuel the lifelong passion for books that he had first acquired from his father. Later, at the sieges of Caen and Meaux, he would take special pains to secure books in his share of the booty, and by the time of his death he had built up an extensive library, which included texts on law, logic and history, along with Seneca's letters, Cicero's *Rhetoric* and various patristic writings. Though the books concerned look somewhat old-fashioned in comparison with those of his brother Humphrey who had a liking for the latest humanist works, they still reflect a keen and well-trained intellect.

Henry's childhood was not, however, entirely filled with country walks and reading. He appears, for example, to have become seriously ill in the spring of 1395, at which time a London physician by the name of Thomas Pye was despatched to Leicester to tend him. And the previous year had already produced traumas of a much deeper and more lasting kind. Indeed, 1394 appears in retrospect to have been nothing less than a turning point in his whole development – a time during which his early security and evolving self-image are likely to have been shaken to the core.

In December 1387, just over a year after his initial decision to exclude the Lancastrian line from the succession, the king had buckled under pressure from the group who would become the Appellants and once more acknowledged John of Gaunt as his heir in line with Edward III's arrangements of 1376. Young Henry had consequently grown up in the understanding that he, like his grandfather and father, was a rightful heir to the throne of England. In 1394, however, Richard resisted John of Gaunt's attempt to have Henry Bolingbroke recognised as heir presumptive by appointing him lord keeper of the realm, and gave the post instead to his own uncle, Edmund of Langley. For the time being, therefore, Langley appeared to assume priority in the order of succession, leaving both Bolingbroke and his son on the political sidelines. Even for a seven-year-old – especially one as astute as Henry – the impact is likely to have been significant.

Worse was to follow, however, for Henry's mother also died in the same year, depriving him at the age of eight of the only parent with whom he had enjoyed sustained contact. Furthermore, Mary de Bohun's death coincided with the next stage of his education – doubtless a time of some disorientation in its own right. From now on the boy would be deprived of the company of his sisters and two youngest brothers and live in the household of his grandfather, along with his brother Thomas whom he did not very much like. Certainly, Henry's actions after he became king leave little doubt about the affection he felt for his deceased mother. She had been buried in the great Lancastrian chantry of St Mary in the New Work at Leicester, although her husband had spent little money on her grave and eventually chose to be buried far away from her at Canterbury. Soon after his own accession, therefore, Henry V paid a London coppersmith £43 for a figure of his mother to be placed on her tomb.

By comparison, Henry's relationship with his father was undoubtedly more distant and somewhat cooler, too. Between 1390 and 1393, in fact, Bolingbroke was wholly preoccupied with forging the military reputation that meant so much to him and as a result he saw little of his son. In the spring of 1390, for instance, he took part in the famous tournament of St Inglevert, not far from Calais, where he became acquainted with many of the leading lights of European chivalry. And soon afterwards, with his wife expecting the birth of their fourth child, he was on crusade with the Teutonic knights against the forest-dwelling Lithuanians. Then, in 1392, he made his way through northern Germany, Austria and Venice – where he was received in person by the Doge – and onwards down the coast of Dalmatia and Corfu, before heading finally for Rhodes and the Holy Land.

Absences of this kind were far from unusual and, in the context of the age, young Henry is likely to have taken such separation in his stride. It was assumed, after all, that the sons of nobles would be brought up 'among the women' until at least the age of seven, and, if anything, his father's exploits are very likely to have served as a further source of inspiration for the kind of lifestyle that the boy himself would later lead. But Henry would now be brought up largely among the knights and men-at-arms of John of Gaunt's household. And if the father himself was not exactly neglectful, he may well have come in due course to represent a figure of competition as well as love – someone, perhaps, to be both revered and surpassed. The nineteen-year age difference between the two was, of course, minimal. Moreover, the fact that Henry troubled to adorn his mother's tomb, while neglecting eventually to carry out his father's will and testament remains striking.

The 'triumph' of the House of Lancaster

If 1394 had been a year of trauma and transition in Henry V's life, then 1398 would usher in a number of even more drastic changes. Predictably, perhaps, Richard II had never put the effrontery of the Lords Appellant behind him and he now decided to avenge himself once and for all. In the event, his first move was to arrest his youngest uncle, Thomas of Woodstock, in July 1397 and an assault upon the earls of Warwick and Arundel followed soon after. In

September, Arundel was beheaded and his brother, the Archbishop of Canterbury, exiled. Meanwhile, the Earl of Warwick was imprisoned, and to complete the first wave of retribution Woodstock was then secretly strangled while in captivity at Calais.

In the aftermath of this purge, Bolingbroke and Thomas Mowbray, the former Earl of Nottingham, became the only remaining Appellants both alive and at liberty, and Bolingbroke in particular posed what Richard considered to be an intolerable threat. Even though his Lancastrian cousin had remained loyal during the comparative political stability of the 1390s, Richard's antipathy to him was well known. Indeed, as John of Gaunt's stabilising influence had declined with the onset of old age and ill health, his son now seemed to loom more and more menacingly. With resources, lands and revenues that were almost comparable to those of the king and solid grounds for a lasting grudge over the succession, Bolingbroke could boast a string of potential heirs at a time when Richard's own marriage to young Isabella of Valois could not yield children for some years to come. In the meantime, the other main claimant to the throne of England from July 1398 onwards had now become a seven-year-old boy, Edmund Mortimer, fifth Earl of March. If, therefore, Bolingbroke were to launch a successful bid for the crown, young Mortimer would be in no position to offer effective opposition.

The king's response to this dilemma was to seize the initiative while time and opportunity allowed. Although Mowbray had been made Duke of Norfolk in September 1397, he had nevertheless mentioned to Bolingbroke not long afterwards that the king remained a threat to both of them. If not outrightly treasonable, such talk was, at the very least, extremely dangerous and when Bolingbroke reported it to his father, Gaunt duly saw fit to stir things by passing the matter on to the king. However, in attempting to damage Mowbray in return for his part in the murder of Thomas of Woodstock, the old man had also furnished the king with precisely the opportunity he needed to attack his own son, and in an episode well worthy of any Hollywood epic, both Bolingbroke and Mowbray were called before a parliamentary commission in March 1398 to plead their respective cases. As accusations and denials flew backwards and forwards between the two protagonists, it was duly decided that they should settle the matter by combat.

It is no exaggeration to say that the proposed trial by battle, which was set to occur on 16 September in the lists at Coventry, promised to be one of the greatest chivalric spectacles of the day. Not only was the duel the first of its kind between two dukes, it also brought together England's two most renowned jousting champions in a fight to the death. As befitted this unique event, it was to be attended by a glittering array of English nobles, not to mention a whole host of other celebrities from throughout Europe, and although we cannot be sure whether he was present, the impact upon Bolingbroke's eldest son may well be imagined. For here, it seems, was chivalry writ large – the firmest possible proof that politics, honour and force of arms were indivisible. It is hard to imagine, too, that the whole protracted build-up to the event would not have made its own particularly vivid impression upon the eleven-year-old boy. Five months of undiluted tension in all elapsed before the actual climax – months in which Milanese armourers shuttled back and forth from Bolingbroke's household and Bolingbroke himself showed increasing signs of strain, as he consulted the stars with his astrolabe and waited anxiously in hope of a favourable outcome.

On the actual day of reckoning, moreover, it seems that a crowd of many thousands gathered to witness the display. Such was the crush that a wet ditch had to be specially constructed around the lists before Bolingbroke duly arrived to receive the constable's challenge. Arriving an hour after his rival, he rode a white war horse, draped in a livery of blue and green velvet embroidered with gold swans and antelopes. Behind him followed his heralds, sergeants-at-arms and six other war horses with exotic trappings in a show that drove the ecstatic crowds to fever pitch on his behalf. But at the critical point when both men were poised on the very brink of combat the king called a dramatic and astonishing halt to the action. Two agonising hours later, it was announced that instead of the proposed trial by combat both men were to be banished – Mowbray for life, Bolingbroke for ten years.

Once again, then, young Henry of Monmouth was to be deprived of his father's company and on 13 October Bolingbroke left London for exile in France. If the sentence were to stand, the father would not see his son again as a boy. Even more disconcertingly, perhaps, the sudden collapse of the boy's political prospects was all too apparent. It is possible, of course, that, at the age of seven, Henry's initial exclusion from the succession had still not hit home fully, but now, at the age of twelve, he would have understood only too well that his position as a potential heir to the throne had been fatally undermined. As if to emphasise the folly and unfairness of the king's action, Bolingbroke's popularity was at an all-time high by the time he took his final leave. According to Froissart, thousands of Londoners lined the streets to bid him a sorrowful farewell, declaring that 'this country will never be happy until you return'.[13]

But neither the drama nor the attack on him was yet finished, for less than four months later, on 3 February 1399, John of Gaunt died at Leicester, leaving Richard free to declare all Lancastrian lands forfeit to the Crown. At the same time, the king announced that the former heir to the Duchy of Lancaster should be banished forever. In one fell swoop, therefore, Bolingbroke's grievance was immediately transformed into a test case for the future security of all noble estates in the land, and he found himself sucked forward into a course of action that was as momentous as it was unexpected, since he could only defend his inheritance from this point onwards by making the crown of England his own.

The consequences of all this for the future Henry V were profound. Aside from the further injustice involved and the prospect of indefinite separation from his father, he was now forced to join the king's household and became, in effect, Richard's personal hostage. Yet Henry was treated with kindness at all times and appears to have reconciled himself to his fate with remarkable equanimity, establishing a genuine bond of mutual affection with his captor. According to the *First English Life of Henry V*, he was 'nourished in the King's Court right honourably in all things' and 'obtained the favour and love of the King'.[14] Richard even, it seems, provided £500 for his maintenance. Not without some irony, perhaps, the boy also had the benefit of receiving his first military experience at the king's own side, for in the spring of 1399 Richard decided to travel to Ireland in person to quell an insurrection with young Henry in tow. If, moreover, the account of the Frenchman Jean Creton, is to be believed, the king's young hostage was soon showing signs of the same military prowess that he would later display so vividly as Henry V.

Creton was, in fact, more minstrel than soldier, but he was still an eye-witness to events and his poetic record of what he saw provides an invaluable record of the Irish expedition itself, as well as an alternative view of the subsequent usurpation of the English throne which helps to balance the accounts of the Lancastrian chroniclers. Even more importantly, the Frenchman gives us our first glimpses of Henry V as a discrete historical figure. And, according to him, the growing boy seems to have acquitted himself admirably in the dense forests and bogs of Ireland, since Richard duly knighted him, along with ten of his companions-in-arms. Indeed, Creton describes Henry as a 'young and handsome bachelor' and also quotes some advice from Richard that has continued, not altogether surprisingly, to resonate down the years. 'My fair cousin', the king is said to have told his enemy's son, 'henceforth be gallant and bold, for unless you conquer you will have little name for valour.'[15]

At the very time that Henry was being taken under his sovereign's wing, however, his own father had decided to break his exile, thus creating a painful crisis of loyalty for the newly knighted boy. It was in early July that Richard first received the news of Bolingbroke's landing at Ravenspur, north of the Humber, and of his triumphal progress through the northern strongholds of the Percy family and his former Lancastrian estates. At this stage, Bolingbroke still talked only of regaining his confiscated lands, but by the time that the king had returned to Wales at the end of the month, he found that the growing swell of frustration confronting him was already gaining an unstoppable momentum. Consequently, by the end of September, Richard would find himself a ruler without either army or throne.

In the meantime, Henry had been left in Ireland for safekeeping at the castle of Trim. According to the chronicler Thomas Otterbourne, Richard had called the boy into his presence upon learning of the rebellion and reproached him for his father's treason, albeit surprisingly mildly under the circumstances – 'Henry, my boy, see what thy father hath done to me ... through these unhappy doings thou wilt perchance lose thine inheritance.' Henry's response – a sincere expression of regret and firm denial of any personal involvement – was, in its way, no less curious. There was no attempt to defend, let alone side with, his father. But nor was he ready to denounce or desert him. Henry seems, in fact, to have exhibited that same mixture of coolness and resolve in adversity that would always be one of his most characteristic features. 'I am sincerely grieved by these tidings', he is alleged to have told Richard, 'and, as I conceive, you are fully assured of my innocence in this proceeding of my father.'[16]

As events swiftly unfolded over the coming days and weeks, Henry's feelings continued to remain, initially at least, somewhat mixed. Bolingbroke had sent a ship to fetch his son from Ireland as soon as he felt sufficiently secure, though Henry had still not fully settled his conscience by the time he arrived in Chester. His father was now, after all, a remoter figure than ever, while Richard was the boy's anointed sovereign and had, in personal terms, shown him considerable kindness and favour. According to one account, Henry actually took his place at first with those attending Richard and was found in this company when his father arrived. He was also said to have been upset by the command that he must leave Richard's service forthwith, and was equally dismayed by the king's final words of farewell to his 'good sonne Henry'. If, moreover, the *Brut* chronicler is correct, he only joined his father when reminded of his filial duty by the king himself.[17]

The boy was, however, soon showing further signs of the man he would become, and once the die was finally cast, any initial unease soon made way, apparently, for the cast-iron conviction that his king and former mentor had been rightfully deposed. On 29 September, Richard tamely resigned the crown and on the following day Bolingbroke was duly elected to a throne that stood conspicuously empty in Westminster Hall, while the teeming crowds outside cheered their fickle approval. And just as Henry now joined them in embracing his father's cause, so he also gladly accepted the stream of honours that swiftly came his own way. At the coronation, which occurred on Monday 13 October, two years to the day since his father had been forced into exile, Henry carried the sword of justice, filling the same role that the new king had played at his fallen rival's coronation twenty-two years earlier. But even this was only a foretaste of his newfound status. Two days later, the new heir was named Prince of Wales, Duke of Cornwall and Earl of Chester and within a fortnight he was made Duke of Aquitaine. Finally, before November was out, the Duchy of Lancaster also became his.

The world was, then, suddenly and wholly unexpectedly the new Prince Henry's. But it was also, as far as he was now concerned, his by right and forever, since God himself had placed his seal of approval upon the Lancastrian cause. If providence had pointed the way, his own religious convictions made it all too easy not only to follow, but to follow with utter conviction, regardless of any previous attachment to the deposed king. And if, after all, his father's 'triumph' was to be marked by nothing more than a dogged reign of nagging doubts and grim survival, it would at least clear the path for his own far greater glory to come.

2 Military and political apprenticeship, 1399–1413

Debt and insecurity

Despite the full weight of Lancastrian propaganda and the careful stage-management of Richard's 'voluntary' abdication, it remained apparent that Henry IV had no real right to the crown of England beyond naked force and Parliament's determination to thrust it upon him at any cost. And surely enough, the manner of his 'triumph' in September 1399 would continue to dog him for at least the first six years of his rule. Henry began, it is true, with much sympathy over his ill treatment at Richard's hands. He was also undeniably head of the richest family in England, with four male heirs to bolster him. But he was not the first king to prove more successful at winning a crown than wearing one, and when the challenges duly arrived they focused unfailingly upon the legitimacy of his rule. In consequence, his heir's first contact with the art of government would occur in the tensest possible atmosphere.

Certainly, the new king could rely on the support of his own family, not to mention the knights, squires and clerks of the Duchy of Lancaster who supplied the bulk of the Crown's administrative and military service in these early years. But perhaps his most distinguished supporter was the Archbishop of Canterbury, Thomas Arundel, who had been banished by King Richard for his part in the actions of the Lords Appellant, only to be reinstated at the very start of the new reign. The Lancastrian cause could also rely upon the consistent support of a number of great men, such as the Beauchamp earls of Warwick, the Nevilles of Westmorland and the archbishop's nephew Thomas Fitzalan, Earl of Arundel. Indeed, most of the major noble houses were initially inclined to support the usurpation, though their loyalty was always likely to be tested over time.

Among these were the Percies, the most powerful family in the north, whose fickle allegiance would soon be stretched to breaking point, with the gravest possible consequences. Their star had long been rising and they now stood out boldly among the very highest magnates of the realm, boasting massive military support for any venture they might choose to undertake. It was with good reason, too, that they saw themselves so confidently as kingmakers, since without their allegiance Henry might never have seized the throne in the first place. And they were led by three highly distinguished military commanders in Henry Percy, Earl of Northumberland, his brother Thomas, Earl of Worcester, and the shining heir to the Percy dynasty, the famous Henry 'Hotspur'.

Another group to be reckoned with was the Mortimer family, whose prowess as marcher lords of South Wales had left them in no doubt about their rightful place amid the high and mighty. In 1397, as we have seen, they were given pride of place in the succession by Richard, and although they were finally forced by circumstance to acquiesce in their master's subsequent deposition, their allegiance to the new regime was always potentially fragile. The Mortimer claim to the throne was, after all, a strong one, deriving from the daughter of the Duke of Clarence, Edward III's second son. And though the nominal head of the family at the start of the new reign was the eight-year-old Earl of March, whom King Henry had already secured in fairly congenial confinement, the real mover and shaper of affairs was the boy's formidable uncle, Sir Edmund.

The House of York, meanwhile, seemed to hover ambivalently in the political balance. They, too, had been placed above their Lancastrian rivals in the line of succession by the previous king and although their head, Edmund of Langley, had given up rather feebly at the appearance of Bolingbroke's army in 1399, his two sons, Edward, Earl of Rutland (also known as Aumale), and Richard, would need to be watched most keenly. The former, who succeeded his father as Duke of York in 1402, had certainly been highly favoured in the previous reign, but he remained, to say the least, a decidedly shifty character who was ultimately lucky enough to die at Agincourt more gloriously than he deserved. His brother Richard, on the other hand, was married – somewhat ominously – to Anne Mortimer.

Then, of course, there were the more overt and outright enemies of the new dynasty, consisting for the most part of displaced Ricardian courtiers who had done well out of the former king's drive towards personal rule and itched for his return. Most important of these were the Holland family and the Earl of Salisbury. John Holland, for instance, was Duke of Exeter and Earl of Huntingdon, and the son of Richard II's mother, Joan the 'Fair Maid of Kent', by her previous marriage with Sir Thomas Holland. Meanwhile, his nephew Thomas also boasted a special relationship with Richard as Duke of Surrey and Earl of Kent, along with John Montagu, third Earl of Salisbury.

By and large, Henry IV adopted a comparatively moderate approach towards these men upon his accession. With the exception of Salisbury, they were stripped of some of their lands, but otherwise left alone. Yet if the new king believed that a policy of partial clemency would win his enemies over, he soon found otherwise when, during the Christmas feast of 1399, the first of numerous conspiracies against the new dynasty shattered the fragile peace. The ringleaders of the plot to storm Windsor Castle and restore Richard II to the throne were predictably the two Hollands, along with John Montagu, Edward, Earl of Rutland, and Thomas Despenser, Earl of Gloucester. Moreover, the plan, which involved smuggling armed men into the castle under cover of a magnificent 'mumming' and tournament to be held on the feast of the Epiphany, came perilously close to success.

Ultimately, indeed, the plot's eventual failure only resulted from Rutland's decision to reveal the scheme to his father, the Duke of York, who then went on to inform the king. But the butchery which followed provided the new Prince of Wales with the bluntest possible introduction to the full rigours of late medieval retribution. After the exactions of the previous reign, any Ricardian rebels could expect little sympathy, of course, and Thomas Holland and Salisbury were both lynched on the spot by a rabid mob, while John Holland was captured at Pleshey and duly beheaded by his captors. Other leading rebels were executed at Oxford by the king's own order before he rode back to London with the rebels' freshly salted heads ready for display on London Bridge. By the end of the bloodletting, Rutland alone had been spared, because of his father's loyalty and influence.

An even more poignant lesson in statecraft for the Prince of Wales was to follow soon afterwards. Before January was out, Richard II had met his end in a dungeon at Pontefract Castle, and although it was claimed at the time that he had refused to eat and died of starvation, the date of his demise was much too convenient to suggest anything other than murder at the king's behest. Yet there is no evidence that the future Henry V shared his father's subsequent torments over this deed. That he was not unmoved by Richard's fate is proven by his early decision as king to arrange for the former ruler's reinterment at Westminster with full ceremony. But as events unfolded at the time, he seems to have absorbed the news with all the calm resignation of someone who had already grasped an all-important lesson – namely, that in a late medieval context political expediency outweighed all sentiment.

This is not to say, however, that the death of Richard II was without unfortunate side-effects. The legend, for instance, that Richard had escaped from Pontefract and that the corpse displayed at St Paul's was a fraud pursued Henry IV throughout his reign, and even outlived him to worry his son. Indeed, by 1402 a man whom some chose to regard as Richard – the so-called 'Mommet' – had appeared in Scotland, while another rumour had it that the former king was alive and well in Wales. To make matters worse, the ugly truth about King Richard's demise was soon being widely circulated. And such legitimist propaganda proclaiming the rights of the dead monarch or, if necessary, the young Earl of March was ideal material to serve the interests of ambitious men who had their own grievances against the House of Lancaster.

Throughout 1400 and 1401, in fact, the predominant atmosphere was one of tension and foreboding – a situation made all the worse by the high price of bread and the spread of rumour at every turn. At Dartmouth, a tax collector only narrowly managed to save his life by escaping in a boat, while at Norton St Philip the cloth-dealers refused to pay their tax, before the royal agent was eventually murdered. Elsewhere, a certain William Clark, who had slandered the king, was sentenced to lose his tongue, his right hand and later his life. Then, in September 1401, it was reported that an infernal device called a 'caltrappe', consisting of poisoned spikes guaranteed to kill anyone unfortunate enough to lie on them, had been found in the royal bed.

Not altogether surprisingly, the Council's response to these and similar episodes reflected the gravity of their concerns. Its members were alarmed, for instance, that the judiciary might now struggle to enforce law and order, 'for fear of the unruliness and pride of the Commons who do not wish to be under any governance'.[1] As a result, the king was advised to retain soldiers in the counties to maintain peace and also warned against summoning Parliament, on the grounds that there would be too much opposition to any requests for taxation. At the same time, the Council feared the possibility of war with Scotland and France, which would be bound to exacerbate the already considerable fiscal problems facing the Crown.

And finance would indeed remain the foremost problem besetting the king, not only now but throughout his rule. 'Kings are not wont to render account', he later declared, and this was hardly surprising, perhaps, coming from the heir of the richest man in England.[2] But unlike Richard II who had enjoyed an annual revenue of £116,000, Henry could now only count upon £90,000 at a time when the financial pressures upon him were greater than ever. Furthermore, in order to consolidate support, he found himself freely distributing grants of land and annuities, confirming virtually all those of his predecessor, and rewarding, as he was bound to, his own Lancastrian supporters to the tune of £22,000. He also kept an open household, the costs of which soon soared above even the level of the previous reign.

The result was nothing short of a continual state of panic among Henry's treasurers. Yet in spite of the rewards that he lavished upon his supporters, the king was still unable to satisfy all the promises he had made during the march from Ravenspur. Nor was he able to redeem his pledge to cut taxes. 'There is not enough in your treasury at the moment to pay the messengers who are to bear the letters which you have ordained to the lords and knights who are to be of your council', wrote Lawrence Allerthorpe in 1401.[3] Indeed, even years later in 1411, Henry's heir was explaining to the Council that the books would simply still not balance.

Naturally enough, such grinding hardship had serious political consequences, not least of all because it led the king to make demands on his aristocratic supporters, which strained their sympathies to the limit – and in some cases beyond. The Percies, for their part, were continually complaining in the early years of the reign that they had not been paid what was due to them. In their view, they were in constant danger of being deserted by their own men for lack of pay and would be forced to resign their offices unless the king offered some remedy. Lord Grey of Codnor, meanwhile, would write in 1405 that even his own harness was in pawn for his soldiers' wages.[4]

But if Henry IV's magnates groaned and grumbled sullenly, his parliaments clamoured. Though they were not niggardly, they were nevertheless resolute that the king should curb his spending and, where necessary, stretch his own resources to the very limit. In 1404, for instance, they passed a stiff act of resumption asking for a one-year postponement of all fees and annuities from the Crown. In the same year, too, Parliament demanded and secured the removal from office of four members of the royal household. However, it was in 1406 that the situation reached its climax. Addressing Parliament on behalf of the Council, Archbishop Arundel declared that he and his colleagues were ready to take up their duties only 'if sufficiency of goods could be found to carry on government properly; otherwise not'.[5] Accordingly, the king was forced to surrender much of the direction of royal finances, and even grants of royal favours, to a council of which the Prince of Wales became the nominal head.

Owain Glyn Dŵr and the Percies

For Henry IV and his young heir the so-called 'Epiphany Rising' of January 1400 had been merely a foretaste of things to come – and a comparatively mild one at that, since revolt and disorder were ever-present over the next few years. In August the king marched against Scotland, where border raiding had intensified since his accession, and at his side rode the Prince of Wales in command of seventeen men-at-arms and ninety-nine archers. But though the English force of more than 13,000 men actually outnumbered the armies that crossed the Channel in 1415 and 1417 and left little doubt about the inherent strength of England's military infrastructure, the campaign itself was largely frustrating. The king, it is true, reached Edinburgh, but gained little glory in doing so and after a few weeks of raiding and burning in the company of the Percies, much more ominous news arrived from Wales, which would have momentous consequences not only for the king himself, but even more so for his eldest son.

When young Henry was first made Prince of Wales, the chronicler Creton had no doubt about the scale of the task confronting him, since in his opinion 'the Welsh would on no account allow him to be their lord, for the sorrow, evil and disgrace, which the English, together with his father, had brought upon King Richard'. As such, war appeared to be the prince's only option in Wales. 'I think', concluded the Frenchman, 'he must conquer it if he will have it.'[6] And on all counts he could not have been more right.

The prince had, in fact, inherited both a hostile land and a precarious settlement, which dated from Edward I's Statute of Rhuddlan in 1284. Under the Normans, southern and central Wales had proved easier to conquer than the north, though even in the more tractable areas, with the exception of Pembrokeshire, the superimposition of Norman lords had left the native Celtic institutions and language largely undisturbed. However, when Edward I finally defeated Llewellyn ap Gruffydd, the last prince of Wales, a viable English enclave had at last been established which comprised the northern shires of Anglesey, Caernarvon, Merioneth and Flint, along with Cardigan and Carmarthen in the south. Centred on Caernarvon, it had its own Council, Chancery and Exchequer, and a legal system, which was founded upon a judicious mixture of English law and Welsh custom, firmly reinforced by the imposing presence of the great fortresses of Caernarvon, Harlech, Criccieth, Conway, Rhuddlan and Beaumaris.

Yet even by this stage the area controlled by the Prince of Wales was concentrated on the western side of the country and remained comparatively small. Furthermore, the so-called 'marches', which comprised the rest of the land, were the almost absolute property of powerful 'marcher lords' – warrior barons, such as the Talbots, Charltons, Greys and Mortimers, who were for the most part descendants of the original Norman invaders. Though they owed allegiance to the English crown, each of a hundred or more of these men had his own stronghold in central and southern Wales, and some still saw their powers as '*sicut regale*' – 'like unto a king's'. Nor did their aggressive superiority endear them to the native Welsh whose intense dislike of English laws and taxes was fuelled by stirring bardic sagas of past independence and ceaseless prophecies of a fast-approaching day when the foreign yoke would at last be lifted.

To complicate matters, there existed within the lands of the marcher lords and the principality itself pockets of Welsh territory, located mainly in the highlands, where a class of well-educated and comparatively wealthy native gentlemen – the so-called *uchelwyr* – wielded significant influence. Perhaps the wealthiest and most influential of all such Welshmen was Owain Glyn Dŵr, a forty-year-old landowner, who was descended from the princes of both Powys and Gwynedd. In his youth, he had studied law at one of the London inns of court before serving with distinction in Richard II's Scottish campaign of 1385. Then, during the crisis of 1399, his allegiance had been given to Bolingbroke, after which he appears to have been looking forward to a future of comfortable, peaceable and highly civilised retirement at his idyllic fortified mansion of Sycherth.

A niggling squabble over a piece of land would, however, sweep Glyn Dŵr into the heart of what was to become the last great Welsh rebellion. For years he had been in dispute with his rival and neighbour, Lord Grey of Ruthin, an aggressive marcher lord who had seen fit to occupy a piece of territory belonging to the Welshman near his Deeside home. In less lawless areas, such a dispute would have been settled reasonably in court, but by 1400 it had degenerated into a series of bloody raids and counter-raids. To add insult to injury, Grey was known to be the king's personal friend, and when Glyn Dŵr came to London to plead his case, he not only failed, but was insulted into the bargain when King Henry rebuked him for failing to participate in the expedition against the Scots. On 16 September, therefore, Glyn Dŵr led a force against Grey and proceeded to burn Ruthin two days later, before attacking other English settlements at Denbigh, Rhuddlan, Flint, Hawarden and Holt.

Initially, at least, the king's response was to treat the trouble as one more episode in the time-honoured tradition of Welsh unruliness, which could be dealt with by the usual short, sharp application of force. Certainly, Henry IV had little regard for the Welsh themselves, dismissing them in one of his letters as 'of little reputation'.[7] And he decided to lead a punitive expedition through North Wales, in the company of his fourteen-year-old heir. Arriving at Shrewsbury on 26 September, the English force had returned to the same border town by 15 October with its mission apparently accomplished. According to Adam Usk, the rebels dispersed and Glyn Dŵr himself took to the mountains with only seven companions. Thereafter, his estates were confiscated and before the month was out, the king was back in London, convinced that the disturbances were at an end. Little did he know, however, that from its mountain bases in Snowdonia, Glyn Dŵr's guerrilla army would soon become a major threat not only to English rule in Wales, but to the Lancastrian dynasty itself.

Significantly, the king had left his eldest son behind at Chester with instructions to maintain order under the guidance of a council of marcher lords headed by the Earl of Northumberland's son, Henry Hotspur, who was to serve as his guide and mentor. But the prince was soon to discover that his father and his advisers had grossly underestimated the challenge before them. And on 21 February 1401 Parliament warned the king that a full-scale war in Wales was increasingly likely. For some months, in fact, Welsh labourers and even undergraduates from Oxford and Cambridge had been streaming home to take up Glyn Dŵr's cause, and by the middle of the year the whole of North Wales was engulfed in open revolt. By 1402, moreover, Glyn Dŵr himself had been proclaimed 'Prince of Wales' and was firmly in control, heading a national revolt, which received strong support from, among others, his powerful Tudor cousins in Anglesey.

What followed was to be a long, hard and often frustrating experience for the 'real' Prince of Wales, though he would learn much from his mistakes and forge a loyal band of talented comrades in the process. More importantly still, he would also acquire a battle-hardened edge of ruthless pragmatism, since the conflict itself was a bitter guerrilla war in which outrages from either side were common. Adam Usk tells us, for instance, that after one raid the English abducted a thousand Welsh children to be their servants, while Glyn Dŵr in a counter-raid 'sorely harried the countryside with fire and sword'.[8] Thomas Walsingham, meanwhile, records how after one particular English defeat there occurred 'a crime never heard of before' when certain Welsh women 'cut off the genitalia of the dead, put the member of each dead man in his mouth, and hung his testicles from his chin'.[9]

Clearly, Prince Henry would have ample opportunity in Wales to learn at close hand all the sordid realities of late medieval warfare, and neither he nor his father were any more – or less – inclined to clemency than other contemporaries. Usk, for example, relates how a certain Llewellyn ap Griffith Vaughan, 'of gentle birth and bountiful', was cruelly butchered at the king's command at Llandovery, 'because he was well disposed to the said Owain'.[10] The chronicler also makes it quite clear that the sentence was carried out in the actual presence of both the king and his eldest son. Likewise, when Prince Henry and Hotspur recaptured Conway Castle on Good Friday 1401, nine other Welshmen were similarly sentenced to be hanged until half-dead, before being disembowelled, castrated and beheaded – their innards being burned in front of them.

Perhaps it was hardly surprising, therefore, that as early as his mid-teens the prince was already displaying all the flint-faced detachment of a seasoned military campaigner. In a letter to the keepers of the marches, written after a typical raid, he remarked in passing how he had captured 'a gentleman of the neighbourhood who offered £500 for his ransom to preserve his life and to be allowed two weeks for the purpose of raising money'. But, said Henry, 'the offer was refused and he received the death'.[11] No doubt, the hapless Welsh gentleman had naively assumed that the chivalric code might somehow still hold good with a young prince who had already learned through hard experience that real war had little to do with romantic conventions.

Nevertheless, as the slaughter on both sides mounted, English efforts to crush the rebellion remained unavailing, and in August the Scots crossed the border, only to be routed at Homildon Hill by the Percies who captured five earls. However, from the king's point of view this victory did little to ease his position. On the contrary, his insistence that the prisoners must on no account be allowed to ransom themselves deprived the Percies – to whom he already owed £10,000 – of a valuable windfall and turned them against him once and for all. Moreover, the king's stubborn refusal to ransom Edmund Mortimer from captivity in Snowdonia led Mortimer to marry Glyn Dŵr's daughter and join the revolt. Even more ominously, when Hotspur went to see Henry in person to demand more money for the defence of the marches, the king is said to have concluded a heated argument by punching him full in the face. According to another version of events, Henry half-drew his dagger, only for Hotspur to reply ominously – 'Not here but in the field'.[12]

It was only to be expected, of course, that Hotspur's influence would have left a deep impression upon the heir to the throne. A contemporary of the king, in his late thirties, Hotspur was, in the words of Adam Usk, 'the flower and glory of the chivalry of Christendom' – a darling of the tournament crowds, whose popularity even made the imitation of his stutter fashionable.[13] Yet Prince Henry was quick to adopt Hotspur's successor, Hugh le Despenser, even though the latter's sudden death made the relationship a brief one. Significantly, the letter that Henry wrote to his father requesting a replacement betrays a genuine tenderness, as he speaks of 'a great weight of sorrow to my heart', and acknowledges the very great concern that Despenser had shown for his honour and estate.[14] No less significantly, however, the prince's nominations for a successor were roundly ignored by his father, though by this time the prince, now sixteen, was already being given more freedom in his military activity. On 7 March, indeed, he was officially declared to be his father's lieutenant on the Marches of Wales, with considerably increased military authority.

Two other letters of this period, both undated, illustrate very aptly the contrasting strains now appearing more and more prominently in the prince's personality. His concern for those close to him is apparent in the appeal he made to an unidentified abbot for the services of a particular monk who was said to know the cure for sciatica. The prince's chancellor at Chester was, it seems, a chronic sufferer and was therefore to be sent for treatment.[15] Meanwhile, Henry's hard-headed grasp of fine details is equally apparent in his order that no effort should be spared in apprehending and punishing those Welsh rebels who had murdered one of his officials. If this was not achieved, he wrote, 'from now on no Englishman will wish to be an officer in Wales'.[16]

Henry was increasingly displaying, too, the kind of boundless energy and determination in his new role for which he would become rightly famous. At the beginning of May 1403, for instance, he led a raiding party which burnt Glyn Dŵr's home and his tenants' houses at Cynllaith Owain before marching on to Glyndyfrdwy and destroying a handsome lodge also belonging to Glyn Dŵr. But Henry would soon be complaining about a serious lack of funds to pay his soldiers, who were threatening to abandon him. Indeed, he warned that unless money was forthcoming, the marches would have to be given up to the malice of the rebels once and for all, because 'without manpower we cannot do more than any other man of lesser estate'.[17] To emphasise his predicament, he pointed out that he had pawned his own jewels to sustain the besieged castles of Aberystwyth and Harlech. And in response the king and Council agreed to send £1,000, but offered no further help.

Yet it was not altogether unfortunate that Prince Henry was unable to prolong his Welsh campaign in the summer of 1403, for on the very day that the king announced his intention to join the Percies in a raid on Scotland, Henry Hotspur raised the standard of revolt at Chester. Setting out from the north, Hotspur aimed to raise the men of Cheshire and the northern Welsh marches, with the intention of seizing the Prince of Wales. Once this had been achieved, he would wait at leisure within the fortifications at Shrewsbury for the arrival of his uncle Thomas and father Henry, along with the Welsh hordes of Glyn Dŵr and Mortimer. When everything was in place, he would duly attack the king.

The impact upon the heir to the throne of his former mentor's treachery is sure to have been considerable, and if all Hotspur's forces had indeed combined as planned, there is no doubting their chances of success. Hotspur had not counted, however, on the speed and military skill of the king who was already marching north with a fair-sized army to deal with Scottish raiders when news of the revolt reached him. Marching forty-five miles in a single day, King Henry eventually arrived at Shrewsbury in the nick of time on 20 July. Nor had his son proved lacking, for while he waited the young prince had promptly gathered what forces he could muster.

The encounter that ensued at Shrewsbury on 21 July 1403 was, in fact, the first major battle of Prince Henry's life. And it was not without some irony that the Prince of Wales soon found himself faced with a barrage of arrows from Hotspur's Cheshire archers not dissimilar to the one he would inflict upon French men-at-arms at Agincourt in years to come. As Henry and his men struggled to advance uphill, the enemy were said to have drawn 'so fast that … the sun which at that time was bright and clear then lost its brightness, so thick were the arrows'. And in consequence the prince's men appear to have fallen 'as fast as leaves fall in autumn after the hoar-frost'.[18] Yet to Henry's credit, he did not flinch from his duty, even though he himself was seriously wounded. 'Lead me thus wounded to the front line', he is said to have declared, 'that I may, as a prince should, kindle our fighting men with deeds not words.'[19]

Hotspur, on the other hand, was dead by nightfall, along with at least 1,600 other men. Killed by an unknown hand as he raised his visor to wipe his brow, his soldiers had eventually broken and fled after a close-fought encounter, and by the next day his corpse lay in the pillory at Shrewsbury, propped up by two millstones. Not long after, his head would be on its way to York to be spiked on Micklegate Bar, leaving Thomas Percy, in his turn, to weep publicly over his dead nephew before being beheaded himself. Only Hotspur's father, in fact, was ultimately granted clemency, since he had missed the battle through illness and was still powerful enough to be granted a verdict of 'trespass' rather than treason from his peers.

The Prince of Wales, meanwhile, spent the night after the battle in outright agony, for his wound, which had been inflicted by an arrow to the left of his nose, was a truly grievous one. According to John Bradmore, the surgeon who removed it, the projectile had penetrated to a depth of six inches, lodging in the bone at the back of his skull, and the fact that the prince had continued to fight on regardless of the pleas of his comrades says much about him. Moreover, the suffering involved in the removal of the arrowhead, which Bradmore describes in detail, can well be imagined. Having cut through the prince's face to the depth of the wound, the surgeon applied tongs, which he had specially designed for the purpose. 'I put these tongs in at an angle', Bradmore writes, 'in the same way as the arrow had first entered, then placed the screw in the centre and finally the tongs entered the socket of the arrowhead. Then, by moving it to and fro, little by little (with the help of God), I extracted the arrowhead.'[20]

But although the wound began to heal over the next three weeks, the effect upon the prince's appearance and reputation would be lasting. The picture now hanging in the National Gallery is his only surviving portrait and the fact that he is depicted in profile is unlikely to be coincidental at a time when all other medieval English kings were depicted in three-quarter-face position. Yet that same scarring must also have had much broader consequences, since ambassadors, magnates, men-at-arms and ordinary soldiers alike will now have been immediately stuck – and deeply impressed – by such an authentic symbol of the young man's prowess. Not only was it the strongest possible token of his bravery and endurance, it would also become in due course a powerful talisman to convince his followers of victory against any foe at any odds.

For the time being, however, the prince's deeds against Hotspur had still brought no relief at all in Wales. Indeed, though Glyn Dŵr had been absent at Shrewsbury, the year 1404 would witness a further significant expansion of his influence. He concluded, for instance, a solemn treaty with the French in June and continued to enjoy a series of military and political successes. The great castles of Harlech and Aberystwyth were captured, and French soldiers assisted in an assault on Caernarvon, from where a lowly woman had been sent to warn the Constable of Chester of an impending attack, since no man was willing to take the risk. Glyn Dŵr was, moreover, sufficiently confident to summon his own Welsh Parliament to Machynlleth. And while the Welsh 'Prince of Wales' felt free even to raid and harry Herefordshire, the 'real' one still found himself starved of funds and groping for a foe he could never see.

Worse still, the threat to Henry's father actually appeared to be broadening during the first half of 1405. Around February, Glyn Dŵr forged a 'league and confederation' with Sir Edmund Mortimer and the Earl of Northumberland, who had not long before been granted mercy and ridden out of York at the king's side beneath his son's rotting head. According to the so-called 'Tripartite Indenture', the three conspirators were to divide up England and Wales between them, with Glyn Dŵr receiving Wales and a considerable part of western England, Northumberland taking the north and a large part of the Midlands, and Mortimer controlling what was left.

Yet such giddy ambition on behalf of the ringleaders would

prove misplaced, since two setbacks in Wales wholly undermined their plans. First, on the night of 11 March, Prince Henry wrote hurriedly to his father of the battle waged at Grosmont between some 8,000 Welsh rebels and a much smaller English force led by Lord Talbot. Between 800 and 1,000 Welshmen were killed in the encounter and in a phrase which would have particular significance in the light of his own later exploits, Henry declared how the incident had demonstrated that 'victory was not in a multitude of people, but in the power of God'.[21] Not long afterwards, in a battle fought at Pwyl-Melyn, the English also killed Glyn Dŵr's brother Tudor and captured his son Griffith, summarily beheading three hundred captives in the process.

Even so, there was still one last great conspiracy for Henry IV to overcome, involving the apparently irrepressible Earl of Northumberland, who had now, in his late sixties, contrived yet another scheme to avenge his family's honour. Thomas Mowbray, the Earl Marshal, was heavily involved in the plot, along with Lords Bardolf and Clifford. More spectacularly still, Richard le Scrope, Archbishop of York, also lent his support. But even such celebrity was no guarantee of success – or survival – and the rebels were unceremoniously crushed by the Earl of Westmorland's forces at Shipton Moor. In the aftermath, Mowbray was made to ride to his execution facing backwards in token of his ignominy, while Archbishop Scrope, too, was executed, albeit amid general outrage which even extended to Sir William Gascoigne, the Chief Justice. The Earl of Northumberland, on the other hand, once again demonstrated his consummate knack for survival by escaping to Scotland.

1405, therefore, had been a key year in Lancastrian fortunes and though the process of consolidation would be slow and arduous, it now began in earnest. Even luck, it seemed, was on Henry IV's side from this point onwards, for shortly after the savage suppression of the Scrope rebellion, the Scottish king decided to send James, his heir, to the friendly French court, on the grounds that his own land was close to civil war. However, the young prince was captured by Norfolk pirates who quickly despatched their rich prize to the king. In consequence, James of Scotland would remain an English prisoner for the next eighteen years, and the threat that he might be sent home was normally sufficient hereafter to keep the Scottish regent, the Duke of Albany, in check. Nor was this the end of Henry IV's good fortune, for the Earl of Northumberland was forced to leave Scotland in 1406, only to be cornered and killed by the Sheriff of Yorkshire at the Battle of Bramham Moor in 1408.

In the meantime, English pressure in Wales had also begun to pay dividends. On 5 April 1406, Prince Henry had been reappointed to the position of Lieutenant of Wales and now, at the age of twenty, he assumed outright military command. By this point, both he and his captains had realised that cumbersome campaigns conducted by great armies in search of an elusive foe would remain fruitless. Instead, the emphasis was increasingly placed upon the capture of castles and the relentless pressure of small bands of soldiers, with the intention of wearing down and, if necessary, starving the rebels into submission. Where possible, Henry and his men also offered liberal terms of pardon, and this combination of the stick and the carrot now proved increasingly effective. Though the Welsh managed to hold on at Aberystwyth and Harlech during 1407, their losses had been mounting elsewhere. In 1406, for instance, following the example of the South Welsh, 2,000 men of Anglesey, the granary of North Wales, submitted, and by the following year Glyn Dŵr was confined to the mountainous west and centre of the country.

Henceforth, Welsh resistance would remain stubborn but unavailing, though it would be wrong, perhaps, to ascribe too much personal credit to the Prince of Wales. From 1408 the prince continued in nominal command, but was rarely present in person. The king had, moreover, been less willing to give him his head than is sometimes appreciated. Indeed, he had only been forced to, it seems, because of his own physical decline and the conflicting demands on his time. Besides which, the Welsh had outwitted their opponents on too many occasions and the war had dragged on far longer than it should have done – not least of all because of a serious military blunder by Prince Henry at the siege of Aberystwyth in the late summer of 1407.

The king had intended to conduct the assault in person and instructed his eldest son to join him in what was fully intended to be the decisive blow to Glyn Dŵr's insurgents. Ultimately, however, the prince was given full control at Aberystwyth in his first major siege and he duly gathered about him most of his closest associates, including the Duke of York, Richard Beauchamp, Earl of Warwick, Lords Furnival and Carew, and Sir John Oldcastle. Leaving Harlech to the Talbots, he was also joined by large numbers of other knights eager to be in at the end of the Welsh revolt.

Yet the English guns and siege engines, which had arrived by sea in large numbers from Bristol and Haverfordwest, proved surprisingly ineffective, and it was not long before Prince Henry had painfully demonstrated his own rawness and naivety. With assault impossible, he first attempted to starve the garrison into submission and then agreed on 17 September 1407 to lift the siege for more than a month, allowing the defenders free exit and entry, in return for a guarantee that Glyn Dŵr would come to open battle between 24 October and 1 November. If no battle occurred, the castle was to be surrendered without the need to provide hostages.

What followed, however, was to be a source of acute embarrassment to the young prince, for in spite of his wish to win a glorious victory in his own right, no royal army was organised and as a result Glyn Dŵr was able to enter Aberystwyth at the beginning of November, duly expelling those Welshmen who had made the agreement with Henry in the first place. Ultimately, therefore, the stronghold was not captured until September of the following year – and only then by others rather than the prince himself. His mistake had been both costly and humiliating, and needless to say he would not risk the consequences of such extreme clemency again.

On balance, however, the young prince's hard lessons in Wales had still taught him much about the practical and moral principles of contemporary warfare. Not least, Henry had acquainted himself fully with siegecraft and the use of artillery, and he had also mastered the art of controlling large areas of conquered territory by small, carefully placed garrisons. He had learned, too, how to employ ships to supply isolated garrisons in coastal fortresses, just as he would one day exploit inland waterways across the Channel for the same purpose. And he now knew how to employ very limited manpower to maximum effect, combining the lethal firepower of his bowmen with mobility over long distances, by giving them horses and encouraging them to carry their own fodder. Most importantly of all, he had taught himself how to use a potent mixture of systematic terror, artificially induced famine and cunningly conceived shows of conciliation to both cow and win over an enemy. In short, he had gained his first grounding in the kind of warfare that he would later hone to perfection in France.

The condition of France

While Henry IV was struggling so desperately against all manner of weakness and division at home, it was hardly surprising, perhaps, that his kingdom was reduced to virtual impotence abroad. Indeed, throughout the first half of his reign, Henry's French enemies probed and goaded at every opportunity, while he in turn was left with little choice other than to hold and endure as best he might. Though the truce of the previous reign was not officially broken, its renewal was nevertheless purposely delayed and, even afterwards, the French stubbornly refused to acknowledge Henry as King of England. To add salt to the wound, the Dauphin had been named 'duc de Guienne' in January 1401 – a direct affront to English overlordship in that territory under the peace of Brétigny.

Nor did the French hesitate to aggravate matters over the next five years. They chose, for instance, to continue their alliance with the Scots, sending armed support in 1402, and in October of the following year Charles VI's brother Louis, Duke of Orléans, was behind a direct incursion into Gascony. At the same time, English shipping found itself under constant attack from French-condoned acts of piracy, many of which were launched from the port of Harfleur. In July 1404, moreover, the French even saw fit to recognise Owain Glyn Dŵr as Prince of Wales and ally with him against the common enemy, whom they insultingly dismissed as 'Henry of Lancaster'.[22] One year later, they were ready to land troops at Milford Haven to assist their Welsh allies, and from October 1406 they duly began to threaten the very heartlands of Gascony, when the Duke of Orléans besieged the castle of Bourg-sur Gironde.

But if appearances suggested that the political and military initiative lay firmly with England's enemy, a subsequent twist of events would soon prove otherwise, for the King of France was actually in effective control of no more than two-thirds of his realm and was now increasingly threatened by the actions of his own subjects. The mightiest French dukes, after all, controlled huge conglomerations of rich estates, along with large armies of vassals.

If the king was strong, he might control his most powerful fiefs. But if he was weak or indisposed in any way, then his strongest nobles had every opportunity to push for greater autonomy. In consequence, while England was racked by internal dissension at the start of the fifteenth century, outright civil war was just around the corner for France.

The central source of France's weakness was, in fact, the intermittent madness of her king, which first manifested itself suddenly and violently in the summer of 1392. On 1 July, the amiable, dreamy and sentimental Charles VI – known to his subjects, for good reason, as 'Well-beloved' – had set out with a military force to punish a would-be assassin by the name of Pierre de Craon, who was taking refuge in Brittany. Observers noted at the time of Charles's departure from Paris that he was already suffering from a fever and speaking disjointedly, but as the journey progressed he became increasingly disturbed until he was driven into a near frenzy by the slow progress of his army through a forest, to the west of Le Mans. It was at this point, it seems, that a barefoot leper dressed in rags rushed up to him, grabbed the bridle of his horse and added to his agitation by warning him that he had been betrayed. Shortly afterwards, when a page startled him by dropping his lance, the king's mind appears to have broken irrevocably in the blinding heat, and in a state of utter panic, he proceeded to kill no less than four of his knights before collapsing and falling into a coma.

Thereafter, in spite of a range of desperate remedies which included exorcism, crude trephining of his skull and seclusion in dark and heavily shuttered rooms, Charles would continue to suffer from bouts of mental illness throughout his life. During one attack in 1393, for instance, the tormented monarch could not remember who he was. On some occasions he also ran wildly through the corridors of his Parisian residence, the Hôtel de Saint Pol, so that the entrances had to be walled up in an effort to keep him inside. At other times he believed he was made of glass and ordered that iron rods be inserted into his clothes to prevent him from breaking. Then in 1405 he refused to bathe or change his clothes for all of five months. And yet, perhaps worse still, there were also times when Charles's sanity returned, adding to the political instability and making any permanent solution impossible.

The impact of Charles's derangement could not therefore have been more profound. Most obviously of all, when the king was 'in his malady' it was never clear who should assume the reins of government, and this led to particularly bitter enmity between two men above all others. On the one hand, there was Charles's younger brother Louis, Duke of Orléans – a depraved libertine in his late twenties, who was suspected, among other things, of fathering several children by the queen, and of using her to secure a political advantage when the king was ill. And then there was the king's uncle, Philip the Bold, Duke of Burgundy – an imposing veteran in his fifties, who had married the richest heiress in Europe, Margaret of Flanders, and now ruled a great principality stretching from the Somme to the Scheldt, together with his wife's lands in Burgundy. Holding court in regal splendour at his two capitals of Dijon and Brussels, his aim was to acquire by any means the land separating the two great blocks of territory he controlled, for if he could do so his power would increase enormously.

With so much at stake, the potential for open aggression was always considerable, though it was only some time after Philip the Bold's death in 1404 that events finally spiralled out of control. By that point, the Duke of Orléans had assumed firm control of the government and established a stranglehold on finance and patronage, which was rapidly plunging the already over-stretched administration of Burgundy's disparate lands into crisis. To compound matters, Orléans had also earned the bitter resentment of the people of Paris for his high taxes and scandalous immorality. He had, it was said, raped the wives of several knights and now maintained a private portrait gallery of the women he had preyed upon. On one occasion he had even paraded the masked and naked wife of a Picard knight before him and asked the unwitting husband to judge her beauty in the presence of an assembly of onlookers. Yet Philip the Bold's successor, John the Fearless, had little more to recommend him. Indeed, the new Duke of Burgundy could not have been more poorly named, for far from being a knightly paragon, he was, in fact, an ugly, cynical and treacherous little man whose prestige had never fully recovered from his capture by the Turks at Nicopolis in 1396.

But if Duke John's moral credentials for leadership were virtually non-existent, it was precisely this that made him such a formidable foe and enabled him to give a new and bloody edge to the power politics that his father had already been pursuing so assiduously before him. It was around eight o'clock on the evening of 23 November 1407, in fact, that Louis of Orléans was cruelly hacked to death by his rival's paid assassins in an ill-lit Paris street near the Porte Barbette. He had been travelling in the company of only five attendants when a group of seven or eight assailants, led by the Norman knight Raoul d'Anquetonville, dragged him from his horse and hacked at him with their swords before finally despatching him with a blow to the head from a halberd. Thereafter, his body was left lying in the gutter, its hands crudely removed to prevent necromancers from raising the devil with it.

Next day, while the *prévôt* of Paris began his investigations, Louis's servants found the severed hands and scattered brains of their murdered master, and placed them in a lead box in his coffin. As news spread, the full implications of the deed were soon apparent. When the King of England had secretly murdered his cousin seven years earlier, all France had condemned him in the most uncompromising terms. But that, at least, had been done in the name of political stability, while Louis's murder could only be interpreted as the most blatant act of opportunism on the Duke of Burgundy's part. Moreover, the perpetrator was soon feigning full mourning as he accompanied his victim's remains to the church of the Celestines, in the company of the dukes of Anjou, Berry and Bourbon. He had struck in cold blood and if his enemy was hardly deserving of undue sympathy, the subsequent pretence of grief fooled no one and settled nothing. On the contrary, it was merely one more shameful episode in a tale of murderous rivalry that would ruin France for more than a generation and provide England with her long-awaited opportunity.

The threshold of power

Since the summer of 1405 Henry IV had been suffering from an agonising and disfiguring affliction of the skin, which both he and others took to be a divine judgement for the execution of Archbishop Scrope. The first attack, which produced an intense burning sensation, had left him screaming in agony, and though it soon subsided, it continued to return regularly in the years ahead. Worse still, early in 1408 Henry suffered an epileptic fit, which left his attendants convinced for some hours that he was dead. Once again he recovered, but now a further physical and mental decline set in. According to Adam Usk, Henry suffered 'an infection' from this time to the end of his life, which resulted ultimately in 'festering of the flesh, dehydration of the eyes, and rupture of the internal organs'.[23]

So at the very time that the heir to the throne was freshly returned from his frustrations in Wales and more eager than ever to make his mark, his father was stricken by a debilitating illness, which would leave him only spasmodically fit to govern. Yet the king still had no intention of forsaking his crown and, in consequence, the prince found himself alternately de facto head of state and political bystander. Not altogether surprisingly, therefore, rumours of tension and disagreement between father and son were soon common, and nowhere more so, perhaps, than with regard to developments across the Channel.

Charles of Orléans, son of the murdered Duke Louis, had been married in 1409 to the daughter of Bernard VII, the mighty Count of Armagnac, and by the following year Orléanist opposition to the Duke of Burgundy had crystallised into a powerful 'Armagnac' party, which took its name from Charles's hard-bitten and overbearing father-in-law. The new Duke of Orléans, a poet of some distinction, was in fact of an altogether nobler mould than both Count Bernard, his main supporter, and the man whom he now implacably opposed, John the Fearless. But this would mean little in the struggle that lay ahead.

From the English perspective, of course, the key consideration was which side to support. A Burgundian alliance would, for example, allow England to secure and consolidate her great bridgehead at Calais with its links to the Flemish cloth trade. The Armagnacs, however, could ensure the security of Gascony as an English appanage and the safety of its profitable wine trade, centred on Bordeaux. Both, moreover, might ultimately provide an English king with free entry into the heart of France, or so at least it seemed.

In theory, therefore, the two sides had much to offer, and neither the King of England nor his heir could reasonably be expected to spurn such a tempting opportunity. Indeed, as the civil wars in France intensified, English demands would grow exponentially.

Initially, there was the prospect of marriage between the daughter of the Duke of Burgundy and the Prince of Wales, and before long there was also the option of Catherine, the daughter of the King of France, with an even greater dowry. Then there was the balance of the ransom of John II, captured at Poitiers in 1356, to be bargained for, along with the whole of Aquitaine, or even, for that matter, the entire Angevin empire, including Normandy. By the early years of Henry V's reign, in fact, the English would be demanding the crown of France itself, though such dreams still lay in the future, and for the time being the King of England and his heir were divided – the former more inclined to keep his options open, the latter firmly supporting a Burgundian alliance.

The prince, meanwhile, had every confidence in his ability to press his case against his ailing father. Young, strong and brave, with a flair for showmanship, he now lived in a 'right fair and stately house' called Coldharbour in Eastcheap and was praised from all directions.[24] Parliament extolled his courage and good sense. Tradesmen were encouraged by his extravagance. His friends, in their turn, bathed in his generosity and protection. Certainly, his surviving correspondence leaves no doubt about his willingness to help those close to him. In one letter, for instance, he asks pardon from a bishop for one of his servants, who had been excommunicated for carelessly allowing one of the prince's hounds to kill animals on the bishop's estates in Sussex. On another more famous occasion the heir to the throne was even said to have struck the Chief Justice in the face as a result of some false charge laid against a member of his household.

But in demonstrating loyalty, young Henry also commanded it, and by 1409 he was assisted on the Council by a talented core of supporters who would back him resolutely in his struggle with the older councillors favoured by his father. Most prominent among the prince's allies were his Beaufort uncles, Henry and Thomas. At the same time, two young friends were also emerging as key figures in the prince's party: the Earl of Warwick, a renowned jouster who was steadily confirming his reputation as 'the master of courtesy', and the Earl of Arundel who had fought with distinction alongside Prince Henry in Wales. Another friend and supporter enjoying increasing visibility was Henry Chichele who had already risen to become Bishop of St David's.

To this group, too, should be added Henry's two brothers, John and Humphrey. The former in particular, though still in his early twenties, was an especially valuable prop to his elder sibling's cause. Highly competent and wholly trustworthy, he was already serving as Warden of the East March against the Scots and steadily establishing a firm reputation for caution and prudence. Well-educated and sensitive, he possessed, it is true, all the pride, drive and hauteur associated with the warrior caste to which he undoubtedly belonged. But the potentially fiery streak in his personality was also tempered by compassion, piety and total loyalty.

By contrast, Prince Henry's eldest brother Thomas stood out firmly against him at this time. A year younger than Henry, the future Duke of Clarence was, in fact, a handsome, brave and energetic competitor who was seen by many as the more natural leader of the two. As such, it was not altogether surprising, perhaps, that Thomas would spend most of his life attempting in dramatic and courageous ways to outshine his older brother – though not, it must be said, by compromising his loyalty. Very much a sportsman and a soldier, with a bastard son upon whom he doted, he had already served as the King's Lieutenant in Ireland. Equally significantly, he had also quarrelled with the Beauforts over the inheritance of his wife, who was the widow of their eldest brother. Moreover, as the row raged over the 30,000 marks that Bishop Beaufort had received as his brother's executor, Prince Henry had taken the bishop's side.

But Thomas was not the only source of resistance that Henry and his followers now faced on the Council. Composed of a minority of conservatives like the king's brother-in-law, the Earl of Westmorland, the opposing party was headed by Thomas Arundel, Archbishop of Canterbury, who had accompanied the king into exile after the lists at Coventry and had stood by him just as firmly since his appointment as Chancellor on 30 January 1407. Now in his mid-fifties, Arundel's presence had helped to ease Henry IV's relations with the nobility and given a greater aura of legitimacy to the king's actions. Yet he, too, had fallen out with Henry Beaufort when the latter fathered a bastard child by his niece, and he had subsequently been behind the decision to bar both Beauforts from the succession. To compound matters, he had also quarrelled with his nephew, the Earl of Arundel, over their lands in Sussex.

There were, moreover, concerns about policy as well as personal differences to fuel the growing divisions. Though the threat from Glyn Dŵr and the Percies gradually subsided during Archbishop Arundel's three year stint as head of the Council, frustration had still increased over the government's failure to exploit the growing political chaos in France. There was increasing concern, too, over the Crown's ongoing financial plight. While customs revenue from wool had by now increased to an average of £36,000 per year, this was still 20 per cent less than for Richard's reign, and the long arrears of the Calais garrison had only been paid ultimately by a large loan from Richard Whittington, Lord Mayor of London. To make matters worse, government was seriously disrupted during the winter of 1408-9 when the king became so ill that he made his will and prepared for death.

The long autumn Parliament of 1406 had, in fact, already forced a series of articles upon Henry IV, which reduced his control and left the balance of power firmly in the hands of his Council. From this point onwards his ability to seek advice from men who were neither recognised nor in many cases paid as councillors was strictly curtailed. Instead, he would have to rule with the advice of a known group of men who were sworn to observe clear instructions laid down by Parliament for their conduct, attendance and responsibilities. Above all, however, the Council was given full power over financial policy in an effort to bring expenditure on the royal household under control.

Significantly, 1406 also witnessed the first signs of growing political prominence for the Prince of Wales. At the end of November, for example, he is known to have witnessed one of his father's charters, and at the beginning of December he made his first recorded appearance on the Council. The following year, he was present at about two-thirds of Council meetings and also received the thanks of Parliament for his efforts in Wales. During 1408 and 1409, moreover, his attendance at Council meetings continued to increase.

But this was still only the start of a process, which would ultimately bring the heir to the throne into direct competition with his father. In February 1409, for instance, he was appointed Constable of Dover and Warden of the Cinque Ports, before being named as Captain of Calais – one of the most important of all

Crown appointments – on 18 March of the following year. Indeed, by 1409, as his commitments in Wales continued to subside and his father succumbed increasingly to the ravages of his illness, the prince began to assume a position of outright primacy on the Council.

It was of no little significance either that both Archbishop Arundel and Sir John Tiptoft, the treasurer, resigned their posts in December 1409. Both were dominating figures, and though the reasons for their departure were never stated in the conciliar records, they seem to have been connected with parliamentary pressure concerning finance and the problem of law and order. Now, therefore, the Prince of Wales and his supporters were well placed to seize the initiative, and by the time Parliament convened at the end of January, they were firmly in control. Bishop Beaufort delivered the opening address, and four days later his brother was installed as Chancellor.

For all of 1410 and most of 1411, therefore, the prince dominated the Council and made every effort to impose his personal stamp upon policy, especially in the sphere of finance, where he pressed for a much-needed programme of sustained retrenchment on terms that suited the Crown. He did so, too, in the face of what would prove to be very significant opposition, and during 1410 he was involved in heated exchanges with MPs over the issue of supply. Yet the decision in the same year to devalue the currency in response to the endemic bullion crisis in Europe gave a foretaste of the prince's willingness to undertake any measure necessary for the long-term health of the realm irrespective of the short-term unpopularity he might incur. And even if his overall efforts were neither wholly fruitful nor entirely warmly welcomed, they at least demonstrated an integrity and realism that would eventually cause Parliament to record its thanks to him in November 1411.

In the meantime, the prince displayed characteristic craft and boldness in his treatment of the Earl of March, who remained potentially the most dangerous individual in the realm. As the rightful heir to Richard II, the now seventeen-year-old noble had been kept in constant custody by Henry IV, but the king was by this stage too ill to demur when the prince chose to accommodate the earl in the comparative freedom of his own household. Interestingly, such carefully calculated gestures of conciliation would become an established tactic in the early stages of the next reign when, as Henry V, the prince sought to win over potentially hostile magnates to his cause.

And while his father lay stricken, Henry also inflicted his first significant blow in defence of religious orthodoxy. In March 1410, the heir to the throne presided at the trial of a Lollard tailor called John Badby who had denied transubstantiation, saying that the consecrated Host was an inanimate object more abhorrent than any toad or spider. The prince was responsible, too, for a curious attempt at clemency when the sentence of burning was finally carried out at Smithfield. Placed in a flaming barrel, Badby began at one point to groan miserably, whereupon the prince had him removed. Even at this late stage, Henry was, it seems, prepared to stretch the law to the limit by considering a pardon, and even offering a grant of three pence a day into the bargain, if the heretic duly recanted. Nevertheless, when Badby's spirits revived and he stubbornly maintained his heretical beliefs, the prince showed no hesitation in once more consigning him to the flames until he was dead. Clearly, where justice, necessity and matters of state were concerned, there were already definite limits to the prince's compassion.

The same remorseless logic was also focusing Henry's attention more and more intently across the Channel. His attempt to rectify the royal finances was underpinned in no small measure by warlike thinking, and while he was urging economy in government, he was already drawing up estimates for the cost of maintaining Calais in time of conflict. By now John the Fearless of Burgundy was in full control of Paris, where he had persuaded the Sorbonne to condemn the late Louis of Orléans as a tyrant, so that he could obtain a pardon from the king on the grounds that the assassination had been tyrannicide rather than murder. The pardon had indeed been granted and Louis's son Charles, the new Duke of Orléans, was left with little choice other than to forgive his father's murderer at an acrimonious ceremony at Chartres on 9 March 1409. Before April was out, however, the anti-Burgundian League of Gien had been formed, consisting of Charles of Orléans, the dukes of Berry and Brittany, and the counts of Alençon, Armagnac and Clermont.

In such circumstances, the Duke of Burgundy had no real option but to seek assistance from England, and in August 1411, in return for immediate military aid, he finally offered Prince Henry the hand of his daughter, together with four Flemish ports and the promise of future compliance in the English conquest of Normandy at some later date. The English, in their turn, demanded reciprocal military aid in recovering lands and possessions in Guienne. And though there is no evidence that the Burgundians eventually agreed to it, Prince Henry and his Council even went so far as to demand Duke John's full commitment to fight against his own sovereign when required.

Accordingly, on 3 October an expedition of 800 men-at-arms and 2,000 archers sailed from Dover under the leadership of Prince Henry's friend, the Earl of Arundel. Although comparatively small, the force nevertheless included both Gilbert Umfraville and Sir John Oldcastle – two knights of particular distinction – and eventually acquitted itself with no small merit. Arriving at Sluys, Arundel's men then marched to Paris where, after a sharp encounter at St Cloud, they assisted the Burgundians in securing the capital. The Armagnacs, on the other hand, were subsequently left with no choice but to retreat beyond the Loire. By the end of the year, therefore, the first overseas campaign associated with the prince had been completed with considerable success and the episode left him in little doubt of what a more impressive army might achieve in future.

Yet the claim that Arundel's force was a private one sponsored by the Prince of Wales against his father's will is open to question. For in mid-August the king himself had ordered all those holding royal annuities to muster in London on 23 September – a strong sign that he was on the road to recovery and preparing to press home the advantage against the French in his own right. Ironically, therefore, Arundel's expedition actually marked the imminent end of Prince Henry's dominance of the Council and the start of a period in the political wilderness that would not end until his father's death. It also served to fuel a growing tension between father and son, which would result ultimately in ominous rumours of an outright struggle for the crown itself.

In October six knights, including the steward of the prince's household, were arrested on an unspecified charge, while the prince himself left London on a progress that seemed to some an appeal for wider support. By November, moreover, the king had recovered sufficiently to dismiss Henry Beaufort as Chancellor and reappoint

Archbishop Arundel. In the process, Prince Henry too was removed from the Council, and to compound his frustration, his brother Thomas now replaced him as the key figure at the Council table, effectively excluding him from any part in government.

The most obvious sign, however, that the king had recovered his old decisiveness was an outright and complete reversal of English allegiance in France. Though he seems to have had no intrinsic objection to his heir's previous alliance with Burgundy, the Armagnacs now made an approach that was simply too good to refuse. And on 18 May, by the Treaty of Bourges, their leaders not only surrendered extensive territory in Aquitaine, but also agreed to do homage to the King of England for any land they held there, in return for an army of 4,000 men. Nor was this the end of Prince Henry's embarrassment. For in June his brother Thomas was appointed to head the planned campaign across the Channel, and one month later, at a Council meeting in Rotherhithe, he was also created Duke of Clarence. As a further twist of the knife, the younger brother was named King's Lieutenant in Aquitaine, even though Prince Henry had been Duke of Aquitaine since his father's coronation.

Nevertheless, Clarence's expedition was not ultimately the military and political triumph that he and his father had hoped for. A force of 3,000 archers and 1,000 men-at-arms would sail from Southampton on 10 August with good reason for high hopes. Among Clarence's commanders, after all, were three particularly distinguished figures, all of whom were members of the extended Lancastrian family and all of whom would feature prominently in the Agincourt campaign three years later: the king's cousin Edward, Duke of York; the king's bastard brother Sir Thomas Beaufort, who had recently been made Earl of Dorset; and the prince's uncle by marriage Sir John Cornwaille, who was renowned as one of the greatest knights of the day. But even before the English force had arrived in France, the Armagnacs and Burgundians had secretly come to terms, leaving Clarence with little option, after he had been duly bought off with 210,000 gold crowns, to vent his frustration in a spate of pillage and slaughter as he marched south to winter in Bordeaux.

Back in England, meanwhile, ugly rumours were circulating that the Prince of Wales might be intending to seize the throne.

Fourteen years later, Bishop Beaufort would deny before Parliament that any such plans had ever existed, and his refutation was duly accepted. But at least one contemporary English chronicle, as well as the early sixteenth-century account, the *First English Life of Henry V*, gave credence to the rumours.[25] Moreover, if the French chronicler Monstrelet is to be believed, Beaufort had actually been sent to Paris as early as 1406 to negotiate a marriage treaty with the French, involving Prince Henry and Richard II's widow Isabella, as a result of which Henry IV would 'lay down his crown and invest his son with the government of the kingdom'.[26]

Prince Henry's actions in the summer of 1412 did little to quell suspicions. After his removal from the Council, he withdrew from the court to the north midlands, where he busied himself raising soldiers – in support, or so he claimed in a letter written at Coventry on 17 June, of his father's wish to make good his rights in Aquitaine. At the same time, he also proclaimed his utter fidelity to his father, though his subsequent decision to ride to London with a host of supporters to protest his innocence seems to have had the opposite effect initially. The capital was, in fact, tense and unsure of the outcome when the heir to the throne arrived at Westminster to deny the accusations of his enemies. And even after he had knelt before his father and offered him his dagger for 'my life is not so desirous to me that I would live one day that I should be to your displeasure', the matter was still not disposed of entirely neatly.[27] Though King Henry duly embraced his son, he concluded that the slanderers should be dealt with by Parliament rather than himself.

The sources of all this tension between father and son are not, in fact, especially difficult to trace, though the question remains whether some of the allegedly more excessive aspects of the prince's behaviour may well have been the result rather than the cause of his difficulties with the king. Curbed, cowed and politically neutered by the man who had become a jaded caricature of the role model he had once been, it was hardly surprising, perhaps, if the prince sought some solace in wayward behaviour. And although there is no clear-cut historical justification for Shakespeare's depiction of Prince Hal's wild youth, too many chroniclers mention it for it to be entirely dismissed. Bastards there were not, but the otherwise hagiographic *Gesta* acknowledges that the heir to the throne was no saint. 'Passing the bounds of modesty', we are told, 'he was the fervent soldier of Venus as well as of Mars; youthlike he was fired by her torches.'[28] Nor is such a claim in any way implausible. For the prince had lived shoulder to shoulder with fighting men since the age of thirteen.

And if Wales or Chester offered meagre pickings for loose living, the many temptations of London were all around him during the winter months when medieval warfare froze to a halt. Coldharbour, the former town house of the Black Prince, where he now resided, lay conveniently near to London Bridge and the Hay Wharf, and it seems that he spent a good deal of time there – occasionally beating up and robbing his own household officials, if some of the tales of the day are to be believed. Certainly, his brothers Thomas and Humphrey were involved in a midnight brawl at a tavern in Eastcheap, as a result of which the Mayor himself had to be called out to restore order. Yet just how far Henry himself really was Falstaff's 'good shallow young fellow' remains uncertain, not least because the real Sir John Fastolf was a flint-faced professional soldier who had little time for frivolity or excess of any kind.

In any event, it was clear by the end of 1412 that Prince Henry's long period of waiting and frustration was finally edging to a conclusion. During December the king was unconscious for a period, and though he recovered sufficiently to celebrate Christmas at Eltham, from February onwards the business of the Council was assented to by the prince – even though he was still not officially a member of that body. Moreover, another seizure now proved the king's last, leaving him to die on 20 March 1413 in the so-called 'Jerusalem chamber' of the abbot's lodging at Westminster.

For almost a decade, in fact, Henry IV's health had rendered him a pale shadow of the dynamic knight who had captivated Londoners in the crisis of 1399 and gone on to seize the throne. But his resourcefulness and sheer tenacity had made him the consummate survivor at a time when survival was, perhaps, the most that could be asked of any English king. He had faced invasion from Scotland, a prolonged rebellion in Wales and three internal revolts led by his most powerful nobles and even an archbishop. Yet he had largely outlived the stigma of usurpation by the time of his death and handed over a viable, if uneasy, inheritance to his eldest son.

As for the heir himself, the urge to succeed, in both senses of the term, was now stronger than ever. From his own perspective, he had never been given the role he believed was rightly his. He had, it is true, gained substantial military experience in Wales, but his campaigns had mainly been small-scale, inconclusive and underfunded. Likewise, his work at the head of the Council had never been completed and when the time arrived for him to prove himself against the French, that opportunity, too, had been snatched away. Even his father's final breaths were to be tantalisingly drawn out. If Monstrelet is to be trusted, the king rallied at that very point when the prince assumed him dead. As the heir lifted the crown from a bedside table to try it on, the stricken king was said to have stirred once more and asked his son what right he had to it, since he himself had none. However, if the crown was not quite his even now, the prince's reply to his father's question could not have been more decisive, or, for that matter, more prophetic. 'As you have kept it by the right of your sword', he is said to have declared, 'so I will keep it while my life lasts.'[29]

3   Unity and honour, 1413–15

The new king and the new regime

What Henry V had not yet gained in terms of glory, he was now well placed to acquire on the back of hard-earned experience and a burning desire to transform both his own and his kingdom's fortunes. Some chroniclers speak, in fact, of an immediate and lasting change in the new king's behaviour once the throne was finally his. 'As soon as he was invested with the emblems of royalty', wrote Thomas Walsingham, 'he suddenly became another man.'[1] In Tito Livio's account, too, he at once 'reformed and amended his life and manners so that there was never no youth nor wildness that might have any place in him, but all his acts were suddenly changed into gravity and discretion'.[2] On the very night of his father's death, it was said, Henry sought out a hermit at Westminster Abbey. And here, over the course of several hours, he apparently confessed his sins and pledged himself to the heavy tasks that lay before him – the clearest possible sign of a new intensity and sense of purpose that would characterise the reign to come.[3]

Yet even allowing for the obvious tendency of so many contemporary and near-contemporary commentators to worship at his shrine, there seems no compelling reason to doubt that Henry V cut a genuinely regal figure from the outset. Though he was lightly made and may have seemed more like a prelate than a soldier to the French astrologer Jean Fusoris, who met him in the summer of 1415, many accounts bear witness, for instance, to Henry's physical prowess.[4] He excelled, it seems, as an athlete and could hurl great iron bars and heavy stones. He was also a tireless huntsman.[5] And on campaign he showed similar endurance, bearing extremes of weather without complaint and displaying an indomitable will in the presence of pain or danger. In the thick of battle, he often preferred to fight without a helmet and wore a suit of heavy armour 'as though it were a light cloak'.[6]

From other perspectives, too, the new king appears to have had much to recommend him. According to the author of the *Gesta*, he was, at the time of his accession, '*etate iuvenis set maturitate senex*': in age a young man, in maturity an old.[7] Having apparently dismissed all but four of the wilder members of his household and replaced them with twelve gentlemen specially selected by his grandmother for their sobriety and good sense, he now came to embody all those qualities befitting a ruler anointed by God himself. In the words of a monk of Westminster Abbey, he was 'devout, abstemious, liberal to the poor, sparing of promises – but true to his word, once given; a quick, wide-awake man, though at times reserved and moody, intolerant of laxity in priests, chivalrous towards women and rigid in repressing riot and crime'.[8] He was also, we are told, accessible, just and generous to his subjects, and neither proud in victory nor downcast when misfortune came.[9] 'As you know', he would later tell his soldiers, 'the fortunes of war vary: but if you desire a good outcome, you must keep your courage intact.'[10]

Henceforth strict self-discipline would be one of the new king's most striking features. It was said by Bishop Courtenay that from the day of his father's death until his marriage to Catherine of France in June 1420, Henry 'never had knowledge carnally of women' – something which has prompted at least one commentator to speculate about Henry's general uneasiness with the opposite sex.[11] Certainly, he spent little time in the company of females and it is true that of the forty individuals mentioned in his will, only two were women – his stepmother, Queen Joan, and his grandmother. It is also true that unlike some of his forebears, Henry did not tolerate prostitutes at court, though nothing here is essentially inconsistent with the traditional image of a godly, chivalrous ruler strenuously applying the high standards of his office – especially when the ruler concerned would, in any case, spend so much of his life on campaign in the sole company of other males.

A man who said little and listened much, Henry would remain an enigmatic and highly potent mixture of kingly qualities. Unlike some leaders, he avoided casual profanity and did not engage in lengthy speeches. His answers were short and to the point and delivered mostly in 'a low tone of voice'.[12] In his letters, meanwhile, there are glimpses of a certain intensity and brusqueness, which might well be expected from any man of action. His instruction to Sir John Tiptoft, ambassador to the Holy Roman Emperor, is perhaps typical in this respect. 'Tiptoft', the letter begins curtly, 'I charge you by the faith you owe to me that ye keep this matter, hereafter written, from all men secret save from my brother the Emperor's own person ... Keepeth this charge as ye will keep all that ye may forfeit to me.'[13] Yet the lack of frills is indicative, too, of a controlled and analytical mind.

And if Henry V did not waste words, he neither altogether lacked nor disdained them. Though never a scholar, he was certainly well read and maintained a large library to which he was always adding. His copy of Chaucer's *Troylus and Cryseyde*, for instance, still survives and he kept other contemporary works, such as Lydgate's *Life of Our Lady* and Hoccleve's *De Regimine Principum*, both of which were dedicated in his honour. Histories of the Crusades and a range of devotional treatises were also in his possession, as well as a complete set of the works of Gregory the Great.

There were other accomplishments, too. According to Tito Livio, the king 'delighted in song and musical instruments' and in years to come he would carry his harp with him on campaign, along with his band of minstrels and musicians of the chapel.[14] On the other hand, Henry was also able to look as well as play the part of the king, for although he seems to have preferred a simple, almost austere way of life, he nevertheless cared about his appearance. His clothes were elegant and rich – sometimes stunningly so when occasion demanded.

Yet Henry V's reputation would ultimately stand or fall, of course, on the basis of his political talent. And like many exceptional leaders, he lost little time in demonstrating extraordinary self-confidence, especially when it came to laying aside old enmities and setting his personal stamp upon government. From the very beginning of his reign the new king employed a shrewd policy of calculated conciliation with his enemies, not unlike the one he had already employed on a more modest scale in Wales. The young earls of Salisbury, Huntingdon and Oxford, for instance, all had their lands restored, in spite of their fathers' involvement in the Epiphany Rising of January 1400, and all, in due course, would repay the king's mercy with loyal service. Similar steps were also taken to allow Hotspur's son to return from Scotland, so that he could inherit the earldom of Northumberland.

But this was by no means the limit of Henry's willingness to forget old scores. Lord Mowbray, brother of the rebel magnate who perished with Archbishop Scrope in 1405, was even invested as hereditary Earl Marshal of England, while a special licence now allowed votive offerings to be made at the disgraced archbishop's shrine in York Minster. Likewise, at the very start of the new reign, the Earl of March was finally released from his long confinement by an amnesty. And to further confirm the new climate of trust, the brother and heir of the shifty Duke of York was created Earl of Cambridge. March, in fact, would die of the plague as a devoted and energetic Governor of Ireland in 1424.

Most dramatically of all, the new king decided in December 1413 to transfer the body of Richard II from its inglorious resting place at King's Langley to the magnificent tomb that the murdered king had originally commissioned for himself at Westminster Abbey. The gesture was prompted, according to the *Brut*, by Henry's desire to atone for his father's sin, and confirmed the new ruler's recognition that, in the words of Thomas Walsingham, 'he owed as much veneration to Richard as to his own father in the flesh'.[15] However, it was also another act of sublime self-confidence and a further indication of Henry's considerable political instinct. As French chroniclers were quick to point out, there were still those who believed that Richard remained alive in Scotland and his reinterment would do much to dispel such rumours.[16] In such circumstances, the son of a usurper had every bit as much to gain by proving the death of the man who had been deposed by his father as by honouring the kindly and cultured patron of his youth.

This is not to say, of course, that Henry's security was now guaranteed, or that all potentially dangerous individuals were treated equally generously under the new regime. Henry took no chances, for instance, with Owain Glyn Dŵr's son, Gruffydd ap Owain, or the Regent of Scotland's heir, Murdoch, Earl of Fife, who were both recommitted to the Tower. And the King of Scots was to be even less lucky. Already a prisoner for seven years since the age of eleven, he was not released until 1423, by which time Henry was already dead. Later he wrote poignantly how he had despaired 'of all joy and remedy' and how much he had envied the liberty of birds, beasts and fishes of the sea during his 'deadly life full of pain and penance'.[17]

But by and large the danger was limited, and generosity befitted Henry's circumstances. The potential rivalry with his eldest brother, for example, was dealt with once again by a judicious combination of firmness and conciliation, leaving the interim heir to the throne duly diminished, but with honour nonetheless intact. Certainly, there were at least two bitter pills for the Duke of Clarence to swallow. First, he was deliberately deprived of his office of King's Lieutenant in Aquitaine, which was given to his uncle Thomas Beaufort, Earl of Dorset. Then, to leave him in no doubt at all of his elder brother's primacy, the duke also lost the captaincy of Calais to the Earl of Warwick. The compensation for all this, however, was an unusually handsome pension of 2,000 marks, which allowed him to welcome the new regime without demur and settle smoothly into his new role as trusted commander and deputy to his elder brother.

There were, it is true, whispers originating in France that loyalty to the old dynasty persisted in some quarters. The Monk of Saint-Denys, for instance, told how some of those present at the coronation favoured the Earl of March and considered civil war likely.[18] But much more importantly, England's senior nobles showed no appreciable sign of opposition. Ralph Neville, Earl of Westmorland, was already safely married to a Beaufort bride, while Richard Beauchamp, Earl of Warwick, stood out as a talented royal servant who had distinguished himself as both crusader and diplomat. In the king's inner circle, too, was a group of lesser lords who were all, as yet, equally free of suspicion. Richard Grey of Codnor, Thomas Lord Camoys and Henry le Scrope of Masham gave no hint whatsoever of opposition at this time. Indeed, the nobility had rushed to take the oath of allegiance even before the king had actually been crowned.

And in spite of blizzard conditions which some interpreted as an omen that the new king would be 'a man of cold deeds' and severity, the coronation itself appears to have been an unqualified success.[19]

The act of consecrating a new king had actually taken on an even deeper significance at the start of the previous reign, with the 'discovery' of a sacred oil, which was said to have been given to St Thomas Becket by Our Lady herself. If, moreover, such a tale was purely designed to underpin Lancastrian legitimacy, none of this detracted from its impact upon the king's subjects – not to mention the king himself. For Henry did not hesitate to use the oil at his own coronation. Nor, it seems, did he take his oath of office with anything other than the utmost seriousness. On the contrary, his commitment to 'good governance' seems to have become nothing less than a divinely ordained mission.

As luck would have it, Henry's bishops were also men he could trust implicitly. In addition to Henry Beaufort, the king had the enthusiastic support of Henry Chichele, the brilliant Bishop of St David's whose appointment as Archbishop of Canterbury in 1414 would send a clear message to Beaufort and others that old hands close to the king could not be guaranteed advancement over other more suitable men. Fifty-two at the time of his elevation, Chichele already possessed a wealth of experience in civil law, ecclesiastical administration and diplomacy. Furthermore, there was nothing of the proud prelate about him. Instead, he was a humble, friendly and merciful man whose first-rate practical efficiency would make him an invaluable servant of the Crown for years to come.

Likewise, Thomas Langley, Bishop of Durham, had already served with distinction as Chancellor, while Bishop Hallam of Salisbury would prove to be one of the most distinguished representatives at the forthcoming Council of Constance. Only the aged Archbishop Arundel could, in fact, give Henry any possible cause for disquiet at the outset of the reign, and only then insofar as he embodied the policies of the king's dead father. Besides which, Arundel's own death in February 1414 was not long in coming. Provided, therefore, that the new king could be relied upon to root out heresy and rule as God's anointed should, the episcopacy's compliance was largely guaranteed.

And Henry V's intense, almost ostentatious, religious devotion was indeed what seems to have impressed observers above all else at this time. Strictly conventional in his beliefs, he heard mass at least three times a day, recited the psalms as part of his regular religious routine and made a special point of discouraging even his most powerful magnates from disturbing him while at prayer. The new king was also a keen devotee of the Virgin Mary and St George, as well as a string of specifically English saints, such as St Edmund, Edward the Confessor and St John of Beverley, under whose banner several English kings had marched against the Scots. His special patron, however, was St John of Bridlington, a wonder-working Yorkshireman who had died as recently as 1379 and possessed a reputation for walking on water and curing physical deformities. More than this, the saint was said to have been especially adept at casting out demons – no small matter for a king who retained till the end of his life a darkly superstitious preoccupation with necromancy and witchcraft.

Naturally enough, the king's choice of personal spiritual advisers also tells us much about him. In all cases, he seems to have favoured a steely combination of high intellect and strict orthodoxy in the men who cared for his soul. The first confessor he appointed after his succession was Stephen Patrington, provincial of the Carmelite 'white friars' and an academic of high standing, who had been one of John Wycliffe's most passionate opponents at Oxford. After Patrington's death in 1417, Henry then chose Thomas Netter of Walden, another Carmelite, who was known to his own order, not without good reason, as 'the swiftest fire that ever smote the trunk of heresy'.[20]

Perhaps it was hardly surprising, therefore, that the reign should have begun with a flood of ecclesiastical endowments, in an effort to place the monarchy at the very centre of English spiritual life. The royal manor of Sheen, for instance, which Richard II had demolished in grief after the death of his first wife there, now became the location of a Carthusian monastery named Bethlehem, while in Twickenham, across the river, another more famous monastery, known as Syon at Henry's particular insistence, was built for the Bridgettine order. Both were intended to serve, in effect, as mighty powerhouses of prayer for the Lancastrian dynasty.

Significantly, there were also plans for the foundation of another monastery – this time for an order of vegetarian hermits known as the Celestines who had been brought to England by Bishop Courtney of Norwich after his travels in France. But the monks concerned were soon refusing to swear homage to a king who was planning war on their own kingdom. Nor could they ultimately accept the English king's wish to fund their monastery with money confiscated from French abbeys. In consequence, Henry found himself hoist squarely on his own petard and, in spite of considerable perseverance on the king's behalf, all plans for the thirty-one-acre site on the north side of the Thames, upon which work had already begun, were eventually abandoned.

But if Henry had taken surprising pains with the bold French Celestines, it would soon be clear enough that his patience was by no means limitless. He had, it is true, built up a well-deserved reputation for the common touch, which dated back at least as far as his days on campaign in Wales. Even lowly soldiers might be treated to Henry's time and close attention, as he empathised with their predicament and offered comradely exhortations. Yet Henry also possessed another sterner side, which allowed him to stir those around him by awe no less than affection. Indeed, the forthright and companionable 'Harry' could swiftly become the cold and haughty autocrat if ever treated to anything less than due deference. This, after all, was a king who would not hesitate before long to demote his French marshal for having the temerity to look him in the eye. Clearly, the bottom line was always boldly drawn wherever Henry V was concerned – and woe betide those unfortunate enough to cross it.

Parliament, finance, law and order

For much of the two previous reigns, relations between Crown and Parliament had been a sorry mix of conflict and recrimination. In both 1376 and 1386, for example, the weapon of impeachment had been used against Richard II's principal ministers, and in 1388 and 1397 Parliament went on to support 'appeals' of treason against leading courtiers. Ultimately, MPs had even endorsed charges of misgovernment against King Richard before underwriting his deposition and approving his murder. Similarly, in both his reign and the next, Parliament saw fit to complain about the size and character of the royal household, and to suggest administrative reforms and restrictions on the king's control of patronage. Even more humiliatingly, the king was forced in 1406, as we have seen, to accept the appointment of a special council with powers to oversee royal government and control its expenditure.

In all these cases, Parliament had encroached heavily upon the royal prerogative, and in doing so it had launched a further barrage of attacks against corruption in local and central government, as well as Henry IV's failure to maintain law and order, defend the realm and suppress rebellion. There were nagging fears, too, about the Crown's possible insolvency. Parliament was, in fact, under no obligation to grant the monarch taxation, other than in exceptional cases for the defence of the realm, and the current anxiety was firmly founded on past experience. The strains of war finance had, after all, already bankrupted Edward III in 1340 and ruined the two Florentine banking houses on whose loans he defaulted.

Worse still, there were now additional pressures, which made the situation especially ominous. Henry IV's need to muster support had led him to 'purchase' it by means of large-scale grants of annuities and the alienation of substantial portions of royal land. He did this, too, at the very time that the Crown's financial resources were already stretched to the limit. On the one hand, customs revenue from wool and cloth was in temporary decline, while a decrease in European mining activity, occasioned mainly by civil war in Bohemia, had led to a serious shortage in the availability of silver coins. In consequence, the king became increasingly dependent upon parliamentary support to carry out those basic functions of government that he was normally expected to fund himself.

It came as no small relief, therefore, that Henry V had already established a well-deserved reputation for financial prudence even before the crown had been placed on his head. He had, for instance, gained first-hand experience of the government's dire financial predicament while Prince of Wales and taken various steps to place his own finances in good order. As early as 1403, he had enacted a series of measures to improve revenues from his duchy of Cornwall and earldom of Chester, increasing rents, taking back under his own management lands that had been rented out, and substantially reducing the number of annuities he paid from local revenues. He had also used the gradual reconquest of his Welsh lands to make a steady and increasing contribution to his income, so that after 1409 he was in receipt of around £1,800 annually from southern Wales and a further £1,300 from the north, compared with a paltry £500 when he first received the principality.

During the later years of his father's reign, moreover, Henry had committed himself to a programme of 'good and substantial governance', and though, as we have seen, his record at the head of the Council during 1410–11 was mixed, he had nevertheless established a working relationship with Parliament and gained praise in the process.[21] He had been a firm advocate of financial discipline, strong defences and good counsel, and had also, unlike his father, taken pride in keeping his word. At the same time, he had been keen to gauge the opinions of the Commons and to ensure that his own views were presented as persuasively as possible.

But though the prince had been sensitive to Parliament's concerns, he had left no doubt about his absolute determination to resist any incursions upon the executive and prerogative authority of the Crown. In 1406, for example, he had refused the oath binding the Council to the articles of reform proposed by Parliament. As Prince of Wales, he had also affirmed that the Council's commitment to financial restraint should be accompanied by guarantees of revenue from taxation. Overall, he had made it abundantly clear that the next King of England would not be faced down easily in any future trial of strength.

So when Henry V's first Parliament eventually assembled in the Painted Chamber at Westminster on 15 May 1413, there was mainly optimism, but also a perceptible undercurrent of apprehension in the air. In what was now to become the standard fashion, proceedings were opened by an oration from Henry Beaufort, which indicated that the new king would be guided by those same precepts that had guided him as prince. Taking the text 'Ante omnem actum consilum stabile' as his theme, the bishop emphasised Henry's commitment to his coronation oath and told MPs that they should provide regular taxation in return for 'bone governance' or, in other words, the effective maintenance of law and order at home and stout resistance to the king's enemies abroad. And as with all his other addresses to the next five parliaments of the reign, Beaufort made every attempt to present his master as a man who fulfilled the concept of kingship in every way and stood for a programme approved by God himself.[22]

The general tone was therefore both authoritative and hopeful – and not without reason, for by the time that he became king, Henry V had already developed a keen appreciation of Parliament's

political potential, both as a national boc
influence in local affairs. He had, moreover, iss
to his first Parliament on only the second day
indication of his desire to establish a working
earliest opportunity. Nor was this a token gestui
Parliament was to be called eleven times durii
every year except 1418 and 1422, and twice a ye
and 1421. And though the king was only presen   or these
meetings, this was simply a result of his absence on campaign and
the confidence he had in his two youngest brothers to conduct
proceedings effectively.

Certainly, there was much about the first Parliament of the reign
that augured well for the future. Henry agreed, for instance, to
reduce the payment of annuities by £10,000, and Parliament, too,
was prepared to make sacrifices. The usual subsidy on wool for the
defence of the realm was granted for four years, along with customs
duties on wines for a year from Michaelmas. Likewise, a generous
sum was earmarked for the royal 'hostel, chamber and wardrobe',
and the Commons' speaker, William Stourton, was received
without dispute by the new king who also listened patiently to the
usual litany of petitions and complaints.

However, any notion that an entirely new and easy relationship
had been forged from the outset is more than a little misleading,
since Parliament was keen to affirm that direct taxation should be
confined to time of war and not granted for the maintenance of
permanent garrisons. Furthermore, Stourton even reminded the
king how often his father had failed to deliver on his promises, and
when Henry asked for the Commons' grievances to be presented in
writing, they bluntly refused. Clearly, there was genuine concern
that a forceful new ruler, however amenable initially, might soon
come to threaten their hard-earned rights and privileges. Besides
which, MPs were still seeking action from their sovereign rather an
attentive ear.

Yet if Parliament was circumspect, the king himself was already
hard at work providing the kind of lead on law and order that was
the hub of any credible programme of good governance. And it was
here that some of Henry's most convincing early work was carried
out. Violence, riot and disorder were, in fact, endemic in late
medieval England, not simply because society was intrinsically

...inal, but rather because justice was so difficult to obtain. ...udicial process relied, after all, on local officials serving as ...eriffs and justices of the peace, and these, as well as jurors, were frequently susceptible to corruption and intimidation as a result of their dependence upon the power and patronage of powerful magnates and nobles.

Indeed, the landed class was often most inclined of all to flout the law, especially in the more outlying regions of the realm. In May 1411, for instance, Sir Robert Hilton had ridden into Sunderland 'in warlike manner' at the head of a considerable body of men and insulted a certain John Duckett.[23] At Hilton's orders, an arrow had then been fired into Duckett's throat, after which the victim was pommelled with the butt of a sword as he lay dying. Yet only a few days later, Hilton's father paid the Bishop of Durham 1,000 marks in assurance that there would be no repetition of such behaviour, and a pardon for the murder was duly granted the following year.

Elsewhere in the north, as well as in East Anglia, the Midlands and especially Shropshire, rioting and serious crime abounded. By 1410, Parliament was complaining bitterly about the collapse of good order and requesting the issue of general oyer and terminer commissions as a remedy. At the same time, petitions were submitted alleging a series of attacks on Lancastrian retainers and tenants in Staffordshire. Then, in 1411, there were further complaints from Northumberland concerning the prevalence of thieves and robbers and the rarity of judicial visitations. It was even brought to Parliament's attention that Robert Tirwhit, a justice of the King's Bench, had tried to intimidate none other than the Chief Justice himself, William Gascoigne, by attending an arbitration at the head of some 500 armed men. Meanwhile, another source of continual anxiety was the vendetta raging in the Channel between English and continental pirates, which was disrupting commerce and undermining relations with Flanders and Brittany.

The question of public order was therefore one of the most pressing problems confronting Henry V upon his accession. And true to character, he lost little time in demonstrating a subtle combination of firmness and generosity. One of his most notable early acts as king came in December 1414 when he offered a general pardon for all crimes committed during the previous reign.

'Whereas we are mindful of the many great misfortunes which have risen out of faction ...', he proclaimed, 'we have firmly resolved, since it would be pleasing to God and most conducive to the preservation of good order, that as God's pardon has been freely bestowed on us, we should allow all the subjects of our kingdom ... who so desire, to drink from the cup of our mercy.'[24] The main aim was actually to reconcile former political opponents of the Lancastrian cause and the results were striking. Over the next three years, nearly 5,000 grants of clemency were issued.

Within a few days of his accession, moreover, Henry had despatched Thomas, Earl of Arundel, to Wales with instructions to pardon those former rebels who deserved mercy. The outcome here was arguably more impressive still. Some 600 men of Merionethshire admitted their guilt as traitors and begged forgiveness, while more than fifty others from Kidwelly were merely fined and given back their lands. Even though the Welsh rebellion had involved a particularly bitter struggle and Owain Glyn Dŵr remained at large in the mountains of his homeland, Henry had demonstrated his magnanimity. And, in the process, he had also turned good will and good sense to good profit, since the fines he gathered from his Welsh lands over the next two years would bring him more than £5,000.

This is not to suggest, however, that Henry was unconcerned with delivering punishment to those who most deserved it, for there followed a concerted effort to prosecute corrupt officials who had abused their powers as representatives of the Crown. The chamberlain of north Wales, Thomas Barnby, at first eluded royal commissioners only to find himself confronted by thirty charges of extortion and embezzlement three months later. Similarly, Sir John Scudamore, the steward of Kidwelly, found himself deprived of his post, even though it had been granted to him for life in the previous reign.

Nor was Henry afraid to bring his own friends to book. The most powerful magnate in Shropshire was Thomas, Earl of Arundel, whose support had been essential in crushing Glyn Dŵr's revolt. But a small group of Arundel's retainers had thereafter established a stranglehold on the Welsh border, terrorising the countryside and freely engaging in all manner of extortions. By the spring of 1414, in fact, Shropshire's local administration had effectively lost control as increasing numbers of travellers and merchants were waylaid and more and more cases of large-scale larceny, homicide and assault were recorded in coroners' rolls. But while Henry IV had chosen largely to ignore such incidents for fear of making powerful enemies, his successor showed no such qualms.

Perhaps the new king's boldest move, however, was the appointment of a special commission of justices from the King's Bench at Westminster to suppress the disorder in Shropshire and neighbouring Staffordshire. As a result, almost 1,800 indictments were received during the summer of 1414. Among those prosecuted were seven of Arundel's chief lieutenants, most of whom were leading members of the gentry, such as Sir John Winsbury and Robert and Roger Corbet. All were found guilty and made to pay the considerable sum of £200 as a surety that they would keep the peace in future. Arundel himself, moreover, was made to provide a bond of £3,000 as a further guarantee of their good behaviour.

In the previous two reigns, such action might well have resulted in much stiffer resistance. But in spite of his firmness, Henry had also acted judiciously and even Arundel's notorious cronies were given a second chance. All received pardons and all were allowed to redeem themselves through military service at a later date. Six of them, for instance, went on to serve in Arundel's retinue during the Agincourt campaign, while the seventh was entrusted with the guardianship of the Shropshire march in the king's absence. At the same time, many of their own servants, who had indulged in similar offences, would fight in France as loyal archers of the king.

Even so, Henry's measures were not always successful or unopposed. The maintenance of law and order demanded, after all, a partnership between the Crown and political society in the localities – including those who might be called upon as jurors – and medieval communities, particularly remote ones, were intensely suspicious of central authority. When, therefore, a whole area closed ranks, even a king as forceful as Henry V might find himself unable to prevail. In February 1414, for example, an oyer and terminer commission was despatched to Devon to investigate piracy and counterfeiting. But of the thirty or so juries summoned, all but a handful refused to make returns of any kind. Nor was such behaviour altogether surprising when the local community concerned was reaping such rich rewards from the pirates who used their ports.

On the other hand, of course, the royal pardon of December 1414 might well be construed as little more than an outright surrender to the tidal wave of disorder that had been engulfing the realm for so long. By Michaelmas 1414, the Court of King's Bench was being stretched to breaking point by the sheer number of cases confronting it, and the decision was taken merely to issue pardons from Chancery at a cost of 16s 4d, which entitled the holder to exemption from a variety of financial liabilities and to immunity from a comprehensive range of criminal offences. Indeed, the terms of the 1414 pardon even included cases of treason, murder and rape – offences that had been expressly excluded from the 1390 Statute of Pardons. As a result, the number of convictions plummeted in some areas, since so many of those appearing in court were now able to escape punishment.

Yet such instances of failure or retreat served mainly to heighten Henry's resolve, and the policy of centralising law enforcement would continue steadily throughout the first phase of the reign and beyond. It was, in fact, at the Leicester Parliament of April 1414 that the main campaign 'for the chastisement and punishment of the rioters, murderers and other malefactors who more than ever abound in many parts of the kingdom' actually took shape.[25] The Statutes of Riots, which had originated with Richard II and Henry IV, were now to involve the Court of King's Bench more directly, and the same court was also encouraged to intervene more effectively in the localities under its guise as a 'superior eyre'. Furthermore, the king's signet letters from around this time leave no doubt about Henry's very direct involvement in legal business. In the case of William and John Mynors of Staffordshire, for instance, both brothers were summoned to appear before him and later, on the king's own instruction, they were duly pardoned.[26]

The importance of this kind of personal intervention is, moreover, something that can never be overestimated at a time when it was so essential for a ruler to be seen to uphold the law both formally and informally – at court, in Parliament and in his everyday behaviour and relationships. The *Brut* chronicles tell how Henry summoned two feuding northern knights to his presence at Windsor. Upon their arrival, it seems, the king was about to consume a dish of oysters, and after squarely reprimanding the two men for their misdemeanours, he made it clear that the dispute must be resolved by the time he had finished his meal. If not, they would be hanged. Predictably, the knights concerned did not delay in reaching a settlement, though even afterwards they were warned that 'whatsomeever they were, they should die according to the law', if they transgressed again.[27]

On balance, then, the significant fact is not that problems of law enforcement persisted, but that public order gradually ceased to assume anything like its former importance. Furthermore, the long-lasting nature of this transformation was not only impressive, but also achieved with the slenderest of resources. Throughout Henry's long absences abroad between 1415 and 1422 there was, in fact, no serious disorder in England and at no stage did he feel the need to interrupt or curtail his military campaigns. On the contrary, the evidence of his reign seemed to confirm that foreign wars – or at least successful ones – actually eased the problem of endemic disorder for any medieval ruler. It was, after all, no coincidence that the muster role for the Earl of Arundel's retinue at the siege of Harfleur closely resembled an earlier indictment list for the Court of King's Bench.

By sheer force of personality and an abundance of plain good sense, therefore, Henry V was already establishing a well-deserved reputation for the pursuit of justice. And it was a reputation that would ultimately extend far beyond the shores of his native land. 'He was', wrote the Burgundian chronicler Georges Chastellain, 'a prince of justice, not only in himself, for the sake of example, but also towards others, according to equity and right; he upheld no one through favour, nor did he allow wrong to go unpunished.'[28]

Lollardy

Though the second Lancastrian king might pardon common criminals and be reconciled to former enemies, there was one particular group to whom he would remain implacably opposed. The so-called 'Lollard' heretics, who had already gained such notoriety during the previous two reigns, were closely associated with the sweeping programme of ecclesiastical reform first proposed by the Oxford theologian John Wycliffe during the 1370s and early 1380s. Recruited originally by John of Gaunt to challenge the theoretical basis of papal supremacy, Wycliffe had gone on to formulate an altogether broader and more radical critique of the Church, which soon spread well beyond the walls of the university where he taught. And as abstract academic debate turned to full-blown heresy in the country at large, so the very term 'Lollard' came to acquire an ominous resonance all of its own among both secular and ecclesiastical authorities alike.

The potentially subversive elements of Wycliffe's ideas were not hard to identify. In emphasising the primacy of scripture as the basis of all true religion, for instance, he had gone on to suggest that it was the right of all to worship as they chose without the need for clerical intermediaries. And since the salvation or otherwise of all mankind was supposedly predestined in any case, it followed that the very existence of bishops, priests, monks and friars was not only unnecessary but actually a direct affront to God. Indeed, on this basis all hierarchy within the Church was to be vigorously condemned, while ultimate responsibility for the spiritual welfare of any realm resided solely with the secular ruler.

This, however, was by no means the limit of the Lollard assault on Roman orthodoxy. Among a multitude of other targets were auricular confession, indulgences, prayers to the saints, clerical celibacy, the all-male priesthood, warfare and ecclesiastical wealth. Pilgrimages, meanwhile, were casually dismissed as a superstitious confidence trick, which served, in the words one female Lollard from Norwich, merely to enrich priests 'that be too rich and to make gay tapsters and proud ostlers'.[29] Even more disconcertingly, there was unstinting hostility to the principle of transubstantiation. One heretical blacksmith from Lincolnshire, for instance, struck a characteristically strident note by proudly boasting how he could make 'as good a sacrament between two irons as a priest does fashion upon his altar'.[30]

Yet for all the vigour of its rhetoric, the threat from Lollardy seems to have remained more apparent than real. It possessed no specific creed, nor any significant central organisation, and its emphasis upon the primacy of the individual conscience not only robbed it of coherence, but alienated it from many of those who might otherwise have been most effective in propagating it. Not surprisingly, Lollardy's support among the nobility was never widespread, and even the humble tradesmen, artisans, graziers and husbandmen who made up the bulk of its membership were comparatively few in number. Most Lollards, moreover, sought not so much to destroy the Church as to regenerate it upon the kind of ascetic and evangelical principles that were largely in keeping with the more moderate elements of contemporary lay piety.

So why, then, did the authorities continue to brood so uneasily upon Lollardy's perceived threat? In part, the answer lies in timing. Between 1308 and 1377 the papacy had found itself under French domination during its residence at Avignon. But the end of this so-called 'Babylonish Captivity' only served to mark the onset of even greater difficulties. Within a year, in fact, the Church was torn asunder by the establishment of rival popes in both Rome and Avignon, and the resulting 'Great Schism' was still dominating ecclesiastical affairs more than thirty years later when Henry V mounted the English throne. By that time, indeed, no fewer than three individuals – John XXIII, Gregory XII and Benedict XIII – were all claiming to be Pope. And with the Church more divided than ever, the spread of any form of heresy was certain to be greeted with the utmost concern, especially in England where strict orthodoxy had always been the norm.

But there were other more substantive reasons why the danger from Lollardy, however negligible, could never be wholly discounted. There was, after all, an occasional boldness about Lollard activity that fuelled the many stubborn myths of conspiracy then in circulation. In 1395, for instance, the so-called 'Twelve Conclusions' had been brazenly nailed to the doors of Westminster Hall and St Paul's while Parliament and Convocation were still in session. And though Lollards may have been few in number, their influence nevertheless encompassed a disconcertingly wide geographical area, which included the Midlands, the Welsh borders, the Chilterns, London and East Anglia. Most worryingly of all, Lollardy was powered by a small but energetic section of the gentry and associated with a number of key doctrines that posed a potential threat to some of the defining principles of late medieval society. If, as Wycliffe's theory of '*dominium*' implied, property could be justly expropriated from the Church on account of its sinfulness, might not the same logic also be applied to secular wealth?

To compound matters, Wycliffe's teachings had also won the sympathy of a small circle of knights whose influence persisted throughout the reigns of Edward III, Richard II and Henry IV.

Individuals such as William Neville, John Montagu, William Beauchamp, Thomas Latimer, Lewis Clifford and John Clanvowe were, in fact, all less concerned with Wycliffite theology or the Church's departure from apostolic practice than with the prospect of replenishing an empty national treasury with ecclesiastical riches. But as a result of their influence, heretical activity at the lower end of the social scale came to gain a more menacing reputation than it might otherwise have deserved.

In consequence, Henry V's almost obsessive concern with orthodoxy and order meant that he wasted little time in affirming the fateful connection between heresy and the more general political subversion that had been confronting his dynasty. In 1406 he had sponsored a petition which emphasised the threat to secular lordship if the clergy were stripped of their temporalities, and a strong proclamation against 'the pestilent seed of Lollardy and evil doctrine' was duly issued in August of the first year of his reign.[31] More importantly still, Henry was soon reinforcing this proclamation with direct action against the individual who had been emerging for some time as the unofficial leader of Lollard opposition. The irony, however, was that the figurehead for these 'cursed caitiffs' and 'heirs of darkness' was none other than a man of 'great popular reputation' who had long been one of the more intimate members of the royal circle.[32]

Sir John Oldcastle of Almeley in Herefordshire – a well-known hotbed of Lollard heresy – had made his name chiefly as a soldier. Around ten years older than the king, he had served in Henry IV's Scottish expedition of 1400 and also performed good service in the wars against the Welsh, as a result of which he joined the Prince of Wales's household. Equally importantly, he became, after his marriage to Joan de la Pole, not only Lord Cobham, but one of the most important landowners in Kent. And by 1412 he had been accorded a position of high command on the Duke of Clarence's expedition to France. It was also abundantly clear from the references in his correspondence to the likes of Isidore of Seville, John Chrysostom and St Augustine that he was a man of no mean intellect.

In short, Oldcastle was a difficult individual to ignore. But even before the new reign had begun, suspicions about his religious beliefs were growing. By the spring of 1410, in fact, one of Oldcastle's chaplains was already preaching heresy in several Kent parishes, directly beneath the devoutly orthodox nose of Archbishop Arundel. And though the decision to interdict the offending churches was soon reversed, mainly out of respect for Oldcastle's wife, the knight from Herefordshire was soon flaunting his Lollard sympathies as brashly as ever. On 8 September, for instance, he wrote a letter of congratulation to Woksa von Waldstein, a Bohemian noble who was in open support of the heresiarch Jan Hus, and a year later he entered into correspondence with King Wenceslas of Bohemia on a similar note, even offering him military support in the seizure of Church lands that he was currently conducting.[33]

It came as little real surprise, therefore, when Archbishop Arundel informed the new king in March 1413 – just after his accession – that heretical tracts belonging to Sir John had been found in the shop of an illuminator in Paternoster Row. Thereafter, Oldcastle was duly summoned to Kennington and asked to listen to the tracts' most offensive passages in the presence not only of the king himself, but also an imposing array of ecclesiastics and magnates. Doubtless, Henry had been mortified by the discovery of his former comrade's religious leanings, but he remained typically keen to give him every opportunity to save himself. For when the hearing was over and Arundel pressed for Oldcastle's condemnation, a final decision was postponed. Instead, the king now attempted in person to make the heretic knight see sense, indicating that he would only be made to stand trial if he persisted in his error.

Nevertheless, Henry's protracted efforts proved fruitless, and when the king pointed out the consequences of further resistance, his antagonist merely retired from court to his castle of Cooling in Kent, thereby committing an act of blatant political defiance, which gave the whole dispute an altogether broader significance. Moreover, when Oldcastle was brought before his inquisitors one last time at Blackfriars on 25 September, he chose to speak his mind more boldly than ever. This time he openly proclaimed that the Host remained nothing more than bread at the consecration. And when asked his opinion of the Pope, Oldcastle was even more outspoken, declaring him to be the head of the Antichrist. Now, then, without further ceremony, the king's former comrade was at last condemned as a heretic and handed over to the secular authorities for burning.

But what should have been the end of a largely unremarkable footnote in the history of Henry V's reign proved to be nothing of the kind. For on the night of 19 October, Oldcastle escaped from the Tower with what appears to have been outside help and hid with a Lollard parchment maker called William Fisher who lived near St Sepulchre's in Smithfield. Significantly, both Henry and Arundel had made further vain efforts to persuade their captive to recant during the usual interval of forty days between condemnation and execution. But though Henry had deeply regretted Oldcastle's stand and done his best to save him, he still knew a bottom line when he saw one. For his former friend's continued defiance had not only flouted royal authority more and more blatantly, but also appeared to confirm the clergy's suspicions that he was the 'chief harbourer of Lollards and their main supporter, protector and defender'.[34]

This is not to say, of course, that the king did not stand to gain in certain ways from Oldcastle's intransigence or by emphasising the strength of Lollard opposition in general. Not only would the scale of his triumph seem all the more impressive to his own subjects if the challenge before him appeared a substantial one, there was also the broader European context to consider. Henry's wish to displace the French monarchy from the leadership of Christendom was, for instance, already taking shape, and as Hussite resistance gathered pace in Bohemia, the potential benefits of decisive action against heresy in England were far from negligible.

Nor, for that matter, can there be much doubt that the evidence surrounding the so-called 'Oldcastle Rising' of January 1414 remains fragile. From the time of Oldcastle's escape, in fact, the main testimony to his actions and intentions is largely limited to the official indictment brought against him after his eventual capture three years later. His treatment in other contemporary and near-contemporary sources is, moreover, equally problematic – so much so that it is virtually impossible in many instances to distinguish fact from fantasy at all. In the accounts of all the main chroniclers, including Thomas Walsingham, Adam Usk, John Strecche, Thomas Elmham and, above all, the author of the *Gesta*, the theme is unwavering. On the one hand, Oldcastle and his confederates are crudely vilified as agents of the devil, subverting the one true faith and betraying their sovereign master, while the king is lionised as the Christ-like protector of all true religion, order and justice.

To complicate matters further, the judicial records of the Court of King's Bench, which contain the official account of the events that now unfolded, are littered with exaggerations, emendations and apparent contradictions, while the Issue Rolls of the Exchequer even provide some evidence that implies an orchestrated attempt by the government to 'manufacture' a Lollard plot for propaganda purposes. Jurors are summoned before the rebellion has occurred, informers rewarded and convenient confessions extracted, all of which can be glossed to suggest a conspiracy. Equally curiously, a proclamation against illegal Lollard gatherings was issued to sheriffs some three days prior to the actual rising. Perhaps it is small wonder, then – particularly when the speed of the authorities' eventual response is taken into account – that at least one eminent commentator has suggested that the treasonous events of January 1414 were nothing more than a 'fabrication' designed to consolidate royal authority and confirm the king's role as defender of orthodoxy.[35]

Yet such claims, however tantalising, are stubbornly circumstantial. And whether the king really did have either the inclination or the means to concoct such an elaborate conspiracy remains doubtful. The Lollard 'threat' was, after all, an established 'fact' insofar as successive rulers had reacted to it over time, and recalcitrant individuals like Oldcastle had done nothing to dispel it. Richard II's relative indifference to religious matters in the early stages of his reign had, for instance, certainly evaporated by the mid-1380s, and by 1389 he had become the vigorous enemy of Lollardy that he would remain until his death. From then onwards, he did not hesitate to arrest and interrogate traffickers in heretical writings, and he proved equally energetic in his use of royal writs to purge heretics like William James and Robert Lechlade from Oxford University. If, then, the menace of Lollardy was indeed an illusion produced by governments, it was by no means purely a creation of Henry V or, for that matter, his father.

Meanwhile, 'thought control' on the scale required to concoct a fictitious rebellion for propaganda purposes would have necessitated a degree of bureaucratic sophistication that still seems curiously out of kilter with the late medieval English state as we know it. Exaggeration and refashioning of the truth for political gain were, of course, time-honoured tools of government and Lancastrian rulers were, perhaps, more prepared than most to use them. But the consciously co-ordinated invention of a rising such as Oldcastle's is altogether something else. If, moreover, contemporary chroniclers were 'complicit' in reinforcing the official interpretation of events, the means by which their co-operation was guaranteed remains far from clear-cut.[36] Nor is it implausible to suggest that the main accounts actually reflected rather than manufactured the general consensus. And if the courts of justice did indeed spin events to suit the Crown in 1414, they, too, were hardly departing from normal practice in times of rebellion.

By the end of the previous year, Thomas Walsingham was confidently asserting that the opponents of the king were 'lifting up their tails' to bring about the final 'subversion of the orthodox faith and the destruction of holy Church'.[37] And if the widespread demonisation of Oldcastle and his followers should be treated with some caution, it should not be forgotten either that the propaganda value of any Lollard insurrection was directly proportionate to its credibility. It was by no means necessarily the government's doing that Oldcastle and his leading associates were widely rumoured to be planning to dissolve the abbeys and share out their riches as soon as Henry – the so-called 'prince of priests' – had been captured. So when word went out that bills were being posted on church doors in almost every county, proclaiming that a hundred thousand men were ready for action, the resulting shudders of fear, if not the facts themselves, were firmly rooted in hard historical reality.

It might be added, finally, that the eventually pathetic outcome of Oldcastle's rising actually emerges only with hindsight. The plot's strategy, it should be remembered, was modelled upon the Epiphany Rising of 1400, which had already shaken Henry's father and led to his own near capture as a boy. Armed Lollards, disguised as mummers were to be smuggled into Eltham Palace where they would seize both the king and his brothers. Nor, indeed, was the alarm engendered by the second phase of the plan altogether unwarranted. Four days later, on the night of 9 January 1414, men from all over England were to assemble in London at Fickett's Field, just outside Temple Bar in St Giles's Fields at what is now King's College Hospital. And the judicial proceedings following the revolt, such as they were, still suggest that times of arrival, billeting arrangements and doles of money as well as bribes had all been arranged with some thoroughness by the rebels, particularly in counties like Derbyshire, where disaffected clerics such as Walter Gilbert and William Edrick were especially diligent.

In the event, no overwhelming Lollard force was ever forthcoming and the king was, in any case, wholly prepared for all contingencies, since he had made full use of the extensive spy network at his disposal. Indeed, the Lollard plot had, it seems, been revealed to him in full by one Thomas Burton, who was eventually paid 100 shillings for his efforts. And in consequence the Mayor of London, supported by a strong force of soldiers, was able to raid the shop of a Lollard carpenter at the Sign of the Axe near Bishopsgate at around 10 o'clock on the evening of Twelfth Night. There, if official accounts are to be believed, they found the carpenter and seven other Lollards, dressed as mummers – and among them a squire of Oldcastle's.

Even so, small groups of unsuspecting Lollards from Essex, Buckinghamshire, Yorkshire, the Midlands and the West Country made the fatal error of heading, as planned, to St Giles's Fields throughout the grey hours before dawn on the day of the proposed rising. In the meantime, the king had ordered that the gates of the city be closed and then stationed himself with a considerable force just north-west of the rebels' proposed assembly point. Lacking leadership, each Lollard group was, in fact, utterly helpless before London's barred gates, and as individual groups arrived they were promptly intercepted and disarmed.

A rising that had raised such fears ended, therefore, in outright ignominy, though the widespread locations from which the rebels came, if not their actual numbers, still lent a certain symbolic significance to the whole episode. Furthermore, the speed of the government's response was actually a measure not only of its efficiency, but also of the seriousness with which it viewed the rebellion. The very same day that the Lollard rising foundered, a special commission was appointed to carry out the eradication of rebel elements and over the next fortnight, the grim work of execution proceeded inexorably – though Oldcastle himself, who remained something of a spectral figure in contemporary accounts, managed to make good his escape to become, in the words of the *Gesta*, 'a vagabond and a fugitive upon the face of the earth'.[38]

For the king, meanwhile, the episode had proved another significant success – and not only in terms of his personal security. Indeed, in the unlikely event that the rising really had been little more than a cynical propaganda ploy, it could not have been more skilfully managed. By March 1414, Henry's victory was so complete that a general amnesty was offered to those remaining prisoners in return for heavy fines, and by December the offer of amnesty had even been extended to Oldcastle himself. At the Leicester Parliament of the following month, moreover, there followed an item of anti-Lollard legislation, which would arguably influence the whole nature of church-state relations in England for years to come.

Hitherto, when the government had intervened at all in religious affairs, it had done so mainly in self-defence against what were perceived to be papal encroachments upon its authority. At Leicester, however, all officers of the Crown were now directly ordered to 'exert their entire pains and diligence to oust, cease and destroy all manner of heresies and errors vulgarly called Lollardies'.[39] In practice, this meant that all secular officials, from central court justices and lord mayors down to the king's bailiffs, were henceforth compelled, under oath, to seek out and if necessary arrest and imprison those suspected of heresy. At the same time, it was also officially confirmed that Lollardy threatened not only 'to annul and subvert the Christian faith and law of God', but also 'to destroy our sovereign lord the king himself'.[40]

The impact of heresy therefore seems to have encouraged a convergence of interest between state and church, which Henry's strict orthodoxy and commanding presence was always likely to push to the limit, particularly when Lollard heretics were fixed in the king's mind as only one feature of a broader threat to law, order and his own legitimacy. Whether he really was giving, as one commentator has suggested, early notice of his wish to act as 'supreme governor' of the 'Church of England', more than a century before those terms were actually in use, is perhaps doubtful.[41] But after the Leicester Parliament of 1414, both Henry and his successors were more inclined and better equipped than ever to pose as the protectors and upholders of true religion in their own right.

More generally, the successful suppression of Oldcastle's rebellion had furnished conclusive proof of the king's decisiveness, close attention to detail, coolness under pressure and unbending commitment to both political and religious conformity. His resounding victory over heresy had also placed the Church under an obligation which he would not hesitate to exploit when he was later most in need of prayers, blessings and, above all, money. At the same time, the propaganda potential of the Church's support could now be milked no less keenly than its coffers. Henceforth, the King of England was duly hailed on all sides as 'the Champion of Christ, the Pillar of Faith, God's Holy Knight, a new Constantine, a Maccabeus come back to life and the Worthy Bearer of the Sword of the Lord'.[42]

Within only a single year of his succession, in fact, Henry V was being widely presented as the guarantor of unity and honour in both church and state. Even Archbishop Arundel, for that matter, commended him as 'the most Christian king in Christ, our most noble king, the zealous supporter of the laws of Christ' – and not, it must be said, without good reason. Henry had, after all, proven every bit as effective in tackling religious divisions as he had in managing Parliament and encouraging public order. He had, moreover, triumphed over adversity by offering mercy to those who merited it and by vanquishing those who did not. And in doing so, he had demonstrated courage, imagination and pragmatism. In short, he had already dispelled most of those lingering doubts about the usurpation of 1399 and was now duly poised to pursue his most cherished dream of all – that of foreign conquest.

The approach of war

If there was any initial uncertainty at all about Henry V's overriding priority, it was soon dispelled. As early as June 1413, he had written to the people of Salisbury asking for money to aid his 'forthcoming expedition', and the following month London's Lord Mayor, Richard Whittington, saw fit to add a further £2,000 to the king's intended war chest.[43] In September, Henry was also hiring oxen and heavy horses to bring guns from Bristol to London, and by February 1414 a team of blacksmiths – which included a woman by the name of Margaret Merssh – had been commissioned to assist in the production of cannons at the Tower. Meanwhile, according to the chronicler John Strecche, Henry was steadily accumulating 'hauberks, helmets, shields, corselets, bucklers, lance-heads, gauntlets, plate-armour, swords, bows' and 'many thousands of arrows', along with every other conceivable implement for 'felling and splitting wood and mining walls'.[44]

A war policy was not, of course, without considerable risks. Even an unrivalled optimist like Henry was acutely aware that English adventures abroad during the previous century had ultimately ended in failure. He knew, too, that the strategy of exploiting internal divisions in Flanders, Normandy, Brittany and elsewhere had so far been of short-term value only. Similarly, the time-honoured English tactic of the *chevauchée*, designed to terrorise the native population while wreaking piecemeal economic havoc, was never likely to yield anything more than minimal gains politically. By the 1380s, in fact, this grim method of fighting had even encouraged a reaction in some circles against the chivalric exploitation of war and the wastefulness and moral corruption it entailed.

Yet if a handful of poets like Thomas Hoccleve and a smattering of scholars and churchmen were beginning to look anew at the almost casual destruction that had been accepted so readily for so long, they remained, as yet, lone voices. Indeed, in girding his realm for war, Henry V was not only defining his style of rule in the clearest possible terms, but also firmly securing the early good will of the vast bulk of his subjects. 'The English', wrote Froissart, 'will never love or honour their king unless he be victorious and a lover of arms and war against their neighbours, and especially against such as are greater and richer than themselves.'[45] Though the expense was never welcome, a convincing display of what contemporaries termed '*virtus*' could thus be guaranteed both to stir and reassure those many Englishmen who still had no doubt that 'to fight and to judge are the office of a king'.[46]

Certainly, the Leicester Parliament had provided ample evidence of growing hostility towards the old foe. For while there is no record of open debate on the subject, the Commons now made its first direct reference to the king's 'adversary of France'.[47] The Statute of Truces, meanwhile, represented a conscious attempt to stamp out the many acts of piracy, which were continuing to undermine relations with Burgundy and Brittany – two of England's most likely allies in any impending struggle. And loud complaints against lords and their retainers who made a mockery of the royal writ left the king in no doubt about the beckoning opportunity to refocus the energies of England's unemployed soldiery. There had been precious little booty from the marches of Wales and Scotland in recent years, and many appetites had already been whetted by the small continental expeditions led by Arundel and Clarence in 1411 and 1412.

The financial problems of many magnates had, moreover, become particularly acute by the end of the previous reign. Edward, Duke of York, for example, was heavily in debt, and his younger brother Richard was landless and heavily dependent upon annuities granted by the Crown. Thomas Beaufort, in his turn, had inherited nothing as John of Gaunt's youngest son, and Richard, Earl of Oxford, as well as Thomas, Earl of Salisbury, were both impoverished as a consequence of forfeitures and attainders which had permanently damaged their family fortunes. James, Earl of Ormond, on the other hand, had recently acquired his Irish inheritance, but had little property in England. Even the king's brother, Thomas, Duke of Clarence, had been forced to marry his uncle's widow, Margaret Holland, in order to gain access to her great wealth.

Clearly, if the Lancastrian dynasty could firmly establish itself at the head of a victorious and enriched aristocracy, any residual doubts about its legitimacy might well be banished once and for all. And now more than ever, the tumultuous situation across the Channel was simply too tantalising for any, even moderately, ambitious English ruler to resist. On 28 April 1413, the uneasy peace that had held between the Armagnacs and Burgundians throughout the previous autumn was abruptly shattered when the Parisian rabble, led by a skinner with Burgundian sympathies called Simon Caboche, seized the Dauphin at his palace in the Rue de St Antoine. Soon afterwards, the rebels went on to capture the king and his wife before murdering, executing or imprisoning most of the Armagnac nobles who held senior positions in the royal household.

If, however, the Duke of Burgundy had initially welcomed Caboche's rebellion in the hope of constraining his sixteen-year-old son-in-law, the Dauphin Louis, he was soon to regret the excesses that followed. On 18 May, King Charles was forced to wear the symbolic white hood of the Cabochiens in public, and, before long, the ultra-democratic agenda of Paris's artisans and shopkeepers became much more menacing still. The ordinance submitting the capital to the control of elected committees was worrying enough. But it was accompanied by numerous acts of gross violence, which reached a singularly unwholesome peak when the corpse of the Dauphin's chamberlain, who had committed suicide in prison by hitting his head repeatedly with a wine jar, was publicly beheaded. With the suppression of the revolt on 4 August, therefore, John the Fearless was left with no option but to flee the capital as the initiative swung once more in favour of the king, the Dauphin and the Armagnac lords.

Yet if Henry V was busily eyeing France's current turmoil with thoughts of glorious conquest in mind, he was also no less keen to fulfil God's will and serve the cause of justice as he saw it. In his eyes, after all, the validity of English claims had already been demonstrated decisively by the naval victory at Sluys in 1340, as well as the later triumphs at Crécy and Poitiers. On all three occasions, it seemed, God himself had intervened directly and unequivocally on England's behalf. And if modern observers may baulk at Henry's unconditional belief in trial by battle or his adherence to a code of justice that flowed directly from the Old Testament, it should not be forgotten that both were intrinsic to the age in which he lived.

Throughout the maze of negotiations that now unfolded, therefore, Henry's belief in his rightful claim to the French throne would remain utterly unshakeable. At a meeting in Leulinghen on 1 September 1413, for instance, both sides produced evidence for and against the English case, which had been made originally by Edward III on the strength of his mother Isabella's status as daughter of Philip IV of France. While the French brought forward the treatise of Jean de Montreuil, which challenged the whole basis of the Treaty of Brétigny, the English, in their turn, produced extensive antiquarian evidence to counter the French argument for Salic Law, which allegedly established a bar to any succession through the female line.

With hindsight, much of Henry's ardent legalism was of the plainly romantic variety. But there still remained more than enough genuine provocation by France to gall and galvanise a king like Henry, not to mention his entire court and family, into the sincerest sense of mission. There was an abundance of lawyers on hand to denounce the seizures of 'English' land by Philip Augustus in the time of King John and to condemn the more general *violentia Gallorum* that had continued to separate the kings of England from their 'rightful' inheritance. There was too, of course, the non-fulfilment of the treaties of Paris and Brétigny to consider, as well as the abrogation of a number of more minor interim pacts. More recently, the broken promises of the Armagnac lords had also become a particular bone of contention – and none more so than the unfulfilled offer agreed by them at Bourges prior to the Duke of Clarence's expedition of 1412.

Nor, for that matter, was there necessarily any inherent contradiction in Henry's wish to end the long-drawn-out conflict with France by means of further fighting. In his view, there could be no lasting peace until the two kingdoms were finally united by military means once and for all. 'The king', wrote the author of the *Gesta*, 'applied his mind with all devotion to encompass what could promote the honour of God, the extension of the Church, the deliverance of his country, and the peace and tranquillity of the two kingdoms of England and France.'[48] From such a perspective Henry's conflict with France was therefore no mere act of wanton self-aggrandisement. Rather, he was seeking to wage a 'war to end wars' – not only between France and England, but also between those same French factions which were currently tearing their land apart and causing untold suffering in the process.

And this, of course, was something which contemporaries fully understood and openly commended. The Book of Deuteronomy, as well as the Book of Joshua and numerous other biblical texts, clearly sanctioned the use of violence against the unjust and ungodly, and it was no coincidence that English diplomatic pressure over the coming months would be richly adorned with an unselfconscious dressing of religious quotation and imagery. In contemporary terms there was nothing intrinsically wicked about bloodshed in defence of a king's 'rights and inheritances'.[49] On the contrary, this moral justification for conflict had been firmly embedded in official Church teaching since at least the time of Hostiensis and Pope Innocent IV in the thirteenth century. Nor should it be forgotten that as Henry's own conflict with France gathered momentum, he would come to see it increasingly as the necessary prelude to a crusade in the Holy Land itself.

This is not to suggest, however, that in hoping for peace eventually, Henry was actually expecting it in the short term. By offering to negotiate with his enemies, Henry was always seeking maximum advantage for the inevitable struggle ahead, just as his determination to maintain legal forms sprang mainly from his keenness to convince his fellow European princes of his cause. In reality, the numerous embassies he despatched, as well as those he received, were all part of a familiar web of calculated manoeuvre, prompted by the conventions governing 'godly' warfare at this time, which emphasised the need for lengthy discussion prior to any outbreak of hostilities. And in quite literally fighting for peace, Henry would certainly feel no compunction either in forging those offensive alliances with the highest bidder that were so central to the internal logic of late medieval diplomacy.

The first exchanges of the new reign were therefore largely aimed at extending the existing truce arrangements, so that a façade of peace seeking could be sustained while the main business of extracting concessions and preparing for war continued unimpeded. Accordingly, a delegation headed by Henry Chichele, the Earl of Warwick and Lord Scrope arrived in France in September 1413 and agreed a general truce shortly afterwards, which was to be extended in subsequent meetings until January 1415 and thereafter from April through to June of the same year. As something of a formality, Henry's claim to the French throne under the Treaty of Brétigny was affirmed at the outset by the English envoys, though neither side wished to push its case too energetically in what amounted at this stage to little more than a preliminary sparring session.

By early 1414, moreover, the dominant Armagnac party at the French court was still anxious to continue talks as the Duke of Burgundy pursued his campaign to recapture Paris and an Anglo-Burgundian alliance became increasingly plausible. During the previous autumn, there had already been tentative talk of marriage between Henry and one of the duke's daughters. But for the time being at least, the French willingness to continue negotiations also suited England, and in late January a further English embassy was empowered to treat for peace – this time on the basis of a marriage between Henry and Charles VI's twelve-year-old daughter Catherine. The result was another exercise in probing and posturing which yielded little more than an assurance on Henry's part that he would not contract any other marriage – whether Burgundian, Castilian or Aragonese – before the beginning of May.

But while English and French ambassadors were dutifully angling for best advantage and the King of England was committing himself to a marriage that would ultimately become one of the mainstays of his whole diplomatic strategy, France's drastic descent into civil war was soon altering the whole drift of affairs and further stiffening Henry's conviction that now was the time for decisive action. After the Armagnac army left Paris in March in pursuit of the Duke of Burgundy, it carried all before it. By May, Compiègne had surrendered and that same month Soissons was sacked amid such outrageous carnage that some French chroniclers were later left to reflect how nothing the English inflicted upon northern France ever exceeded the miseries wrought by their fellow countrymen.[50]

The Burgundian need for English help had thus become especially pressing, and it was at this point that Henry opted, no less surprisingly perhaps, for a policy of conspicuous double-dealing. During the Leicester Parliament of 30 April to 29 May 1414, Burgundian envoys had little difficulty in securing an English promise for a force of 500 men-at-arms and 1,000 archers. Though John the Fearless himself refused a request to ally against either his own king or the Dauphin, he agreed nevertheless to help Henry conquer any English lands currently held by Armagnac lords. Only two days after this arrangement had been reached, however, ambassadors from England were despatched across the Channel not only to negotiate for the hand of Princess Catherine, but also to press the French king for those territorial claims that had so far been merely asserted rather than demanded. For good measure, Henry's ambassadors were also encouraged at one and the same time to seek the Duke of Burgundy's homage, as well as marriage to one of his daughters.

In the interim, John the Fearless's predicament continued to worsen significantly, as Bapaume surrendered in June and the French king and his Armagnac allies began to besiege Arras at the end of the following month. In consequence, the English were now even better placed to turn the screw on their prospective Burgundian allies. And according to a draft treaty drawn up by Henry's advisers on 7 August 1414, the Duke of Burgundy was duly requested not to resist any attempt the King of England might make to seize the crown of France itself. Though there is no evidence that the draft was ever ratified or even seriously considered, its very existence is ample proof of the growing scale of English ambitions in the face of Burgundy's increasingly desperate plight.

Elsewhere, the embassy appointed by Henry on 31 May was now pressing the French more strenuously than ever in the hope that the prospect of an Anglo-Burgundian alliance would force them to offer the most generous concessions possible. At the outset of the negotiations, Henry's envoys once again affirmed his claim to the crown and realm of France, but soon offered to settle for less in an increasingly unconvincing effort to maintain at least the appearance of a willingness to compromise. In reality, the territorial claims of the English remained impossibly ambitious as Bishop Courtney and his fellow emissaries asked for what amounted to the whole of western France: Normandy, Anjou, Maine, Touraine, Poitou and the lands between Flanders and the Somme, along with Aquitaine as it had been in 1360 and Provence. Furthermore, as if to add insult to injury, they also demanded the payment of 1.6 million *écus*, along with the still unpaid ransom of King John II, and a dowry of 2 million *écus* for the hand of Princess Catherine.

By now, then, the scope for further hollow discussion was rapidly diminishing. The French, for their part, were only prepared to concede Aquitaine in lordship rather than sovereignty, and the dowry of 600,000 *écus*, which they now proffered, was a further sign that the time for talking would soon be at an end. The following month, moreover, English hopes for a breakthrough evaporated once and for all when an outbreak of dysentery among Charles VI's besiegers at Arras left him no alternative but to seek peace with the Burgundians. And though Charles's hopes of outright victory over John the Fearless were frustrated by this turn of events, he still had the distinct consolation of facing the impending attack from England without the immediate likelihood of civil war at home.

When Parliament met on 19 November, therefore, all diplomatic routes were hopelessly blocked and war was closer than ever. Indeed, the opening declaration of Henry Beaufort could not have sent a clearer signal of his king's intentions. Just as a tree responds to the seasons, Beaufort explained, 'so, too, man is given a time of peace and a time of war and toil'. 'The king', he continued, 'understands that a suitable time has now come for him to accomplish his purpose with the aid of God', especially since the realm was now blessed with peace and tranquillity 'by God's grace'.[51]

Yet even now, there was still some further persuasion required at home, for although Lords and Commons contributed a double lay subsidy and committed themselves to the service of the king 'with their bodies', they also requested unanimously that a further embassy be sent to France.[52] To add to Henry's frustration, the subsidy on offer could not now be collected quickly, since he would have to wait until the return of the new embassy, which was finally appointed on 5 December 1414. Moreover, the money raised, though generous, would not generate sufficient funds for a campaign on the grand scale that was being envisaged. Instead, Henry was forced before long to pawn most of the valuables in his possession.

Ultimately, then, the path to war had become as much a test of endurance as of nerve and guile. But it was not until this point that Henry appears to have achieved his most impressive diplomatic manoeuvre of all. To all appearances, the subsequent negotiations of March 1415 seemed to confirm that the King of England was in the midst of his first major setback. Certainly, the French were now in much less need to concede territory after the Peace of Arras, and the English ambassadors were accordingly instructed to submit significantly reduced demands. With regard to territory, for instance, Henry's representatives now asked only for the lands transferred under the Treaty of Brétigny, along with Provence, Nogent and Beaufort, all of which had specific Lancastrian connections. Similarly, the English expressed their willingness to accept a reduction of Catherine's dowry, first to 1.5 million *écus* and then to 1 million.

Far from retreating, however, Henry was actually strengthening his case immeasurably before Parliament, as well as on the broader international stage, which meant so much to him. When the French inevitably queried even these more modest territorial claims and merely offered lands in Guienne as fiefs – conditional upon the English dropping their claims to outstanding payments of John II's ransom – there could be little further doubt where right lay. Even on the subject of the dowry the French offered only 800,000 *écus*. And as the English delegation finally withdrew on 29 March, Henry was therefore perfectly poised for a final push to war, which would now at long last have the full force of domestic and international opinion behind it.

At a Great Council summoned to assemble on Monday 5 April, the king was able to announce with all sincerity that he had fulfilled Parliament's request for a second embassy and had even offered to let his adversary keep the greater part of what rightfully belonged to the crown of England. Under such provocation, Henry argued, he had exhausted all possibility of progress by means of diplomacy and was now left with no alternative but to conduct a military expedition. In other words, like any skilled combatant, he had used his enemy's strength as leverage to gain the outcome he desired. And with checkmate complete, indentures for the recruitment of an English army were duly sealed before the month was out.

Across the Channel, meanwhile, the French were also squaring to fight – and with greater willingness than is often recognised. With the prospect of a united front against the English once again restored, Charles VI had ordered a substantial tax levy to defend his kingdom on 13 March. And to boost French confidence further, their king was currently enjoying a period of comparative mental stability, which had allowed him to participate in the jousts arranged as part of the hospitality for the second English embassy. Above all, however, it was the Dauphin, who was raring to come to grips with the King of England. By now he was calling the tune in his relations with the Duke of Burgundy and was also firmly in control of both royal finances and the appointment of royal officials. Indeed, he may even have felt sufficiently buoyant to deliver a personal taunt to Henry, though not in all likelihood the one immortalised by Shakespeare in the famous tale of the tennis balls.

If such an egregious insult had actually been delivered, it is hard to see how negotiations could have continued. Yet one final set of talks did indeed begin at Winchester on 30 June. Like previous meetings, these talks were driven by ulterior motives. In this case, however, it was mainly the French who were driving the deceit, since they were determined to delay the invasion until the last of their tax collections had been completed on 1 August. The talks also provided an opportunity for their ambassadors to gauge Henry's military preparations. Fully aware of his enemies' ploy, Henry was, however, powerless to press ahead with his invasion if he was to maintain his chosen pose as the aggrieved party.

What passed at the weeklong meeting in the bishop's palace at Winchester is in fact unclear, since there was no official record of proceedings. But it appears from one incident at least that the usual diplomatic pretence was by now wearing particularly thin. Dressed in cloth of gold from head to foot and flanked by Chancellor Beaufort and various prelates, Henry seems to have finally cut loose and warned the Archbishop of Bourges that if Charles VI did not meet his demands, he would be responsible for 'a deluge of Christian blood'. The archbishop's response, however, was more provocative by far. 'Sire', he retorted, 'the King of France our sovereign lord is true King of France, and regarding those things to which you say you have a right, you have no lordship not even to the kingdom of England which belongs to the true heirs of King Richard.' At which point, Henry is said to have stormed from the conference chamber.[53]

Thereafter, on 6 July, war was formally declared. Henry called once more on God to witness that it was the fault of Charles for refusing to do him 'justice' and also, according to the author of the *Gesta*, ordered copies of 'pacts and covenants entered into between the most serene prince the King of England Henry IV, his father, and certain of the great princes of France on the subject of his divine right and claim to the Duchy of Aquitaine'. Transcripts were then sent to the Council of the Church that had recently convened at Constance, and to the Holy Roman Emperor Sigismund, as well as other monarchs, to explain why the English ruler 'was being compelled to raise his standard against rebels'.[54]

Even now, however, there was still time for one last ultimatum, which was sent to Charles by Henry from Southampton on 28 July. The themes, of course, were mostly familiar enough. On the one hand, the usual religious images were employed, including a reference to the law of Deuteronomy, whereby a man who continued to be refused justice after offering peace was entitled to attack his wrongdoer. The letter also offered to reduce the demand for Catherine's dowry by 50,000 *écus* – 'to show that we are more inclined to peace than avarice' – though this, like the rest of the letter, was not so much a serious offer as a further pretext for war. It was, however, in his final personal appeal to the King of France that Henry best betrayed all the controlled intensity and absolute confidence in his cause that would soon be carrying him to his greatest triumphs. Having done everything he could to ensure peace, he declared, he had nevertheless been barred from his lawful inheritance for too long. Nor, he continued, did he now lack the courage to fight to the death. As such, there was only one prudent course for his French counterpart to follow. 'By the merciful bowels of Jesus Christ', ran Henry's final plea and warning, 'friend, render what you owe.'[55]

4 God's chosen warrior, 1415

Logistics, finance and war aims

Towards sunset on Saturday 6 July, Henry V and his courtiers had finally left Winchester to join the greatest fighting force assembled on English soil since the siege of Calais in 1347. Throughout the previous week, the night skies for more than twenty miles around Southampton were brightly lit by campfires, as the king's men gathered for action. On Southampton Common and in the fields around Portsmouth, not to mention a host of other mustering points like Wallopforth, Hampton Hill and Swanwick Heath, royal officials had been busily checking the retinues of Henry's captains, while all along the Hampshire coast, opposite the Isle of Wight, every suitable creek and inlet continued to fill with ships. Henceforth, as the final tired moves in the diplomatic game were being dutifully played out, the king would be gearing his troops for war and closely supervising the many complex movements and preparations now nearing completion.[1]

These preparations had been gathering pace since at least 22 September 1414 when Nicholas Merbury, the king's master of ordnance, had first been commanded to employ a variety of craftsmen for the manufacture of guns and other engines of war. Iron, timber and other necessary materials were duly ordered, and four days later the export of gunpowder from any English port was strictly prohibited. By the end of October, moreover, 10,000 gunstones were heading for London and in the early months of 1415 the navy was also placed in a state of heightened readiness. Under the supervision of William Catton, who became clerk of the king's ships in July 1413, the six royal vessels that Henry inherited from his father had now grown to twelve. But in all as many as 1,500 ships were now needed for transport, many of which were seized in English ports from foreign owners, or hired from Holland and Zeeland.

As always, the king left little to others that he could reasonably do himself. He was prepared, it is true, to delegate where necessary, and a number of individuals were assigned specific responsibilities. Henry Beaufort, for instance, was instructed to array men in each county for the defence of the realm and arrange for the monitoring of any Lollard activity, while the Earl of Arundel was asked to obtain and transport victuals to Southampton. It was also decided, more importantly, that the keeper of the realm in the king's absence was to be his brother John, assisted by a handful of peers, such as the Earl of Westmorland and Lord Grey of Codnor, who were to protect the marches and act as his advisers. Yet almost everything else – from the provision of iron nails for his horses' hoofs to the purchase of bread and ale – remained under Henry's direct supervision.

Nor was the king prepared to tolerate any abuse of authority by those requisitioning on his behalf. On 24 July, in an innovation without parallel in Europe, he gave notice that any individual aggrieved by his captains or his soldiers should present their complaints before either the seneschal of the treasury or controller of the king's household.[2] Every writ that the king issued to obtain provisions was, moreover, to be read aloud in both the county courts and the marketplaces of the shires involved – encouraging not only fairness, but also the more direct involvement of non-combatants in the struggle to come. For this was to be presented as a new type of conflict – one involving not only the honour of the king and the military elite who served him, but also the interests and efforts of the whole realm.

Clearly, such a war could never be waged effectively if it was not well funded, and here, as elsewhere, Henry's bitter experiences of campaigning on a shoestring in Wales had taught him a number of invaluable lessons. His approach to finance was, in fact, characteristically level-headed. By restoring central control and auditing, for instance, he set out to monitor unnecessary expenditure and reduce fraud and waste. He also made a point of reviewing rents on Crown lands. Above all, however, the annuities and pensions, which his father had been so eager to bestow, were now halved, while those earning them were compelled in return to serve on the king's expeditions. By such means, the Crown had already doubled its income from the previous reign. And now Henry was keener than ever to depart for France with his finances in good order – 'to the comfort of his lieges' and as a 'well-governed Christian prince'.[3]

Yet the military campaign of 1415 could not be paid for by retrenchment and good bookkeeping alone. The primary indirect taxes at this time were levied on wool and wine, and the clergy were also liable to pay subsidies, granted to the Crown by Convocation. Such sources of income still remained inadequate, however, and this meant that Parliament would now be made to stand and deliver, for since 1407 the House of Commons had boasted sole authority to grant taxation. The main types of direct tax, on the other hand, were levied on moveable goods at the customary rate of one fifteenth in the countryside and one tenth in the towns, and somewhat worryingly perhaps, the king had already been granted a full fifteenth and tenth in his first Parliament of 1413.

Henry's keen political instinct had, however, deterred him from asking for more at the next Parliament of April 1414, so that when his third Parliament met in November of the same year, he was well placed to seize the financial initiative once again. This time, indeed, he asked for and received two whole fifteenths and tenths, which yielded the mighty sum of £76,000, thanks in no small measure to the efforts of Henry Beaufort and the Speaker, Thomas Chaucer. Not to be outdone, the clergy, too, obliged him with generous grants of two tenths, no doubt partly in gratitude for the king's successful suppression of the Oldcastle rising only a year earlier. And wealthy church leaders also willingly played their part. Archbishop Henry Chichele and Bishop Repingdon of Lincoln lent £200 and £400 respectively, while the wealthiest clergyman in all England, Henry Beaufort, was particularly bountiful. In June and July alone he supplied his nephew with almost £2,630.

This is not to say, of course, that all was plain sailing. The money could not, for instance, be collected in one fell swoop. Half would be due in February 1415 and the rest a year later. And though Henry wisely shunned the temptation to borrow from foreign banking houses in the way that his great-grandfather had done, he was forced, nevertheless, to look to his own subjects for the necessary funds. For this reason, therefore, there was little choice but to mortgage the most precious items of the royal jewel house as security for a series of massive loans, which began on 10 March with an approach to the City of London for an advance that would eventually amount to £10,000. In return, Henry was prepared to offer one of his most treasured possessions, the so-called 'Pusan d' Or' collar, weighing 56 ounces and richly decorated with jewelled and enamelled crowns and antelopes.

Nor were other transactions of this kind long in following once Richard Courtenay, treasurer of the king's chamber, had been given overall responsibility for arranging them. In one instance, Richard II's gold crown was pawned for a loan of 1,000 marks from the people of Norfolk. On another occasion, a richly bejewelled golden tabernacle, once belonging to the Duke of Burgundy, was offered as security for 860 marks loaned by a consortium of laymen and clergymen from Devon. Bristol, in its turn, provided £582, York £200 and Dartmouth the humbler sum of £13 6s 8d – all in return for appropriate sweeteners. Prominent individuals, too, were no less willing to support the patriotic cause and thereby curry favour with their sovereign. The biggest single contribution, worth £10,936 3s 8d, came from Roger Salveyn, treasurer of Calais, who would have to wait more than six years for full repayment.

Naturally enough, there were occasional protests, most notably from those towns that had already paid the first instalment of the taxes granted by Parliament towards the end of 1414. At Salisbury, for instance, the sum of £100, which had been requested at first, was finally reduced by a third after popular unrest. The Venetian Antonio Morosini also complained that many Italian merchants were being seized along with their goods, and forced to pay huge fees for their release.[4] But by capturing the mood of the day and applying a potent mixture of moral pressure and naked intimidation, Henry nevertheless managed to generate the lion's share of the funds needed to make good his assault on France. Writing thirty years after the actual campaign, Enguerrand de Monstrelet estimated the amount at well in excess of 500,000 gold nobles.[5] And although the actual figure remains uncertain, the fact that sufficient money was raised at all is a testament not only to the king's tenacity, but to the faith of his subjects in the overall worth of his cause.

If, moreover, Henry V's initial military planning was largely unaffected by financial worries, he was no less fortunate when it came to the reserves of manpower at his disposal – so much so, in fact, that he was ultimately forced to leave men behind in England for lack of transport. By this time the old feudal system of military service, relying on grants of land in return for personal loyalty and obligation, had largely broken down under the pressure of almost constant fighting in France during the reign of Edward III. And though traces of it still remained, the emphasis now was upon legally binding contracts of service, known as 'indentures'.

Almost all of those agreed between Henry and his captains – some 320 in all, according to Exchequer accounts – seem to have been signed on 29 April. Each laid down arrangements for length of service, the size and composition of specific retinues, the payment of wages and general conditions governing the allocation of prizes, booty and ransom money. Wage rates, meanwhile, were finally fixed on 18 April at the level for a campaign in Guienne, which was higher than that paid for service in France itself. Here, however, the aim was twofold – to confuse the enemy and to encourage men to enlist – since Henry's eyes were already firmly set upon a campaign to the north. Nor is there any doubt that the king's inner circle was fully aware of his real intentions. For in the Issue Rolls for 19 April there is a tell-tale payment to a certain William Hoklyst for the cost of a *jantaculum*, or breakfast, at the palace of Westminster, so that the king could be advised 'on his present expedition towards Harfleur and the region of Normandy'.[6]

If so, then Henry's war aims may at first appear contradictory. His final ultimatum to Charles had implied a desire for little other than the terms laid down by the Treaty of Brétigny or, in effect, those offered by the Armagnac princes under the recent Treaty of Bourges. And it was copies of the latter agreement that Henry would send to the Council of Constance and the Emperor Sigismund on 10 July as proof of the justice of his cause and the need for him to act 'against rebels'.[7] Yet his military preparations were now directed towards Harfleur, the key to Normandy – a territory to which Edward III had explicitly surrendered all rights, and one, moreover, that could only be justly attacked in the event of Henry pressing a claim to the crown of France itself. To complicate matters, the *Gesta* interpreted the military campaign of 1415 as an attempt 'to recover the Duchy of Normandy, which belonged to him by right from the time of William the first, the conqueror'.[8]

Significantly, though, the only mention of Henry's claim to Normandy in 1415 appears in the *Gesta*. Henry Beaufort's opening speech to the November 1415 Parliament, by contrast, would specifically refer to Harfleur as 'in France', while Henry's march from there to Calais was described as being 'through the heart of France'.[9] As such, the *Gesta*'s comments are more likely to reflect the king's expanded war aims of 1417 than the actual situation two years earlier before he had routed his opponents and further convinced himself of both his cause and his invincibility. In reality, therefore, Henry's present decision to target Normandy was driven by no more than sound strategy and simple convenience.

It was certainly much cheaper and easier to transport a large army across the Channel than southwards towards Bordeaux, where an invasion would place little real pressure on the enemy. But there were also more specific reasons why an attack on Harfleur was altogether preferable. On the one hand, the capture of this key port would provide the English with a convenient bridgehead on the Seine through which supplies and reinforcements could be brought, and subsequent invasions launched. The town had also been serving as a centre for raids on English shipping and lay on a river leading directly to Paris, through an area that contributed substantially to French royal revenues. Above all, the size and composition of Henry's force made it perfectly feasible for him to capture and garrison further towns, which could then be added to his later demands.

Significantly, archers were to outnumber 'men-at-arms' by a ratio of three to one in most indenture arrangements, although the additional inclusion of some 1,247 archers raised from Wales, Lancashire and Cheshire meant that the overall proportion was probably about 80 per cent. Archers were, after all, about half as expensive as men-at-arms, and they could be raised more easily, since they needed less specialised equipment and multi-faceted training. But they were also highly efficient as well as economical. Quite apart from their potentially decisive impact in set-piece battles, archers were just as useful as men-at-arms when it came to the raids, skirmishes and sieges, which made up most campaign activity. And since they were mostly mounted, their presence did not slow down an army or restrict their use to fixed-point warfare.

The nobility, meanwhile, took up the call to arms with gusto. Indeed, only three of the seventeen members of the higher nobility alive when Henry set sail in 1415 did not fight in person – and of these, two were boys and one blind. When it came to combat, moreover, Henry's nobles were tried and trusted. England had become highly militarised since the usurpation of 1399 and this not only reinforced the predominant martial ethos among the realm's elites, but considerably augmented the pool of experienced and talented commanders at the king's disposal. Men such as the earls of Dorset and Arundel, for instance, had already enjoyed lengthy careers in arms and were totally trusted by the king. Furthermore, eleven of the higher nobility were actually between the ages of eighteen and thirty-two at the start of the new reign – the age when fighting men are normally at their peak. Many, including the earls of Salisbury and Warwick, had already served with the king in Wales against Glyn Dŵr, while others, like Richard Beauchamp, Earl of Warwick, had fought with the Teutonic Knights in Prussia, alongside Lord Fitzhugh, Sir Ralph Rochford and Sir Walter Hungerford.

Such men were also prepared to incur considerable expense in pursuit of glory abroad. For the major retinues in 1415 were sure to have been very expensive indeed. After the 960 and 800 men brought by the dukes of Clarence and Gloucester came the contingents of the Duke of York and the Earl of Dorset, each at 400. Then came the retinues of the earls of March, Cambridge and Norfolk – all at upwards of 200 – followed by the dukes of Suffolk, Oxford and Salisbury at 160, 140 and 120. It should be remembered, too, that these nobles expected to travel in style. The Earl of Norfolk, for example, took not only his master of horse, but also his stewards, his minstrels, his baker and armourer, the yeoman of his robes and even his barber. His pavilion, meanwhile, was equipped with every facility, including a new bed, mattress and bolster, along with a new iron seat for his latrine.[10]

The distinctive feature of the 1415 campaign, however, was the very large number of small and even tiny retinues involved. Three years earlier, the Duke of Clarence's 4,000 strong army had consisted of only three contingents. Now, however, at least 122 individuals contracted to serve with as few as ten men. Not only did this create a more direct link between the king and his army, it also enabled Henry to draw his soldiers from a much wider geographical area than might otherwise have been the case. Larger concentrations of soldiers came, it is true, from London and the Home Counties. A good number also seem to have been recruited from the maritime counties of the south coast. But many more counties were represented in Henry's muster rolls than if he had depended upon a handful of mighty individuals to raise his army for him. And in consequence the force that now stood poised to cross the Channel was much more of a truly national entity than its predecessors.

Nor was the presence of foreign troops especially missed, for the army of 1415 was not only high in morale, but large in size. From the statistics available, 26 peers entered into indentures to provide 5,222 men, while 57 knights contracted for a further 2,573 men. Those indented below knightly rank, on the other hand, produced a total of 1,306 men. Wales, Cheshire and Lancashire, as we have seen, produced 1,247 archers, while around 900 other archers were raised from the royal household, giving an overall total of approximately 11,248 soldiers, of whom 2,266 were men-at-arms. We know, too, from the muster rolls that certain captains exceeded the recruitment totals required by their indenture, and it also seems likely that others indented for whom no information exists, boosting the total number of combatants to more than 12,000 – a force at least triple the size of the one that left England in 1412.[11]

Yet in spite of mounting pressure, the king still found time, it is said, for pilgrimage to the shrine of St Winifred at Holywell in Flintshire.[12] And if so, this was certainly no act of penance for waging war. He had, after all, been in constant consultation with Parliament, the Great Council and his leading churchmen as the countdown proceeded. He had also set out his case carefully, and – in his own eyes at least – given his adversary every opportunity to compromise. Ultimately, he would take the third and final step of consulting international opinion by ordering transcripts of the Treaty of Bourges to be sent not only to Constance, but also to the Holy Roman Emperor and other European princes. By the standards of the age, therefore, Henry's current zeal for conflict was neither hypocrisy nor fanaticism. Rather, it resulted from the remorseless application of cold logic and God's will. For as Christine de Pizan put it at the time, wars and battles waged for a fitting cause were 'but the proper execution of justice'.[13]

The Southampton Plot

On 24 July, Henry V quietly signed his will at Winchester, entrusting his soul to the merciful intercession of the Virgin, the saints and his special patron, John of Bridlington. 'This is my last will', he wrote in English, 'subscribed with my own hand R.H.' And with a final plea for help to 'Jesu Mercy and Gramercy Ladie Marie', he duly concluded a deeply personal document, which was heavily loaded with pious intentions. In all, 20,000 masses were to be said for the repose of his soul, including 3,000 in honour of the Holy Trinity and another 5,000 for the joys of Our Lady. Three masses were also to be sung daily by each and every monk of Westminster Abbey, where Henry was to lay at rest in a fine stone tomb amid the many relics of Edward the Confessor's Chapel. As a further token of the king's devotion, 1,000 marks were to be left to each of his new foundations at Syon Abbey and Sheen.[14]

Amid the lengthy list of bequests to the great and not so great, there was only an oblique reference to 'our successor', Thomas, Duke of Clarence, who was to receive his brother's two best crowns and armour, the sceptre of the kingdom, a queen's crown, an ensign of Spain and two pairs of astrological spheres. The long history of tension between the two was no secret, and it had made their father warn at one point of 'some discord' that might arise after his death. More ominously still, the former king had even warned his heir how Thomas might later 'make some enterprise against thee', since both men were known to be 'of so great stomach and courage'.[15] But though the younger brother had been conspicuous by his absence from the Council between 10 April and 27 May 1415, and had also missed the important meeting with the Lord Mayor of London at the Guildhall in March, his value as a skilled and loyal commander was still beyond all doubt. And it was for this reason that Henry had granted him the castle of Somerton on 15 May as a token of good faith, confirming that there was no desire on his part for petty snubs and point scoring at this crucial juncture.

Yet if the king had any notion that the sealing of his will would clear the way at last for his long-awaited reckoning with France, he could not have been more mistaken. For only one week later, on the very eve of his departure, he was rocked by a revelation which appeared to place everything – his plans, his faith in those closest to him, and even perhaps his supreme self-confidence – in the gravest jeopardy. The bearer of bad tidings was, in fact, Edmund Mortimer, Earl of March, who on 31 July arrived without warning at Portchester Castle to demand an urgent audience with the king. Agitated, fearful and stricken with hollow remorse, March was actually bracing himself for a meeting that would either cost or save his life, since he had come to confess how his very own brother-in-law, the Earl of Cambridge – aided by Sir Thomas Grey and Henry Lord Scrope – had tried to make him the figurehead in a plot to usurp the crown.

As Cambridge later explained in his confession, the initial aim of the so-called 'Southampton Plot' had been to remove March to safety in Wales, after which the entire north would be raised with the help of a Scots army and the added assistance of Hotspur's son, Henry Percy, who had been living in exile across the border since his grandfather's defeat at Bramham Moor in 1408. If the impersonator of Richard II known as the 'Mommet' did not then materialise as planned, the Earl of March would be proclaimed king, just as the royal castles in Wales were being seized, with inside assistance, by followers of Glyn Dŵr. As a finishing touch, the Welsh borders and West Country were also to rise at the instigation of the seemingly irrepressible Sir John Oldcastle and his Lollard supporters.

The involvement of the Earl of Cambridge in such an enterprise was not, perhaps, altogether surprising. He was, it is true, the king's first cousin twice removed, but while his brother Edward, Duke of York, was one of Henry's closest companions, his sister Constance was the widow of Thomas Despenser, the self-same Earl of Gloucester who had been deeply involved in the Epiphany Rising of the previous reign. Nor had the current king done much to cement Cambridge's loyalty. Henry had, in fact, promoted him to his earldom in 1414 and then bestowed upon him the office of 'almoner of England', along with a pension of 350 marks. Yet gestures of this kind were far more likely to insult than satisfy a man of such pedigree – especially when he was not only poor but without prospects. Indeed, unlike his elder brother, who had inherited the dukedom of York, Cambridge himself had no further titles or lands to look forward to, in spite of the fact that his first wife had been Anne Mortimer, sister of the Earl of March, which meant that his three-year-old son stood to inherit all the claims of the Mortimer family – including its right to the thrones of England and France through Edward III's granddaughter Philippa – if the Lancastrian line were extinguished and March himself died childless.

Yet if this particular conspirator had cast-iron grounds for grievance, the same was much less obviously true of another. Henry, Lord Scrope of Masham, was the nephew of Archbishop Richard Scrope who had been summarily executed by Henry IV in 1405, but he was also the grandson of one of Edward III's most loyal knights and had himself faithfully upheld the Lancastrian cause for over a decade. Now around forty, he had fought on crusade in his youth and gone on to wield his sword bravely against Hotspur's rebels at Shrewsbury. More importantly still, he had served the current king so faithfully in Wales that when Henry became temporary regent in 1409, he was quickly admitted to the Garter and appointed treasurer of England. After Henry's succession, moreover, he became a regular member of important English embassies to France, assisting in the most delicate negotiations with both French and Burgundian representatives.

The 'hammer blow' caused by reports of Scope's disloyalty can therefore well be imagined.[16] This, after all, was not only a member of Henry's Council, but also one of the trustees recently nominated to administer the king's private estate, should he fail to return from France. And for Henry the parallels with Oldcastle's rebellion of the previous year must have been particularly galling. Then, too, a trusted lieutenant had betrayed him and sought his death. But this time the implications were even more disturbing, since the nexus of family ties binding the Earl of March to other members of the nobility gave the Southampton Plot an altogether broader significance. Clearly, a good number of high-ranking men stood to gain from his succession, even if most of them, including Cambridge himself, had so far demonstrated no overt opposition. The Earl of Devon's heir, Sir Edward Courtenay, was, for instance, the husband of March's other sister Eleanor, while Lord Camoys was married to the earl's aunt. Members of the Holland family were also related to the Earl of March through his mother. And Lord Clifford, in his turn, was Cambridge's brother-in-law.

Nor was the third of the accused men, Sir Thomas Grey, someone to be casually dismissed. On the contrary, as Constable of Bamborough and Norham castles, he controlled key strongholds in Northumberland, and was also both son-in-law to the Earl of Westmorland, and brother-in-law to the Earl of Northumberland. His son, meanwhile, had already gained the hand of the Earl of Cambridge's daughter. Though not, therefore, a member of the aristocracy in his own right, Grey was nevertheless well connected and highly respected throughout the North Country – 'a knight', according to the *Gesta*, 'famous and noble if only he had not been dishonoured by the stain of treason'.[17]

With such a list of traitors – real and potential – at such a critical moment, it was hardly surprising that the king's response to any conspiracy should be both swift and decisive, though Henry's actions would remain characteristically measured. It is possible, in fact, that his spies had already warned him of the conspiracy and instead of resorting to panic, he seems to have summoned his magnates to Portchester, as though to an ordinary Council meeting, in order to seek their advice. Nevertheless, before nightfall Cambridge, Gray and Scrope were all imprisoned in the new tower at Southampton Castle, and a commission of four earls, four barons and two royal justices had been appointed to hear the case before a regular jury.

The trial, which began next day on Friday 2 August, was held within the castle, and Scrope's confession was duly presented in a lengthy letter drawn up on his behalf. In a humble preamble, he acknowledged that his life lay in the king's hands, but emphasised that he had never offended Henry before, and never would again. Although he had on his own admission known of the conspiracy, he claimed to have been entirely ignorant of any alleged assassination, and also emphasised how he had warned the plotters against their other plans. If, moreover, he had discovered a 'grounded purpose' or concrete plan connected with the plot, he would, according to his version of events, have informed the king immediately. His sole aim, in other words, had been to listen to Cambridge, in order to expose him if necessary. But the Earl of March had ultimately beaten him to it. And this would remain Scrope's story to the very end.[18]

Cambridge in contrast left conflicting accounts of what had transpired over the preceding days. In the first and most badly damaged of his surviving letters, he admitted his plan to take the Earl of March into Wales, and to capture and exchange the Earl of Fife for the fake Richard II and Henry Percy. He also suggested that Sir Robert Umfraville and Sir John Widdrington, as well as Sir Thomas Grey, had been complicit in the plot, but denied any intention to bring about the death of the king, and emphasised Scrope's innocence. Later, however, he admitted to producing a proclamation referring to the king as 'Harry of Lancaster, usurper of England', and also altered his testimony with regard to Scrope's involvement. Although Scrope had remained ignorant of some aspects of the plot, he had, said Cambridge, known of the plan to remove the Earl of March to Wales.

But if the waters were still somewhat muddied after Cambridge's testimony, it was left to Grey to deliver the most damning confession of all. After repeatedly stressing that the Earl of March had wholeheartedly assented to the plot, right up to its very conclusion, he went on to suggest that not only Scrope, but also the Earl of Arundel had supported the idea of deposing the king. And as the earth shifted more and more ominously beneath the plotters' feet, the government now found it easier still to ensnare them with the broader, but unsubstantiated charge of conspiring to murder the king. In spite of their vehement denials, therefore, both Grey and Cambridge were labelled as would-be assassins, while Scrope's failure to inform the king of their intentions was conveniently presented as a capital offence in its own right, even though it fell outside the strict parameters of the 1352 Statute of Treasons.

Grey, for his part, was therefore immediately sentenced to a traitor's death, though Cambridge and Scrope demanded trial by their peers, and in consequence briefly postponed their fate. It was not until 5 August, in fact, that the Duke of Clarence, who presided over the second hearing, finally delivered the inevitable guilty verdict. And while March was merely left to dangle in doubt until 9 August before being granted a full pardon, there was no such clemency for his associates. All three were to be drawn through the streets of Southampton in disgrace, and thereafter hung and beheaded, though the hanging was ultimately remitted by the king's personal intervention, and Cambridge and Grey were also excused the indignity of public display on their way to the gallows. Scrope alone suffered the ignominy of the traitor's hurdle, finally arriving at Southampton's north gate, where he was beheaded just outside the city wall on the same day as Cambridge. Some time later, his head would be duly spiked and displayed at York, while Grey's was hung from the tower at Newcastle as another grim reminder to all northerners of the price of treason.

And there, or so it seemed, the whole unhappy story ended. Yet much remains that continues to baffle and perplex across the centuries. Not least, the accounts of the various chroniclers who reported the event at the time are plainly suspect. Naturally enough, the claim that French gold was at the bottom of the conspirators' treachery was a recurring one. In Thomas Walsingham's account, for instance, sheer greed provided the motivation for 'three powerful men, in whom the king had the greatest trust', while the *Gesta* tells of how 'these men, in their brutal madness and mad brutality' conspired 'not only to prevent the intended expedition but also to inflict disaster by killing the king'.[19] According to the *Brut*, too, the conspirators 'for lucre of money had made promise to Frenchmen', receiving 'a million of gold' for their treachery.[20]

But no such claims were ever corroborated, and baseless conjectures of this kind were also mixed with outright inaccuracies. The *Gesta*, to take but one example, records that Sir Thomas Grey was tried and executed along with Cambridge and Scrope on Monday 5 August, when he had, in fact, met his death three days earlier.[21] And to compound matters, the confessions of all three men, which were hardly freely given, amount to a curious blend of fond hopes and glaring folly. Henry's intended replacement, the Earl of March, was, for example, a limp and uninspiring figure, who clearly lacked the vision, thrust and vigour of the reigning king. It was true that he had been given firm grounds for grievance when Henry unwisely inflicted a shattering fine of 10,000 marks upon him for marrying his kinswoman Anne Stafford without royal permission. But far from being an artful intriguer or man of action, the earl was essentially a political wallflower, more concerned – if his personal accounts are any indication – with the pursuit of pleasure than power. Between the autumn of 1413 and the spring of 1414, we find that he lost £157 at cards, raffles dice and cockfighting, and this, it seems was not his only vice, for he is also known to have made a number of suspiciously large payments to a certain 'Alice at Poplar'.[22]

And if March's main talent lay in self-preservation, his fellow conspirators were hardly more convincing either. Cambridge lacked the territorial power-base to foment political insurrection in his own right, and was therefore forced to place his faith in a series of shaky alliances – not only with March, but also the followers of Glyn Dŵr and the young Henry Percy. Sir Thomas Grey, on the other hand, had been spurred into action by little more than a sordid cocktail of greed and chronic insolvency, while Scrope's involvement was always largely peripheral. It seems certain, for instance, that he was absent from several key meetings between the conspirators, including one at Hamble in the Hook just two days before the alleged assassination attempt was due to occur. At the same time, he was also one of the most deeply religious and orthodox noblemen at Henry's court – something that makes it hard to understand his apparent willingness to join forces with Lollard heretics.

Then, of course, there is the apparent harshness of Scrope's treatment to consider, especially in comparison with the leniency exercised towards others like Lord Clifford and Sir Edward Courtenay, both of whom, arguably, were no less guilty of the same crime of silence. In Henry IV's reign, moreover, 'misprision' of Scrope's kind had sometimes been gratefully condoned. The Earl Marshal, Thomas Mowbray, had, for instance, been readily pardoned in 1405 after failing to disclose his knowledge of Lady Despenser's plot to escape with the two Mortimer boys. And to add a further twist of irony to the proceedings, March would actually sit in judgement of Scrope among the panel of peers appointed to hear his case, while Sir Robert Umfraville, who had allegedly allowed the Scots to pass before finally crushing them at Yeavering, had no further questions asked of him.

Perhaps it is hardly surprising, therefore, that some experts have expressed serious misgivings about official accounts of events and gone on to suggest that the plot had effectively collapsed even before it was finally betrayed. There have been those, too, who have raised much darker questions about the whole handling of the conspiracy. Was Henry, for instance, merely intending to scapegoat a few high-ranking innocents, in order to ensure that there would be no risings against him during his absence, or to discourage all resistance to his decisions whilst on campaign? If so, was the whole episode – richly embellished as it was in contemporary accounts with 'the stench of French promises or bribes'[23] – nothing more than a propaganda ploy, skilfully exploiting the Lancastrian stranglehold on what has been termed elsewhere 'the construction of historical meaning'?[24] Was there, in other words, another Lancastrian rat at the bottom of the Southampton Plot, just as there had allegedly been with Sir John Oldcastle's rising of the previous year?

Plainly, with enough imagination, the 'facts' could well be refashioned to fit such an interpretation. Yet for all its wishful thinking, a plot of some kind – however misrepresented and misconceived – had undoubtedly occurred at a time of critical national importance. It had, moreover, involved a number of key figures, some of whom were primary threats to the Lancastrian dynasty, and some of whom had the potential to be so. Certainly, the fears of the government were real and present, even if the danger itself was not. And the speed and firmness of the government's response must be viewed accordingly. Indeed, to suggest that a ruler in Henry V's particular predicament might have reacted with anything other than cold repression is to ignore not only the specific context in which the plot occurred, but also the more general norms and assumptions underpinning the whole process of government and justice at this time.

Not least of all, the notion that enemy gold had fuelled events was far from implausible at the time. French ambassadors were still in England in July and knew of rumours that there might be a rebellion in favour of either the Earl of March or the Duke of Clarence once Henry had left the country. Scrope, moreover, had played a key part in a number of diplomatic missions in France, affording him ample opportunity to be 'softened' for treason. And both Cambridge and Grey were in severe financial difficulty, which their preparation for the Agincourt campaign could only have compounded. In this connection, too, the leading conspirators were all committed to providing some of the biggest contingents then gathering at Southampton, something that added significantly, of course, to their potential threat.

Nor, for that matter, was Henry Lord Scope quite the sacrificial lamb of modern myth – 'the victim', as one authority puts it, 'of a vindictive and cruel act' at the hands of a king who was 'more interested in exercising authority than justice'.[25] Doubtless, there are tragic elements to Scrope's case. There is no denying, for instance, that he used his influence as best he could to persuade the conspirators to abandon their reckless scheme. In the process, the reluctant and hesitant Earl of March was warned that he faced almost inevitable failure, and the earl's chief adviser at that time, Walter Lucy, was also squarely rebuffed when he first outlined the plan to Scrope. As a result, the reluctant nobleman was not even invited to the meeting at Cranberry at which the details of the whole scheme were eventually finalised.

Yet if Lord Scrope of Masham had the sound common sense to realise that the plot was doomed from the start, the past misfortunes of his family also made it impossible for him to escape suspicion – especially when other aspects of his background are taken into account. For Scrope was a man with a nose for wealth. The bulk of his lands lay in Wensleydale in the North Riding of Yorkshire, but he was also a landowner in shires as far apart as Northumberland and Kent. His second wife, moreover, was the twice-widowed Joan Holland, dowager duchess of York and one of the wealthiest women in England. By marrying Joan in 1411, therefore, Scrope had probably trebled his landed income, becoming one of the most prosperous members of the English baronage. Together, indeed, Scrope and his wife jointly enjoyed a revenue of at least £1,800 a year, allowing the former to enjoy an income rivalling or even exceeding that of his wife's stepson, Edward, Duke of York.

And it was this gift for acquisition that may well lie at the heart of Scrope's eventual undoing. For although the full amount is unknown, the shrewd Yorkshire baron had certainly lent money to the Earl of March, acting as the chief contributor, along with Thomas Arundel, within a syndicate of fifteen creditors headed by Richard Courtenay, Bishop of Norwich. If March suffered a traitor's fate, the prospects for his creditors were therefore far from assured. And in spite of his considerable landed wealth, Scrope was also seriously short of ready cash when potential financial catastrophe struck him in July 1415. Apart from a golden salt cellar, all the other precious vessels that he kept in London – to the value of more than £940 – were in hock to four individuals, presumably as security for the cash he had been obliged to raise for the war. As such, it was probably all the more important for Scrope to be sure of recovering the money he had lent the earl to assist with his exorbitant marriage fine.

Whether this was the whole or primary reason for the noble's failure to inform Henry, we shall never know. But Scrope's behaviour at his trial was both disingenuous and unconvincing, while the king's decision to press home a charge of 'misprision' against him was not nearly as novel or reprehensible as is sometimes suggested. True, there was no precedent in English law since 1225 for regarding the concealment of information as treason, but the 'Great Statute of Treasons' of 1352 was, in fact, ambiguous when it came to the so-called 'imagining' of the king's death.[26] And such cases of 'constructive treason' were sadly typical of the time, encouraging a speedy conclusion to judicial proceedings and acting as a neat and definitive response to the offences set down in the indictment.

When Parliament met in November, it formally confirmed the king's actions. And the logic of the king's case was on this occasion impeccable, for it is hard to picture his long-term survival, had the plot succeeded. Nor, by contemporary standards, was Henry's reaction unduly cruel or vindictive. Unlike Henry IV in 1400 and 1405, however, the current king had nothing to gain and everything to lose from wholesale leniency at this point. With every delay, his chances of a successful campaign were sure to diminish, and with a mission of such importance so imminent, 'justice' would have to be both visible and robust. Scrope's claims about his non-involvement were, in any case, hardly more convincing than the brittle protestations of Cambridge and Grey about their own intentions. And when it came to weighing doubts against certainties, there could, in Henry V's case, be only one outcome.

Harfleur

When the king finally left Portchester Castle on 7 August to join the invasion fleet, his spirits were far from dampened, for though the conspiracy of recent days had doubtless shaken him, the broader significance of its outcome was already apparent. In some respects, the Southampton Plot was little more than a fitful epilogue to the previous reign. Yet it had genuinely threatened to rekindle old enmities to the Lancastrian cause, and the decisiveness of Henry's victory served as a crucial vindication of his legitimacy. No less importantly, the king's conviction that God's hand was both guiding and protecting his affairs had now been affirmed in the most striking fashion possible. Never again, in fact, would Henry's nobles see fit to challenge his rule, and more importantly still, those who had backed him were from this point onwards firmly on course to win the honour and glory they craved.

Though three of his largest ships were utterly destroyed by fire before departure, Henry eventually set sail for France on the fine and sunny afternoon of Sunday 11 August at 5 p.m. The motley assortment of vessels that ventured into the Channel from the shelter of Southampton Water and the Solent may well have been some twelve times larger than the Spanish Armada of the following century. And there was pomp and spectacle to match the occasion, which seems to have lost nothing in the telling by the ecstatic English chroniclers who witnessed it. Huge pennons and lofty banners flew from masts. Painted hulls sliced the waves. Coats of arms and heraldic beasts were everywhere. There was even a flock of swans on hand to provide 'a happy augury' for the task ahead.[27]

It would take all of two days for the fleet to reach its destination at the fishing village of Chef de Caux on the Normandy coast, just three miles from the port of Harfleur at the mouth of the river Seine. And for most of that time, all but the ships' captains and principal army commanders were ignorant of their destination. For as always the king's emphasis upon security left nothing to chance, and some of his troops may well have considered themselves bound for Guienne. Cap de la Hogue on the Cotentin peninsula, where Clarence had landed three years earlier, was also a possibility, as were the prosperous seaports of Boulogne, Dieppe and Fécamp to the east.

Early next morning, however, 'between the sixth and seventh hour' and in the midst of 'a beautiful dawn', Henry duly set foot on French soil at the spot where Le Havre now stands.[28] Although the beach was rocky and offered good possibilities for defence there was no resistance, and the English pitched camp on the side of a hill about a mile north-west of Harfleur in a spot flanked by woods and orchards. 'When all the tents and pavilions and marquees were erected and set up', said the anonymous author of the *First English Life*, 'they seemed a right great and mighty city.'[29] With the road clear, Henry's army moved off to invest the town the following day.

By any standards, Harfleur was a rich prize. Renowned for its salt and weaving industries, it was the 'key of the sea of all Normandie' – second only to Rouen in status.[30] It was also reputedly impregnable, with well-fortified moat walls about two and a half miles in circumference, and three gates, each protected by drawbridge, portcullis and barbican. In all, there were twenty-six towers of massive thickness punctuating the crenellated fortifications, and the river Lézarde running through Harfleur's centre – 'as quarter as wide again as is the Thames at London' – guaranteed its water supply.[31] To compound Henry's difficulties, the flat land surrounding the town was marshy, making it difficult to besiege, while the harbour itself was protected by a formidable chain and huge wooden stakes, driven into the sea bed.

The garrison and citizens of Harfleur were, moreover, prepared to offer stout resistance. The valley of the river Lézarde to the north of the town was, for instance, purposely flooded before Henry could complete its encirclement, and the Duke of Clarence was therefore forced to take a circuitous route to close the northern approaches. In the meantime, the commander of the garrison, Jean d'Estouteville, received welcome reinforcement from the redoubtable Raoul de Gaucourt who lived nearby. Slipping into the city with between 300 and 400 handpicked men-at-arms, de Gaucourt arrived at the critical moment before the town was finally sealed off from the world outside to await the arrival of the considerable French force being mustered by the Dauphin at Rouen.

Ultimately, it was not until 19 August that Harfleur was completely ringed by English forces. But Henry's determination to make Harfleur his own was tempered by a need to convince his prospective Norman subjects that their new ruler was a defender of justice, as well as his own birthright. And with this in mind, he therefore imposed a strict code of discipline upon his men. Though the tactics of Henry's army involved living off the invaded country, as was customary, his declared aim was to avoid the brutal harrying of a countryside that he had promised to rescue from bondage. There was to be no arson, and priests and women were to go unmolested, though any harlot coming within three miles of camp would have her left arm broken after a first warning. Churches and church property were also to be protected, while swearing in camp was strictly forbidden.

Such regulations were, in fact, commonplace among medieval armies, and in spite of any attempts at firmness and humanity on Henry's part, his instructions could never eradicate the excesses which inevitably followed his soldiers' arrival outside Harfleur. The lower ranks were, after all, beset by appalling conditions in marshy country, and they were soon racked by dysentery into the bargain, while king and court kept regal state in the comparative safety of Graville. Henry could therefore whistle against the whirlwind as much as he chose, but this did not prevent the full beastliness of war being visited upon the besieged town. Six years later, indeed, he would have no alternative but to reissue the same ordinances on account of the 'enormous crimes and excesses' that had by then become habitual among some of his soldiers.[32]

Though there is no absolutely reliable chronology for the siege, it seems to have taken up to five weeks for Henry to capture Harfleur. And it was gunpowder ultimately that served as the key to his army's hard-earned success. In all, the English seem to have deployed twelve great cannon of a size never seen before. Some, such as the 'Messenger' and the 'King's Daughter' had already been used by Henry in Wales, and together they wrought havoc day and night. The biggest, which were some twelve feet in length, could shoot stones of up to 500 pounds in weight, and according to numerous accounts, the king personally supervised their activity – carefully positioning them to best effect and spending whole nights in preparation for the thrice daily bombardments which followed.[33] In consequence, wide breaches were made in the walls, while 'really fine buildings almost as far as the middle of the town were totally demolished or threatened imminent collapse'.[34]

Even so, the defenders continued to make good their repairs with improvised palisades and tubs of earth, and though food began to run short within the ramparts, it was not long before those outside had problems of their own to contend with. Marshy air, the night frosts of an early autumn, over-indulgence in young wine and raw cider, excessive consumption of rotten apples and unripe grapes, as well as local shellfish – all were blamed for the dysentery, which now struck high and low alike. 'In this siege', recorded Friar

Capgrave, 'many men died of cold in nights and fruit eating; eke of stink of carrions.'[35] And if he was confused about the causes and wrong about the numbers of dead, Capgrave was not, it seems, far off when it came to the actual scale of infection.

Though the *Gesta* plainly exaggerates in suggesting that 5,000 men were forced to return to England, a figure of at least 1,330 can be guaranteed from the post-campaign accounts and the separate sick lists compiled by the chamberlain and steward of the king's household, while a significantly higher total of around 2,550 – including non-combatants – has also been suggested.[36] Nor was the infection sweeping the English camp any respecter of rank. The Duke of Clarence, for example, became grievously sick and was shipped back to England, along with the earls of March and Arundel, and the Earl Marshal, John Mowbray. Arundel, indeed, died on 10 October. Another notable victim was Michael de la Pole, Earl of Suffolk, who had earlier gone into exile with Henry IV. Sadder still, the king's valued friend, Bishop Courtenay of Norwich, was said to have died in his arms.

We hear, too, of the death of a certain John Phelip of Kidderminster. Phelip was, however, no mighty noble or high-ranking churchman, but a comparatively humble knight who had earned his sovereign's friendship through simple soldierly courage. A nephew of Sir Thomas Erpingham, he had distinguished himself in combat at St Cloud in 1411 and had also fought daringly at Harfleur. For Henry, it seems, this alone was enough to commend him, and today Phelip's tomb memorial still proudly proclaims his personal friendship with the king.[37]

But the flux was working with the English as well as against them, and by 18 September it had played no small part in forcing the citizens of Harfleur to parley for peace at last. Four days later, the garrison's leaders and sixty-six hostages were presented to the king, by his direct order, in only their shirts and wearing halters around their necks. Before entering the great silken pavilion where Henry had decided to meet them, moreover, they had been forced to wait on their knees for several hours. And when they finally entered his presence, the impact was carefully designed to be suitably stunning. Clad in cloth of gold with Sir Gilbert Umfraville at his right hand bearing his helmet, crown and poleaxe, the King of England roundly upbraided them for daring to withhold 'a noble portion of his inheritance' from him 'against God and all justice'.[38] Thereafter, he received the keys of the town from de Gaucourt and other representatives before graciously entertaining them to a lavish banquet. And next day, without any hint of further triumphalism, Henry proceeded to the half-destroyed church of St Martin to give thanks for his victory. Upon reaching the town gates, he duly dismounted and entered the church 'without hosen and shoes' in humble recognition of God's favour.[39]

It was from first to last a classic exercise in the propaganda of display, typical of the man responsible for it and no less typical of the age in which he lived. The surrender terms, too – however regrettable in some of their details – were wholly consistent with contemporary norms and expectations. Sixty knights and 200 gentlemen, along with de Gaucourt, were allowed to depart, because, as de Gaucourt himself later recalled, 'many of us were extremely sick'.[40] In return for this favour, all agreed to present themselves as 'faithful captives' at Calais at Martinmas when they would be taken into custody for ransom. The richer citizens, on the other hand, were immediately sent to England to await ransoming, while people of lower social status were divided into two groups. Those prepared to swear allegiance to Henry were allowed to stay, while around 2,000 others – many of them sick, elderly, or women and children – were expelled 'amid much lamentation, grief and tears' for the loss of their 'customary', but 'unlawful' habitations, as the author of the *Gesta* put it.[41] Churchmen, too, were allowed to leave.

All this – with the exception, perhaps, of Henry's decision not to sack the town – was standard practice. Even the expulsion of the native population on 24 September, for which Henry has received so much criticism, accorded with usual procedures. The women who constituted the lion's share of Harfleur's exiled population, were, it seems, given 5 *écus* each and allowed to depart with their clothing and all they could carry. Des Ursins suggests that there were around 1,500 of them in all, but it is difficult to see how these vulnerable groups could actually have remained behind when the physical state of the town and continuing war are taken into consideration. And after they had been escorted by English soldiers to Lillebonne, they were met by Jean Boucicaut, Marshal of France, who gave them food and drink, after which they appear to have been transferred to Rouen by boat.

Henry's intention was, in fact, to turn Harfleur into a second Calais, and it is this that explains his decision to pack his freshly conquered town with an influx of English settlers, just as Edward III had done with his new acquisition in 1347. None of the surviving financial accounts of Henry's captains mention gains from plunder at this stage of the war, which is, in truth, more a reflection on the extent of Harfleur's destruction than any real indication of the army's good behaviour. But the potential for regeneration and future growth was considerable, and on 5 October the king issued a proclamation in all of England's greater cities, offering houses in Harfleur and cash subsidies to all merchants and artisans prepared to assist. Now, indeed, there was to be nothing less than a carpet-bagging bonanza. 'They put out all the French people both woman and child', said the *Brut* chronicle, 'and stuffed the town with English men', just as Edward III had done at Calais.[42] Ultimately, the title deeds of every Frenchman holding property in Harfleur were publicly burnt in the town's market square.

It was hardly modern statesmanship. Nor, for that matter, was one of Henry's other gestures around this time, which further demonstrates the yawning gap between late medieval and modern attitudes. On 26 September, without consulting his Council, Henry commissioned the Sire de Gaucourt to deliver a challenge of single combat to none other than the Dauphin at Rouen. Written in Anglo-Norman, it proposed 'to place our quarrel at the will of God between Our person and yours'. In other words, the crown of France should go to the better fighter, though not, it should be emphasised, until the present ruler, Charles VI, was dead. In this way, said Henry, two Christian princes might hope to avoid 'the deaths of men, the destruction of countries, the lamentations of women and children and so many general evils that every good Christian must lament it and have pity'.[43]

In fact, such challenges were by now a rarity, and on this occasion the King of England's boldness was no doubt partly intended to boost the morale of his troops at a critical time. When it is remembered that the Dauphin was not only fat and sluggish, but still only eighteen years of age, Henry's chances of acquiring 'the approbation of God and the praise of the world' by his ritual slaughter were in any case remote, and the stirring invitation was indeed declined without reply. Yet such personal clashes still remained an established feature of the contemporary military scene. And this, it should be remembered, was the son of the man who had once faced Thomas Mowbray in the lists at Coventry. In spite of appearances, therefore, Henry's plan was not quite the empty flourish it might at first seem. He had, of course, been thoroughly immersed since boyhood in the most potent ideals of chivalric tradition. And by now, at the age of nearly thirty, he remained both unvanquished and utterly enthused.

Agincourt

Predictably, the capture of Harfleur was reported to the Mayor of London as a resounding victory, but the siege had been unexpectedly time-consuming and Henry's forces had already been depleted by both disease and a spate of desertions, which, it was said, had driven him to rage.[44] Most of the king's advisers were further concerned by the approach of autumn and the number of men needed to garrison Harfleur securely. Indeed, they were begging him, it seems, to return home without delay, lest the French hem them all in 'like sheep in pens'.[45] There were, after all, over 150 miles between Henry and his appointed rendezvous with Raoul de Gaucourt and the other released hostages who had guaranteed to meet him at Calais with their ransom money. Henry's army would also be travelling through difficult and hostile country with many fortified towns, much forest and marshland, and numerous swollen rivers to bar the way. At Rouen, meanwhile, there was the ominous presence of the Dauphin's army to consider.

Yet the alternative before Henry was hardly more attractive. If he followed the advice of his more cautious advisers, he would be returning to England with a tattered army, a tarnished reputation and a forbidding burden of debt, which might well, before long, bring his reign to ruin. If, however, he reached Calais unopposed – or better still at the head of a triumphant army that had achieved a stirring victory along the way – the gains were sure to be considerable. At the very least, Harfleur's credibility as a bridgehead for further conquest would remain intact and he would also have managed 'to see those lands, whereof he ought to be lord'.[46] If, on the other hand, battle came his way, there were not only God's protection and the memories of Crécy and Poitiers to sustain him, but also some 7,000 archers – the largest force of its kind that the French had faced for several decades.

There were precedents, too, for Henry's current strategy. The Battle of Crécy, for instance, had been prompted by the similar march of Edward III's army, which had provoked the French to attack in Ponthieu. So the trek to Calais was no mere exercise in blind egotism – 'the most foolhardy and reckless adventure that ever an unreasoning pietist devised', as J. H. Wylie put it almost a century ago.[47] It was actually the lesser of evils, and the pitched battle that it prompted is likely to have been anticipated by Henry from the very outset. He would, it is true, avoid fighting at various points along his route as a series of unforeseen challenges confronted him. But from the very earliest stages of Henry's planning, the English army had always been too large for the demands of siege warfare alone, and the preponderance of archers, especially of the mounted variety, also suggested a thorough readiness on his part for the demands of mobile warfare and pitched battle.

This willingness to fight also helps to explain Henry's delay of over a fortnight in setting out for Calais – something that is hardly consistent with any wish to pass through enemy territory at lightning speed for fear of conflict. Extra funds were certainly brought across to Harfleur, and there is also the intriguing possibility that the English army underwent significant reinforcement during the same period. The original sick list for the Earl of Arundel's retinue, for instance, names nineteen men-at-arms and sixty-eight archers, as well as three minstrels, all to be shipped home. Yet the earl's post-campaign account suggests that two-thirds of his men-at-arms had been replaced, along with all the archers who had either died or been invalided home. The same account also gives the dates between 24 September and 3 October on which the replacements were made.[48]

Whether these figures are typical or whether they were achieved by reallocation of existing troops from other depleted retinues is unknown. But even without such reinforcement, the numbers of dead and sick – ranging, as we have seen, from 1,500 to 2,500 – were still far from crippling. Nor, for that matter, was the cohort of men left to defend Harfleur any more likely to ruin Henry's prospects for success. In all, 1,200 troops remained behind with the Earl of Dorset after Henry's departure, suggesting that from the initial force of around 12,000 that first left England in August, around three-quarters were still available for the journey to Calais.

This, then, was not quite the ragtag army of propaganda and romance. Nor was it simply cobbled together from leftovers, in order to save the face of a frustrated egotist. But the French, in contrast, were still dogged by faction and indecision. Although the Armagnacs had regained the initiative in 1414, they were now reluctant to march north in full strength to counter the English, lest the forces of John the Fearless should return in their absence to seize Paris. From the Burgundian perspective, meanwhile, the current grand appeal for unity against the foreign invader could only be viewed with the utmost suspicion. It was no coincidence that the decision to place an Armagnac noble in command of Picardy had already been fiercely resisted. And few now had any more faith in the ultimate purpose of the Dauphin's force at Rouen, especially when the Duke of Burgundy himself had been specifically instructed not to join its ranks in person.

As such, Henry's decision to march to Calais was a calculated risk worth taking – a probable 'win–win' situation in which the enemy would either fight and lose, with an army not significantly bigger than his, or more likely opt to let him pass in precisely the way that older, wiser heads on the French Council, such as Marshal Boucicaut and Charles d'Albret, the Constable of France, were actually recommending at that very time. What no one fully realised, however, was the extent to which French enthusiasm for the war would suddenly escalate, and it was this that turned the march to Calais into the dramatic, sometimes desperate adventure it eventually became. On 10 September, Guillaume Martel, Lord of Bacqueville, had carried the symbolic red banner of war – the so-called '*Oriflamme*' – from the abbey of Saint-Denys to Rouen. And in spite of all the deep divisions and recriminations of recent times, the banner's arrival from its home at the burial place of French kings now prompted a surge of fresh recruits which no one – least of all the English force at Harfleur – could possibly have anticipated.

So it was that on 8 October Henry V's army of between 8,000 and 9,000 men duly set out on its fateful march to Calais with rations for perhaps as few as eight days. Divided as usual into three divisions, the vanguard was commanded by Sir John Cornwaille and Sir Gilbert Umfraville, and the rearguard by the Duke of York and the Earl of Oxford. In between, the king himself personally commanded the main body. Travelling with the fewest possible baggage waggons and no artillery, the aim was to make all possible speed, avoiding battle if possible, but meeting it readily should it come. With a view, perhaps, to producing them in some kind of stirring pre-battle ritual, Henry had also chosen to take with him some of his most impressive regalia: a precious crown, a sword of state said to have belonged to King Arthur, a gold cross worth £2,166, a piece of the True Cross set amongst rich jewels, and an orb used for the coronation ceremony itself. In the meantime, he had also instructed a force from Calais to seize the ford at Blanchetaque before his arrival, so that a safe crossing of the Somme could be guaranteed.

As usual, the English army would supplement its rations by plundering the countryside, but while most French chroniclers duly recorded the sufferings of their compatriots, there is no record of any atrocity that could be considered exceptional by contemporary standards.[49] Indeed, the privations now inflicted upon the local populace by Henry's army seem once more to have been no greater than those resulting from the action of French troops. According to the Bourgeois of Paris, the invading soldiers 'devastated and robbed all the countryside'. But so too, it seems, did their French counterparts, 'who did as much harm to the poor people as the English'.[50] There were minor skirmishes at Montivilliers just north of Harfleur and near Fécamp, where the abbey church was allegedly burned after a group of women had been raped inside it. In other cases, however, the threat of fire and sword was sufficient to cow the local populace into compliance.

At this stage, indeed, the army was making good progress. By Friday 11 October it had already travelled some 55 miles to arrive on the outskirts of Dieppe, and was tightly on schedule to reach Calais within eight days, as planned. But if the King of England had been looking forward to a successful crossing of the river Somme around midday on 13 October, he was to be disappointed. For only six miles from the river a Gascon prisoner captured by English scouts suggested – perhaps fraudulently – that the tidal ford at Blanchetaque was blocked by sharp stakes and that Marshal Boucicaut was waiting with 6,000 troops. The force from Calais had evidently been driven off, and to complicate matters, a sizeable

French contingent was said to be moving up from Rouen. Though the Duke of Burgundy still vacillated and preferred to hunt in the forests of the Côte d'Or rather than join his countrymen, Henry therefore chose to veer eastwards along the course of the Somme.

The English, then, were now approaching the moment of truth for which their king had probably been waiting all along. Certainly, the dangers facing Henry's army were considerable, and it was from this point onwards that his leadership would be tested to the limit as the mood among his increasingly famished, exhausted and sickly soldiers shifted from cautious optimism and camaraderie to gnawing anxiety. Now, however, instead of following the river's loop to the north, Henry chose to cut directly across the neck of the loop to Nesle, in the hope of outdistancing the enemy who were left on the other side to take the long way round. Stopping the whole army to execute an English soldier who had stolen a copper gilt pyx from a church, Henry was himself, perhaps, showing signs of inner turmoil.

But he now heard news that two fords had been located at Bethencourt and Voyennes, and after suitable repairs had been made to two causeways damaged by the French, he personally supervised the crossing, exhorting his men as they passed and preventing any rushing and jamming of the narrow passages. In consequence, by an hour after nightfall on 19 October, the English army was at last safely across the Somme, with the way to Calais before them. That night, we are told, Henry's weary soldiers were able to spend a 'cheerful' night in the neighbouring hamlets.[51] But the nearest coast was still some seventy miles away and, far more ominously, the French were close at hand.

Indeed, only six miles away at Péronne there was feverish planning in the enemy camp over how best to proceed. With King Charles and the Dauphin safely to the rear at Rouen, the serious decisions could now be taken. Yet if France's political divisions were temporarily in remission, the military debate rankled with undiminished intensity. On the one hand, Boucicaut and d'Albret were continuing to counsel caution. France's two most senior commanders were, however, overruled by a less experienced, more pugnacious majority, led by the dukes of Orléans and Bourbon, which sought to dispose of the threat from Henry V of England once and for all. And though Orléans and Bourbon were both

Armagnacs, support for a pitched battle was shared with equal conviction by the Duke of Burgundy's own brothers, the Duke of Brabant and the Count of Nevers. Only John the Fearless himself, it seemed, now remained uncommitted to the cause.

With heady optimism, fuelled by superiority in numbers and the social prejudice of a military caste that still disdained the arrows of base-born English archers, the die was therefore cast for battle. And on Sunday 20 October, heralds from the Constable of France and the dukes of Orléans and Bourbon were duly despatched to the English camp. Their message, though wrapped in all the tinsel dignities of the chivalric code, was clear and of deadly intent. But Henry's own response was typically measured – made all the firmer and indeed more menacing by its brevity. 'Be all things according to the will of God', he observed, and then proceeded to warn that any attempt to interrupt his march would not be 'without the utmost peril' for his enemies. 'We do not intend to seek them out', he said, 'but neither shall we in fear of them move more slowly or more quickly than we wish to do.'[52] In other words, Henry was still following the self-same policy of flexible response that he had adopted from the very outset of his journey, while continuing to maintain, as he had throughout, his posture as reluctant warrior.

Battle was indeed still some way off – not least of all, because the reconnaissance of both armies was so primitive. For some days, in fact, Henry's army continued through driving rain and wind, marching in parallel with the enemy whose close proximity was finally made clear by the sight of freshly trampled fields – churned to a muddy mess, as if by 'an unimaginable host'.[53] Yet it was still not until 24 October that the Duke of York was informed by a scout that the enemy were now massed close by. A few miles ahead the French were emerging from a valley on the English right, in three huge contingents filling the area between the villages of Agincourt and Ruisseauville – 'like a countless swarm of locusts'.[54] And the King of England's response – whether through fatalism, cool calculation, or a mixture of both – was appropriately resolute.

Not altogether surprisingly, French chroniclers were inclined to view things rather differently. According to the Monk of Saint-Denys and Jean Juvénal des Ursins, for instance, Henry's confidence waned drastically upon witnessing the French force for the first time, and at some point over the next twenty-four hours – perhaps on the morning of battle itself – he is said to have made a series of abject offers, including the surrender of Harfleur, in return for the prospect of free passage to Calais.[55] In other words, he quietly and cravenly accepted the folly of every detail of his military planning, and in the process betrayed his God-given cause, destroyed his own reputation and consigned his kingship – if not his dynasty – to universal ridicule upon his return.

Such extravagant claims are, however, largely explained by the blame culture that prevailed in France after the war. For if, on this basis, the English king had indeed offered to compromise, how much greater was the folly of the opposing commanders in failing to seize the opportunity? But far from pleading for leniency, Henry now proceeded to display the very highest standards of generalship. The weight resting upon his shoulders at this critical point may well be imagined. He had hitherto fought only one set-piece battle – at Shrewsbury – and there he had almost lost not only the engagement but also his life. By experience, moreover, he remained primarily a gunner, sapper or staff officer rather than an infantry commander. Yet he was now facing an infantry battle of the most crucial significance, and his reading of the Roman authority Vegetius will have made it abundantly clear to him that 'a battle is commonly decided in two or three hours, after which no further hopes are left for the worsted army'.[56]

Nevertheless, from this point onwards Henry read both the situation and, more importantly still, his men to perfection. All were exhausted, sodden and starving after a trek of just over a fortnight, in which they had covered an average of some fifteen miles a day, and all were now ordered to keep silent during the night, under threat of severe penalties: the forfeiture of horse and armour for a knight, the loss of a right ear for any man of lower rank. Clearly, with so many Frenchmen eager to avenge the loss of Harfleur at any cost, Henry's army could not afford to lower its guard, and Enguerrand de Monstrelet's claim that the English played their trumpets and other musical instruments throughout the hours of darkness, 'so that the whole neighbourhood resounded with their music' seems unlikely.[57] Armourers, bowyers and fletchers, it is true, worked tirelessly to service the weapons needed next day. And since the queues for priests were so long, some men chose to make their confessions to each other – but doubtless all in whispers.

As for Henry himself, he did not, it seems, spend the night exhorting his men amid the pouring rain, as Shakespeare so graphically suggested. Instead, he was lodged with his inner circle of advisers at Maisoncelle, from where, around midnight, he appointed a handpicked group of knights to survey the battlefield by moonlight. Moreover, the news they brought with them upon their return could not have been more favourable. The heavy clay soil, which had been newly ploughed and sown with winter wheat, was already turning into a quagmire, even before it had been trampled by French cavalry and heavily laden men-at-arms. Any progress across it would therefore be painfully slow, allowing ample time for English archers to inflict maximum damage before any melee could occur.

But while Henry was not with his men physically, he now demonstrated to perfection his instinctive grasp of how to hone and galvanise a body of fighting men to a peak of readiness – something which both English and French sources readily acknowledge. He was quick to make it known, for instance, that any rumours of his impending capture and ransom were wholly unfounded. He would, he emphasised, either win the coming battle or die in the attempt. At the same time, he is also said to have reminded his troops that this was the eve of the martyrdom of Saints Crispin and Crispinian, the cobbler saints of Soissons where the Armagnacs had massacred both nuns and English bowmen only the year before. And it was made patently clear, too, that now as then, the enemy would proffer no quarter. Death or mutilation were, in effect, all that could be expected from the French, and with this, wrote Thomas Walsingham, 'our men became all the more determined, and took heart, encouraging one another'.[58] Clearly, if perfect love casts out fear, the same may also be said of blind, inveterate anger as well as desperation.

Yet Henry was also able to play upon his soldiers' sensibilities more subtly. The very sombreness and religious tone of the English camp before battle seems to have added to its focus. The priests of the King's Chapel, for instance, were instructed not only to hear the men's confessions but to make themselves visible and pray continually. And the King of England's leadership by personal example was also underpinned by a broader moral foundation. The justice of his cause had been emphasised throughout, and now his men were given to believe that they stood on the threshold of fulfilling a great historic destiny. By invoking the memory of Edward III and the Black Prince, moreover, and by drawing upon the examples of Crécy and Poitiers, Henry was able to emphasise that victory was achievable against any odds.

The English army possessed at this critical moment, therefore, not only a leader who continued to inspire, but a single-minded unity born out of a common cause and the kind of tight comradeship that comes with the hardship of extended campaigning and experience of recent victory. In the case of a certain Thomas Hostell, indeed, the eagerness to fight seems to have transcended all reasonable bounds. A man-at-arms in the retinue of Sir John Lumley, Hostell had already lost an eye and shattered a cheekbone with the aid of a bolt from a French crossbow at Harfleur. But, with the climax of the whole campaign perhaps only days away, he had nevertheless insisted on joining the march to Calais. And now he was preparing to take his place alongside his king at Agincourt.[59]

The French, by contrast, were altogether more vulnerable than their high spirits suggested. In fact, they were cursed by over-confidence and damned into the bargain by an incoherent chain of command. The gathering of so many former enemies, Burgundian and Orléanist, seems to have created a super-charged sense of euphoria. 'Some of them', wrote one chronicler, 'kissed and put their arms around each other's necks in making peace, and it was moving to see this. All troubles and discords which had been between them, and which they had in the past, were changed into great feelings of love.'[60] The unfurling of the *Oriflamme* had, then, both intoxicated and enthused a nation, but in doing so it had also clouded the judgement of that nation's military leaders – Orléans, Bourbon, Alençon and others – who were swept along on the same unthinking wave.

The resulting sense of invulnerability was further fuelled by the French nobility's stubborn insistence that their massed ranks could overcome any obstacle placed before them – or, in other words, by the naive notion that *noblesse oblige* and undaunted military spirit were the sole pre-requisites for domination of any battlefield. It was a notion with a long history and the French contempt for plebeian warriors was by no means confined to English archers. John II had, for instance, dismissed most of the poorly equipped and ill-disciplined foot soldiers raised by the *arrière ban* before the Battle of Poitiers, on the grounds that their earlier presence at Crécy had only hampered the professionals.

And now, according to the Monk of Saint-Denys – who was, it must be said, a keenly partisan critic of his social betters – this same prejudice was as prevalent as ever. The citizens of Paris had, he claimed, proposed to send 6,000 fully armed men to join the royal army. Their offer was, however, contemptuously dismissed on the grounds that 'the help of mechanics and artisans must surely be of little value, for we shall outnumber the English three-to-one'.[61] And if this particular tale is deemed suspect, it should not be forgotten either that 4,000 of France's best crossbowmen would soon be dismissed from the forthcoming battle, on the pretext that there was only room for men-at-arms in the fatefully narrow vanguard crammed between Agincourt and Tramecourt. Clearly, the French had learned little from Poitiers, let alone the battles of Courtrai and Nicopolis.

Nor did the French now possess any really coherent battle plan. Their original intention, it seems, had been to bring Henry to battle near the Somme, with a comparatively small force, consisting of a vanguard led by d'Albret and Boucicaut and a single main 'battle'. An alternative plan was, however, drawn up at Rouen around 20 October, which involved a larger army, consisting of three battles under the command of the Duke of Orléans.[62] The main result, not surprisingly, was confusion, and there was no doubt either that the plan ruffled large numbers of notoriously sensitive aristocratic feathers into the bargain, as French nobles jostled hungrily for seniority in the coming historic encounter. Seasoned campaigners like Boucicaut, who had been so successful in harrying the English army on its long march, found themselves subject to a hastily improvised proposal under the command of a young royal duke who had so far played no role in the war. And many of the French contingents would now, in any case, be coming together for the first time to face a hardened enemy.

The English were an enemy, too, that could not necessarily be relied upon to play the game of war by every rule in the chivalric book. They were, as the French were keen to emphasise, a force made up mainly of common men. And even their king was not above the kind of hard-nosed realism that could never be condoned

– or expected – from a knight of genuine honour. According to the Berry Herald, the French had originally planned to fight Henry at Aubigny on Thursday 24 October, but he had, it seems, broken his initial promise and moved in the opposite direction, causing further general disruption and, above all, making it impossible for some of the French retinues to appear in time for the eventual battle.

Certainly, French numerical superiority on the actual day of battle was not nearly as pronounced as they themselves had been anticipating and many since have believed. The Duke of Brittany was only one of many nobles who failed to attend the encounter, and to compound their predicament, the French were seriously weakened by a string of late arrivals. Hard as it is to believe, the Duke of Orléans, for example, did not present himself until 24 October, and the tardiness of the commander-in-chief was matched or exceeded by a number of other senior commanders. The Duke of Anjou's bladder disease would prevent him from arriving in person at all, while the contingent of 600 men that he sent under the leadership of the Sire de Longny did not arrive in the vicinity of Agincourt until the encounter was effectively all over. And though the Duke of Burgundy's two brothers were both present at the battle, neither had time to prepare adequately. Upon the arrival of the Count of Nevers the fighting was already in full flow, and his journey had been so hectic that the majority of his troops had been unable to keep up with him. Even his equipment had not arrived as intended, and he was forced to seize a banner from one of his trumpeters in order to improvise a surcoat, which would swiftly prove to be the one in which he died.

So how large, then, was the French force that faced Henry V on 25 October 1415? Not altogether surprisingly, English chroniclers were keen to emphasise the huge size of the enemy host. The author of the *Gesta* suggests a figure of 60,000, including a vanguard which was 'thirty times more than all our men put together'.[63] Adam Usk and Thomas Otterbourne, in their turn, also opted for 60,000, while Thomas Walsingham and John Capgrave both referred to a French army of 140,000. Burgundian estimates, meanwhile, though lower, were intended to heighten the scale of the defeat inflicted under a government that was largely controlled by their Armagnac opponents. Monstrelet, for instance, takes the total number of soldiers to be 50,000. Other French chronicles, on the other hand, are much more circumspect, with a figure of 10,000 being suggested by both the Berry Herald and Gruel's *Chronique de Richemont*. Significantly, perhaps, these two sources also suggest that the English force was marginally bigger.[64]

Plainly, such discrepancies raise serious questions about whether any reliable estimates can be achieved. But we are not entirely without other types of evidence. French pay records indicate that at the end of August the intention was to raise an army of 6,000 men-at-arms and 3,000 archers. It is safe to assume, too, that this number will have grown significantly with the arrival of further contingents led by Orléans, Bourbon, Nevers, Brabant and others from the southern and eastern areas, although these are unlikely to have much exceeded 2,500. Then there appear to have been another 500 or so raised by recruitment in Picardy from 20 September onwards. If so, the overall total seems to emerge at around 12,000, with two-thirds of the army's strength consisting of men-at-arms.[65]

Although much smaller than traditional estimates, this figure is, in fact, wholly compatible with what is known more generally about French armies of this period. During the 1380s the French managed to muster larger forces of 15–16,000 men. But these were drawn from the whole kingdom, while in 1415 there was little recruitment south of the Loire. And though Charles VI had intended only the year before to raise an army of 14,500 against John the Fearless, there is no evidence that this was ultimately achieved.[66] In reality, the military resources available to the French remained limited, even after the surge of recruitment that accompanied the unfurling of the *Oriflamme* in September. If, moreover, the Duke of Burgundy had probably raised some 2,250 men in the summer of 1414 for the defence of his lands, these were now unavailable.[67]

Why, then, were such exaggerated estimates of French strength considered so credible at the time? The answer lies, perhaps, in the social composition of the French army and in particular the generally acknowledged predominance of men-at-arms within its ranks. Since every man-at-arms required at least one page, and the number of men-at-arms on the French side was around three times that on the English side, it follows that the number of French non-combatants must have been at least three times greater.[68] When it is remembered, too, that French troops were continuing to arrive and that large numbers of patrols had also been reported in the locality, it is hardly surprising that the author of the *Gesta* was so deeply impressed by the 'grim-looking' host in front of him, or that the scout who had first spotted it returned to the Duke of York 'with trembling heart, as fast as his horse could carry him'.[69]

As battle loomed, therefore, the strength of the French position was largely illusory. And it is here, perhaps, that the real essence of Henry V's achievement at Agincourt is to be found, for far from defeating an invincible enemy in the face of overwhelming odds, he alone seems to have appreciated the weakness of his enemy's position in comparison with his own. The French had, it is true, cornered their prey, but, in doing so, they had both heightened its potency and cruelly exposed their own deficiencies. Put quite simply, it was one thing to force the English to a state of apparent desperation, altogether another to finish the task. And now the King of England's enemies would discover this cruel truth in the starkest and most harrowing way imaginable.

The *Gesta* records how, on the day of battle, the French arrayed themselves 'in that field called Agincourt, across which lay our road to Calais', and that 'the number of them was really terrifying'.[70] The area before the English was, in fact, a vast open field, two miles long and a mile wide, bordered by small woods on either side and narrowing to about 1,000 yards at the end where Henry's army now took up its own position. On the English left, hidden by woodland, stood the village of Agincourt, while to the right, also behind one of the bordering woods, lay the village of Tramecourt. As Henry doubtless realised, therefore, his enemies had already made their first and fatal error.

The French, for their part, were to rely on the crushing impact of their dismounted men-at-arms and the outflanking tactics of their cavalry, which would destroy the archers on Henry's wings and enable an attack upon the English position from the rear. Largely as a result of the battlefield's narrowness in comparison with the number of their men-at-arms, the French would also prefer the column to the line. At the front, in the place of greatest honour, were to stand the massed ranks of the cream of their men-at-arms, all in full plate armour and carrying sawn-off lances to allow for effective fighting in what was intended to be the decisive, over-powering melee with their English counterparts. Fighting alongside them was to be the small but formidable force of French crossbowmen, which would help to harry the enemy before the final deadly impact occurred. Behind this vanguard came a second battle, about twenty men deep, followed by a third consisting of fully armed Bretons, Gascons and Poitevins.

But Boucicaut's original plan, as well as the one improvised more recently at Rouen, had been rendered largely redundant by the hurried arrival of so many battle-hungry nobles, which had played havoc with an already ragged command structure. Indeed, the teeming forest of banners crammed into the French vanguard told its own story. And as deadly crossbowmen now found themselves forced to the rear to make way for their social betters, even Boucicaut and d'Albret could not resist the urge to take their place in the position of honour – at the head, in other words, of an apparently unstoppable phalanx of heavily armoured men-at-arms, some thirty deep. According to the Picard nobleman, Jean de Waurin, who actually fought in their ranks, many of these French knights were also 'weakened by hunger and lack of sleep'.[71]

'The French', said the chronicler Pierre Cochon, 'thought that they would carry the day because of their great numbers, and in their arrogance had proclaimed that only those who were noble should go into battle.'[72] The Monk of Saint-Denys, on the other hand, seems to have viewed this parlous situation with something bordering on black humour. Each of the French leaders, he noted, 'claimed for himself the honour of leading the vanguard', which led to 'the rather unfortunate conclusion that they should all place themselves in the front line'.[73] The dukes of Bourbon and Orléans, the Count of Eu, Boucicaut and d'Albret were all there, along with a teeming host of lesser nobles, all focused on individual prestige rather than tactics and all intent upon a crude and mechanical strategy that amounted, quite literally, to warfare by numbers.

The English also took up their positions just after sunrise, arrayed in a line of three divisions. Wearing a jewelled gold crown upon his helmet and a surcoat displaying the three leopards of England and the three golden fleurs-de-lys of France, the king himself commanded the centre, while the right and left wings were placed, respectively, under the forty-two-year-old Duke of York and the highly experienced Lord Camoys, who had gone on to marry Hotspur's widow after seeing service against the French as long ago as the 1370s. Also on hand to complete the tightly disciplined, determined and deadly team was the reassuring figure of 'old' Sir Thomas Erpingham, a fifty-eight-year-old Knight of the Garter, who commanded the archers.

Like their French counterparts, each English man-at-arms was dismounted and carried a sawn-off lance, but unlike their enemies, they appear to have been supported by projecting wedges of archers four or five deep – each archer equipped with a six-foot bow that could fire with deadly accuracy over 250 yards, as well as a leaden club to deliver speedy and ignoble destruction to any fallen foe. On both wings, meanwhile, protected from outflanking manoeuvres by the adjoining woods, lay further, horn-shaped formations of massed archers. Curving gently forward in order to shoot inwards towards the centre, their task was to deal with the cavalry attack and force the oncoming French to advance in increasing confusion as they approached the killing zone in front of the four-deep vanguard of English men-at-arms.

Flouting strict chivalric convention, the English also relied for defence on a relatively new tactic that had been employed to considerable effect by the Sultan Bayazid in defeating his Christian enemies at Nicopolis. It was either Henry himself or possibly the Duke of York who had instructed every archer at the crossing of the Somme to equip himself with a stout six-foot stake, sharpened at both ends, which could be driven into the ground and pointed in the direction of any approaching cavalry onslaught. If nothing else, the potentially vulnerable English archers could at least take some psychological solace from this particular measure, which was certainly an innovation in Anglo-French warfare, though not new to the likes of Boucicaut and others who had, in fact, fought at Nicopolis nineteen years earlier.

By 7 a.m., then, the scene was set for the final reckoning, though for the next two to three hours, it seems, there was mainly delay and nervous posturing. In such circumstances, the morale of his men was one of Henry's key concerns, and the chronicles are agreed that his role was inspirational. Upon hearing from his companions that the time was now 'prime' – the first canonical hour before sunset – he was apparently heartened. 'Now is it good time', he declared, 'for all England prayeth for us.'[74] Then, riding a small grey pony and followed by a page leading a great war-horse behind him, he is said to have ridden back and forth along the English line, exhorting his men and reminding them of both the justice of his cause and previous victories that had been won against the French by his ancestors.

Nor, in all likelihood, was Henry's show of confidence artificial. For as tension mounted agonisingly from this point onwards, the King of England could also see more and more clearly the possibilities opening up before him. Crucially, the battlefield terrain was perfectly suited to his purposes. On the one hand, the woods to left and right, which narrowed before the English line would have a funnelling effect upon the French if they could be encouraged to move forward, both cramping their advance and neutralising the full effect of their superior numbers. Equally significantly, there was every possibility that if the English line held firm, the French vanguard might well be disastrously crushed by those columns advancing behind it – especially when the battlefield itself was already a quagmire. All depended, however, on whether the enemy could be made to sacrifice their advantage and attack.

What followed is a matter of heated dispute, generated by a tangle of conflicting contemporary accounts and the virtually endless array of theories that these have generated. There is general agreement, however, that the ongoing delay was altogether more beneficial to the French. It was Henry, after all, who needed to pass to Calais, and while the stand-off continued, the enemy's numbers were growing all the time. From this perspective, therefore, he found himself confronted by an apparently insoluble conundrum. With around 1,000 yards of sodden clay before it, the English army had little choice, it seems, but to advance and thereby guarantee its own destruction.

There can be no question, then, that Henry required a ploy of some kind, in order to provoke his enemy into acting first. And according to a long tradition, the desired effect was achieved as follows. After some two to three hours of interminable waiting, the order was supposedly given for the English army to remove its defensive wooden stakes and advance some 700 yards to within bowshot range of the French – at which point the archers once again inserted their stakes and positioned themselves to fire. Then, after riding along the repositioned English line, it was Sir Thomas Erpingham who tossed his marshal's baton high into the air and ordered his men to unleash a deadly arrow storm – after which the French at last surged forward to muddy, bloody disaster.

The crucial question, however, is why the English were able to advance so far so easily when their opponents would struggle so dreadfully over what would have been a much shorter stretch of the same virtually impassable terrain. There is certainly no doubt about the conditions. 'It was', as Thomas Walsingham related, 'extremely difficult to stand or advance', and French accounts make precisely the same point.[75] According to Jean Juvénal des Ursins, for instance, men 'could scarcely move their legs and pull them out of the ground'.[76] How, then, could even archers, let alone the entire English army cover the distance suggested – without any hint of a counter-strike – when it would probably take them at least half an hour to cover the necessary ground and re-establish their line, complete with newly reinserted defensive stakes?

The answer, in fact, is that they could not have done. Much more plausible is an alternative explanation, which not only accords more neatly with common sense, but also confirms the tactical acumen of Henry V more impressively than ever. The key components of this explanation are the occurrence of a provocative ambush staged from the woods on the flanks of the French position, coinciding with a much more limited English advance, designed to lure the enemy into a spontaneous and largely uncoordinated attack of its own. By this means, Henry would have exploited both the over-enthusiasm of his enemies and their inadequate command structure, as well as the natural advantages afforded by the battlefield's terrain. It was a textbook example of military audacity and battlefield psychology. Not only had Henry read his own men to perfection, he had also, it seems, read his adversaries.

Although the ambush is denied by Jean le Fèvre, both Monstrelet and Juvénal des Ursins make specific reference to it. 'The King of England', wrote Monstrelet, 'sent about 200 archers to the rear of his army, so that they would not be spotted by the French. They secretly entered a meadow near Tramecourt, quite close to the rearguard of the French, and held themselves there secretly until it was time to shoot.'[77] If so, then Henry was once again displaying that typically hard-edged, even cynical approach, which made him so formidable. Such surprise attacks were, of course, hardly new. Indeed, they had been used to considerable effect by Sir John Hawkwood at the Battle of Castagnaro, as well as at Poitiers. But to an enemy whose conceptions of combat still remained handily gift-wrapped in chivalric romance, they could hardly have been more effective.

The real secret, however, was to accompany any disorientating volley of arrows with a broader, more threatening provocation – in other words, to stage a fake advance with the sole intention of stirring a dazed, confused and enraged enemy into a precipitate reaction. There is also the possibility that this particular manoeuvre may have been conducted over a much shorter distance, with many, perhaps most, of the defensive stakes left in their original position to provide a fallback option when the French cavalry strike inevitably arrived. On this model, the English army may well have advanced forward just far enough – perhaps as little as ten or twenty yards – to convince their enemy that they had, in desperation, finally abandoned their defences. Then, as the enemy cavalry made their move, spurred on by the surprise assault of Henry's hidden archers, there was scope for the English to effect a measured return to their original location, leaving French horses and riders to impale themselves precisely as planned.

Certainly, the cavalry charge that ensued was nothing less than an unmitigated disaster. Just as the first line of French men-at-arms began its advance, 500 cavalry, led by Guillaume de Saveuse and Clignet de Brabant charged the English on each flank – only to be easily repulsed by massive arrow fire. Most turned back and those that forced their way on only collided with the stake wall. Worse still, a large number of wounded and panic-stricken horses now went crashing back though the advancing ranks of the French vanguard trudging forward on foot. In the resulting pandemonium, the men on the wings proceeded to seek the relative safety of the centre, only to compress the front line further and thereby destroy all possibility of swift and unfettered action. The irrepressible desire of the French nobility to take pride of place at the forefront of a historic victory had therefore guaranteed the most monumental of French defeats.

As the advance continued, the greatest men in France, including the dukes of Bourbon and Orléans, were subjected to further armour-piercing fire from their flanks. 'God and our archers made hem sore to stumble', the *Brut* recounts.[78] And when they did fall, there was little hope of rising again from the clinging mud and the bloody scrum around them. Yet still the French made their way forward, forming as they did so three tightly packed columns with the aim of avoiding the projecting wedges of archers, and smashing through the thinly stretched English front line. If Henry's strongest points could therefore be penetrated by sheer weight of numbers and his standards captured, it might yet be possible to win the day.

In the melee that followed, the English men-at-arms do indeed appear to have been forced back 'almost a spear's length'.[79] But the line proceeded to hold – not least of all, because the French were now so closely crammed that they could hardly raise their arms to use their weapons. They were also, according to one anonymous French chronicler, 'exhausted and much troubled in their advance', while their enemies 'were fresh and unwearied, since they had not moved from their advantageous position'.[80] And to compound its dreadful predicament, the French vanguard now found itself crushed from behind as its second 'battle' arrived. In consequence, the fallen were pressed down in ever growing heaps, many of them suffocated by the bodies above, so that John Hardyng would later recall how 'more were dead through press than our men might have slain in no time less'.[81]

Before long, therefore, the battle had turned to outright slaughter as the piles of dead rose in front of the English position and archers now abandoned their bows to fall upon those still living. Seizing swords, hatchets, mallets, bill-hooks and any other weapon that was readily to hand – including stakes, according to the *Gesta* – the lightly clad bowmen leapt on top of the dead in order to despatch any survivors.[82] The English, wrote Monstrelet, 'were slaying all before them' – in many cases, thrusting daggers into the eyes of the fallen through their visors – while Tito Livio recorded later how 'mountains of corpses' began to pile up before Henry's men.[83] The author of the *Gesta* was also keen to emphasise the same thing: 'Nor, it seemed to our older men, had Englishmen ever fallen upon their enemies more boldly or fearlessly, or with a better will.'[84] Clearly, the King of England's attempts to sharpen his men's spirits to a deadly intensity prior to the battle had not been in vain.

In the meantime, Henry himself was said to have been fighting 'as a famished lion for his prey'.[85] With both the Duke of York and the young Earl of Suffolk slain, the king now found himself at the heart of the fray – losing one of his helmet's fleurets to a French sword blow. This, indeed, was the crisis point of the whole battle as the enemy still sought to capture the English standards before punching their way through the line. And when his youngest brother Humphrey was wounded and brought to the ground by the Duke of Alençon, Henry, it seems, did not hesitate to defend him personally – bestriding the fallen body, which was already 'sore wounded in the hams with a sword', and fighting off assailants. Held at bay by this intervention, the French duke was finally beaten to his knees before surrendering, only to be cut down by a frenzied man-at-arms after he had removed his helmet.[86]

By this stage, then, the tide had turned decisively as the discipline and cohesion of Henry's army allowed him to push his men-at-arms forward for the first time, striking fresh blows against his demoralised enemy. Yet according to some accounts, it was at this very point of triumph that Henry heard unsettling news. Some time before the start of the battle his baggage had already been raided, and now there were rumours of a repetition. Much worse still, a cry went up that the third, mounted French line was 'showing signs of wanting to fight, marching forward in battle order'.[87] The late arrival of the Duke of Brabant may well have been responsible for this impression, but it is also certain that after the rout of the second line, the counts of Marle and Fauquembergue were intending to launch a do-or-die cavalry attack with a mere 600 men, in a final effort to kill the King of England. At a time when his own army was already weary and increasingly distracted by the quest for ransoms, the danger posed by the prisoners already taken was apparent.

With this in mind, then, Henry took the chilling decision to begin the slaughter of French prisoners in cold blood. The order was met by his own men with incredulity rather than horror since it entailed the loss of so many valuable captives, and the threat of hanging was used as an incentive for any soldier inclined to disobey. Thereafter, a group of 200 archers duly proceeded to undertake the bulk of the task. According to John Hardyng, the captives' bodies were 'paunched in fell and cruel wise', while the Tudor chronicler Edward Hall related how the majority were 'sticked with daggers, brained with poleaxes' or 'slain with malles'.[88] Some, meanwhile, were burnt to death in the hut where they had been confined, though Gilbert de Lannoy, the French nobleman who described the event, was able to crawl to safety, since his wounds were comparatively minor.[89]

Not surprisingly, the entire episode continues to serve as a harrowing reminder of Henry V's capacity for utter ruthlessness when circumstances required. It reminds us, too, of this 'true knight's' readiness to discard one of the most basic laws of chivalry in pursuit of ultimate victory. Nor should the comparative silence of both English and French chroniclers be used to conceal this. For Jean de Waurin, at least, left no doubt that each and every victim was 'inhumanly mutilated there in cold blood'.[90] Indeed, Henry's action continues to confirm the inherent danger of assuming that morality can be entirely suspended in the light of practical necessity. The standards of the time were, of course, harsh – the internal logic of the decision to press forward with a spree of bloody murder is easily understood. Yet the slaughter of defenceless men at Agincourt continues to serve as all too sobering proof of the kind of depravity that may ultimately result from unflinching devotion to honour, justice and God's will.

In fact, the murders were halted as soon as the threat from the French third line was over and its remnants had begun to leave the field. By that time English losses could probably be numbered at 500 or less. However, the total number of French deaths in battle was altogether higher. The dukes of Alençon, Bar and Brabant were all killed, along with the Count of Nevers, Constable d'Albret, the Archbishop of Sens and at least eight other counts. Ninety-two barons and 1,560 knights were also among those said to be piled into five hurriedly dug grave pits – each containing, according to the chronicler of Ruisseauville, some 1,200 Frenchmen. The casualty list reads, in fact, like a roll call of the cream of the French nobility, though King Henry claimed, as always, that 'it is not we who have made this great slaughter, but the omnipotent God and, as we believe, for the sins of the French' – a view shared, it seems, by some of his soldiers who claimed to have seen St George himself hovering over the English army during the battle.[91]

The surviving prisoners, meanwhile, had little to cheer them. The dukes of Bourbon and Orléans, as well as the counts of Eu, Richemont and Vendôme, for instance, all faced lengthy captivity in England to await ransom. Orléans, sadly, would not regain his freedom until 1440, and even the redoubtable Marshal Boucicaut now found himself vanquished and impotent in the hands of his captors. Ultimately, he would die at Methley in Yorkshire in 1421

– still awaiting release. Their humbler fellow captives, on the oᴛ hand, were even less fortunate, since many could not pay theı. ransoms and were therefore sold as servants by the Calais merchants who bought them from the English troops.

It was small wonder, then, that many French chroniclers were inconsolable. 'O eternal dishonour! O disaster forever to be deplored', wrote the Monk of Saint-Denys, while Pierre Cochon would describe the battle as 'the ugliest and most wretched event that had happened to France over the last thousand years'.[92] Among Frenchmen, indeed, only the local peasantry seemed to lack the time for rueful reflection as they went to work that night busily stripping the corpses of their betters.[93]

Heroic return

By the evening of 25 October, a large barn at the village of Maisoncelle had been piled high with faggots to serve as a funeral pyre for the English dead. Next day, it was still smouldering as Henry V's army resumed its march to Calais in the steady autumn rain to which it had become so accustomed. Weighed down with items looted from their enemies, still seriously short of food and also lacking horses, England's victorious soldiers faced a far from triumphant journey. In the fields, woods and hedgerows round about lay the scattered bodies of those who had died from their wounds. And in the hamlets through which the English now passed, there was little on offer beyond fear, grief and sullen loathing. There were, moreover, still forty-five weary miles ahead – a distance that would take another four days to cover.

Nor was the greeting awaiting Henry's troops in Calais a warm one. The king himself had paused with his most valuable captives some six miles outside the town, at the castle of Guines. Lodged in suitable splendour, it was here that he told the Duke of Orléans how he had never doubted victory 'for never were there greater disorders, sensuality and vices than now prevail in France, which it is horrible to hear described'.[1] But the common soldiers who preceded him were made to wait outside Calais's walls, since provisions within were running low. Despite their exploits many disillusioned troops were left with little choice but to sell their remaining prisoners and booty cheaply in return for bread purchased at profiteering prices.

Even so, the king's eventual arrival was all that might be expected. Making his way over the Nieulay Bridge, which had been hastily repaired for his entry, he was duly welcomed by the Captain of Calais, Richard Beauchamp, and a vast crowd of ecstatic townspeople. By 11 November, moreover, the Frenchmen who had been released at Harfleur duly presented themselves as arranged to face financial ruin and years in captivity rather than dishonour. And five days after the arrival of his Harfleur prisoners, Henry finally set sail for Dover in heaving Channel seas which sank two ships and led the French nobles on board to suffer dreadfully from seasickness.

Prior to his departure, the king had actually considered a further attack on the neighbouring fortress of Ardres before finally accepting his nobles' advice that such an action with a worn-out army would be both unnecessary and unwise. Now, however, he rode the stormy Channel with all his usual assurance and aplomb. While retching Frenchmen, unused to the sea, compared the ordeal of their journey to the agonies of Agincourt, they were nevertheless deeply impressed by their captor's ability to bear the waves 'without accumbrance and dis-ease of his stomach'.[2]

News of Agincourt had, in fact, reached the capital some three weeks earlier, amid growing pessimism. Indeed, the Letter-Book of the City of London recorded on the very day of the battle how 'a lamentable report replete with sadness and cause for endless sorrow' was in widespread circulation.[3] On 29 October, however, the anxious capital received word of Henry's incredible victory. With the bells of the entire city ringing, the Mayor and citizens made grateful pilgrimage to the Confessor's shrine at Westminster before making for St Paul's where Bishop Beaufort conducted a service of thanksgiving in the presence of Queen Joan.

And by the time that Parliament met the following Monday, the Council had taken immediate advantage of the situation. Predictably, Henry Beaufort's sermon praised the king's capture of Harfleur, 'the strongest city of this part of this world', and 'his glorious and marvellous victory' against all odds at Agincourt.[4] In response, the dazzled Commons took the unprecedented step of surrendering their chief tool for holding the monarchy in check by granting Henry tonnage and poundage for life. As a result, the all-important tax on wines and imports, which the king had previously had to ask for each year, was now guaranteed. Buoyed by the prevailing surge of patriotism, Parliament also sanctioned a whole fifteenth and tenth to be paid in November for the defence of the realm.

Not surprisingly, then, Henry's formal entry into the capital on Saturday 23 November became the occasion for one of the most elaborate medieval pageants on record. As the conduits at Cornhill and Cheapside flowed with wine instead of water, tableaux mounted in the city streets proclaimed the great events of English history. On London Bridge, meanwhile, there stood the image of a gigantic figure, armed with a battle-axe, bearing an inscription formerly attributed to the poet, John Lydgate: 'A gyant that was full grym of sight, To teche the Frensshmen curtesye.'[5] And to complete the impression of a Roman triumph, the king's most distinguished French prisoners, including the Duke of Orléans and Marshal Boucicaut, marched behind him under guard.

The hero himself, however, rode in sombre mood throughout the entire extravaganza – dressed plainly, we are told, with eyes cast down and never smiling once. His gown, in fact, was purple – the colour that English monarchs usually wore in mourning. And he had urged from the outset that his victory be attributed to God and St George rather than himself. Indeed, the figure of St George on London Bridge held in its left hand a scroll proclaiming 'To God Alone Be Honour and Glory.' Nor would Henry allow his crown and armour that had been battered at Agincourt to be displayed to the frenzied crowds.

If this was propaganda on the king's behalf, it was therefore most definitely of the subtler kind, for rarely would a ruler so inclined be likely to miss such tempting opportunities. Certainly, most spectators who watched Henry that day had no hesitation in attributing his bearing to his well-known piety and humility. And the popular 'Agincourt Carol', which was probably of Norfolk origin, appeared to speak for an entire kingdom in praising God for giving England a king who 'went forth to Normandy, with grace and might of chivalry'.[6] Perhaps, then, it was neither mock modesty nor feigned piety that explains the king's demeanour on this occasion. Perhaps, indeed, the man behind the myth was not so utterly unlike the myth itself, which had now already taken root.

French resurgence

While all England effervesced in late November 1415, the mood across the Channel was increasingly one of simmering vengefulness. And French resistance was far from dead, for the army decimated at Agincourt was only a portion of the Armagnac forces now stirring for action. The King of France, the Dauphin and the Duke of Berry still commanded considerable reserves at Rouen, while the main forces of the unpredictable Duke of Burgundy also remained menacingly intact. Significantly, too, there was no mention of Agincourt by the clerk to the *parlement* of Paris until nearly a month later, and even then it was referred to obliquely as 'the affair that the English had against the king'.[7] Far from crippling France, then, or crushing her resolve, Henry's victory was merely the prelude to the inevitable counter-strike, which would not be long in coming.

By now, the formidable Bernard VII, Count of Armagnac, had been created Constable of France in a shrewd move to forestall the machinations of John the Fearless and his supporters, who by December 1415 had penetrated to within sixteen miles of Paris. That same month the Dauphin, Louis, died at the unripe age of eighteen and was replaced by his brother John, husband of the Duke of Burgundy's niece Jacqueline. With the heir to the French throne now firmly in his physical possession, as he had been in Burgundian territory at the time of Louis's death, the duke decided that an immediate attack on the capital was needlessly risky. Instead, it would be better to continue to court England and wait upon events.

But the resulting pause provided a valuable breathing space for the new Constable of France to press forward with his ambitious plans for the recovery of Harfleur. And before the following month was out he was indeed threatening to overwhelm the small English force that had been left under the Earl of Dorset to protect the port. On the one hand, the French forces closing in on the town were very much larger and supplies were already running low. Furthermore, English raids into the surrounding countryside were becoming increasingly difficult to stage, and it was on one such raid in March that disaster nearly struck.

Alerted by the smoke from burning farmhouses, the Count of Armagnac was able to intercept a force of 1,000 English soldiers who had been plundering all along the northern coast. And although Dorset's men were finally able to extricate themselves from the subsequent French attack at Valmont, their escape was achieved only with great difficulty after many casualties. Nor could their lucky victory shortly afterwards beneath the cliffs of the Chef de Caux hide the deeper significance of the new situation. Though Dorset eventually returned with 800 French prisoners in tow, similar raids were now impossible and Harfleur would soon be starving.

By early June, in fact, the Seine was being blockaded by nine carracks and eight galleys hired from Genoa, along with a further sixty vessels of lesser tonnage provided by the King of Castile. In these increasingly desperate circumstances, a relieving force was hastily mustered at Southampton and other locations under the King of England's personal supervision. Extra ships from the Cinque ports were also enlisted to engage the Franco-Genoese warships lodged at the mouth of the Seine. But though it was Henry's original intention to lead the expedition himself, he was by this time heavily involved in diplomatic exchanges with his recently arrived guest, the Holy Roman Emperor. It was therefore left to his brother, the Duke of Bedford, to take command of an operation that would decide at a stroke the permanence or otherwise of any military progress made so far.

Big and ungainly, with fleshy jowls and a long, loping nose to boot, Bedford was by no means the archetypal hero of chivalric romance. But he had already demonstrated his worth as a remarkably effective administrator during Henry's absence in France, and he was no less loyal than capable. This, moreover, was something that Henry, with his keen appreciation of human strengths and weaknesses, was quick to appreciate. Indeed, it was the king's ability to delegate judiciously when occasion demanded that distinguished him from many lesser commanders. This time, the Duke of Bedford's own steadfastness under intense pressure would prove nothing less than vital to Henry's cause.

In the bloody battle that followed on 16 August, the English were seriously disadvantaged by the superior height of the opposing vessels, from which the enemy poured down hails of crossbow fire and blinding clouds of quicklime. Bedford himself was seriously wounded in the fray. However, after five hours of havoc and carnage during which English and Genoese ships were lashed gunwale to gunwale, the duke's force was able to sale triumphantly into Harfleur. Next morning, moreover, the French besiegers were already abandoning their positions, leaving Henry and his subjects to draw the all too obvious conclusion. For how, with another sign of this kind, could God's continuing favour now be doubted? How, too, could the King of England possibly resist the momentum of his own destiny?

Imperial alliance and the Council of Constance

Not altogether surprisingly, the impact of Agincourt on Henry V's European reputation was considerable. Henceforth, he would be widely proclaimed as 'a second Hector' and 'king of kings'.[8] There were comparisons, too, with Moses, David, Cicero and Gawain.[9] And even the Pope did not hesitate to describe him as 'the arm of his strength'.[10] For one contemporary preacher, meanwhile, he was now 'oure maister mariner, oure worthi prince'.[11]

With renown, too, came international influence, for Henry's realm was swiftly acquiring a new and important role in the affairs of Christendom, which he was keen to exploit. The main priority was to ensure the Duke of Burgundy's neutrality in any future invasion of France – something which could best be achieved by exploiting fears of an anti-Burgundian alliance involving England, France and the Holy Roman Empire. At the same time, however, there was also an ongoing need for Henry to confirm the justice of his cause and to persuade his fellow rulers not only of his moderation, but also his concern for the welfare of the Church. As such, the general ecclesiastical council presently meeting at Constance would be crucial, as would the allegiance of the Holy Roman Emperor Sigismund.

The emperor, in fact, had already established a curiously mixed reputation, which made him, at one and the same time, both a paragon and parody of regal qualities. Brother to Wenzel the Drunkard, King of Bohemia, whose daughter had been the beloved wife of Richard II, he was a renowned jouster, a military commander of great enthusiasm – if limited talent – and an incorrigible hunter of women of every class. He was also savagely cruel and ruthless when roused. Yet he was known, too, to be a man of pious ideals and noble ambitions. And now this fine Latinist and patron of learning had set himself the task of eradicating Hussite heresy in his own territories and reuniting the whole Church, so that a grand crusade could then be launched to drive the infidel from the Holy Land.

Such plans were certain, of course, to appeal to England's own ruler. In the years since 1378 when the so-called 'Babylonish Captivity' of the papacy had given way to the 'Great Schism', the heads of European states had sided with rival popes mainly on grounds of political expediency. England, for instance, had supported Urban VI in Rome, simply because Clement VII at Avignon was France's instrument. Flanders, Portugal and the Holy Roman Empire had also joined the Urbanist cause, while Scotland and Christian Spain rallied to Clement. In effect, then, the schism had driven a diplomatic wedge through Christendom which neither Henry nor the emperor could tolerate. And while Turkish control of the Holy Land continued to go unchallenged, the Pope at Rome had become none other than the notorious John XXIII, better known as the condottiere Baldassare Cossa, whose reputation for piracy, murder, rape, sodomy and incest was the source of unrelenting scandal.

It was with all this in mind that on 16 November 1414, Emperor Sigismund had first summoned a General Council of the Church to meet in the imperial free city of Constance, with the express intention of ending the schism, stamping out heresy and initiating a programme of ecclesiastical reform. Moreover, the first of these objectives was duly achieved in November 1417 when all three 'popes' were made to resign in favour of Martin V. Yet if the emperor's success was significant, the King of England had much more reason still to be satisfied. For throughout the negotiations, he had maintained a very high-level embassy under Bishop Hallam of Salisbury, which had managed to establish his realm's acceptance as a voting 'nation' in its own right – no small feat in the face of intense French opposition. And though proceedings had been marred by the burning of Jan Hus after an offer of safe conduct had been cynically reversed, Henry himself had meanwhile emerged to his shining credit as the victor of Harfleur and Agincourt.

Now, therefore, it was crucial to Sigismund that France and England should settle their differences, so that a joint alliance could at last be forged against the Turkish foe, but what met him in Paris early in 1416 was a deeply disheartening situation. The Battle of Agincourt was, as we have seen, already viewed as little more than a temporary setback, while the dominant Armagnac faction was not only gearing for a renewal of conflict, but remained implacably opposed to its Burgundian adversaries who were still apparently intriguing with the English and prepared to sell the crown of France to the highest bidder. Any prospect of Anglo-French reconciliation seemed hopelessly remote, and to add insult to injury, the emperor's hosts were also openly contemptuous of his pretensions, not to mention his dirtiness, his drinking and his whoring. On one occasion, it seems, he invited no less than 600 Parisian 'ladies' to dinner – with aspirations no doubt as inflated as his diplomatic hopes.

Nevertheless, in April 1416 Sigismund duly decided to try his luck with the King of England. And this time, over the four summer months that followed, both Henry and Sigismund played the game of personal amity to perfection. At an investiture at Windsor, for example, Sigismund was made a Knight of the Garter, in return for which he is said to have given Henry the petrified heart of St George. Yet the aim of healing the rift between England and France remained a pipedream. Henry, it is true, while still maintaining his right to the French throne, was prepared to surrender it as long as France would agree to restore all lands and rights surrendered under the Treaty of Brétigny. But Harfleur was to prove an altogether more substantial stumbling block, since it had already cost England dear and Henry was unwilling to give it up. Throughout the spring and summer, after all, it had been retained only after bitter fighting.

Faced, then, with the intransigence of both sides, the emperor now had little choice but to marry common sense with self-interest. And this inevitably meant alliance with the King of England who had played his hand at diplomacy in recent months almost as skilfully as he had wielded his sword at Agincourt. The result was a comprehensive alliance between the two rulers, guaranteeing both offensive and defensive action, which was signed at Canterbury on 15 August 1416. In consequence, Henry now had not only the military support of the Holy Roman Emperor at his disposal, but much more importantly still, a cast-iron warranty for all his claims on France. It was a strategic victory of the first order and another propaganda victory of the greatest significance. Clearly, the King of England's star remained ascendant, and within the week news had arrived of the Duke of Bedford's naval victory at the Battle of the Seine, which guaranteed the relief of Harfleur.

Invasion preparations

On 16 March 1416, Henry Beaufort had delivered to Parliament what amounted to an invasion speech. 'He hath opened for you a way' was his chosen text and under the circumstances it could not have been more apt. Having returned to the time-honoured theme of France's 'unjust' refusal to recognise the King of England as its ruler, Beaufort proceeded to berate the stubbornness of those French subjects who refused to recognise the hand of God in recent events. 'Why', he asked, 'do not these miserable and hard-hearted men see by these terrible divine sentences that they are bound to obey?'[12] It was political oratory at its most persuasive, emphasising England's apparent control of the moral high ground, and marrying the keenest possible sense of righteous indignation with the current surge of national pride.

Yet Beaufort's speech was as sincere as it was compelling, and it captured rather than created the overwhelming mood of the Lords and Commons who heard it. Indeed, this particular session of Parliament was conducted by all concerned in an apparent daze of optimism and goodwill. Although no new subsidy was voted, the grant of a tenth and fifteenth that had been scheduled for November was now brought forward to June without demur. And the king also gave vent to his brimming self-confidence by finally exchanging young Henry Percy for Murdoch, son of the Scottish regent, Albany. The subsequent restoration of Percy to the earldom of Northumberland, along with all his grandfather's other titles and rights, could not have demonstrated more conclusively the progress that had been made in three brief years of rule.

There remained, it is true, latent tensions at the heart of government, which it would require all of Henry's skill and personal standing to overcome. On the one hand, the Council was continuing to press for negotiations with the French on the understanding that Henry should moderate some of his more extravagant claims over and beyond the Treaty of Brétigny. More importantly still, the king's treasury remained sorely depleted and the advance grant agreed by Parliament in March, following on from a similar arrangement the previous December, merely reflected rather than forestalled the onset of Henry's growing financial difficulties. Quite apart from the loans entailed by the Agincourt campaign, the defence of Harfleur was also proving more and more costly, and it should not be forgotten either that the particularly lavish treatment of the Emperor Sigismund was 'all the king's cost'.[13]

At this stage, however, the initiative remained wholly Henry's. On 4 September, he had travelled to Calais for a meeting with the emperor, the Duke of Burgundy and representatives of the Armagnac party. And though there is some obscurity about the precise nature of what transpired, the outcome was certainly favourable from the English perspective. While talks with the Armagnacs foundered mainly over Harfleur, Henry did achieve, in effect, the benevolent neutrality of Burgundy during any future assault on France. And by the time that the King of England returned to meet his sixth Parliament in October 1416, he was already intent upon another invasion of France on a new and altogether more impressive scale.

The cautious response of the Commons was neither unreasonable nor altogether unexpected. In granting a comparatively generous two tenths and two fifteenths, it was made clear to Henry that only three-quarters would be made available to him at Candlemas (2 February), and it was stipulated, too, that there should be no subsequent requests for advances before the final instalment was duly delivered at Martinmas of the following year. In the event, the sums involved were not enough for the king's needs. But he could not have expected otherwise, and would soon make good the shortfall – albeit only by means of further borrowing, which entailed amongst other things the re-pawning of the celebrated Pusan collar to the City of London and a further loan of 21,000 marks from Bishop Beaufort, pledged on the security of the king's best crown.

In the meantime, the more practical necessities of war were once again being attended to with typical energy and thoroughness. While cash was being amassed for the purchase of munitions and stores, estimates of manpower were being prepared, along with indentures for a general muster near Southampton in the spring. On this occasion, master craftsmen from Normandy were enlisted to fashion crossbows, while colossal supplies of food – mainly of corn and bacon – were stored along the southern coast. Detailed instructions were also drawn up for the construction of additional vessels as far away as Bayonne and Barcelona, since Henry now required an invasion fleet of well over 1,500 ships.

Thereafter, all that remained was to clear the Channel of those Genoese ships that threatened the English crossing, and for this purpose Henry chose to select John Holland, son of the self-same Duke of Exeter whom Henry IV had previously executed. Although his father's dukedom had been awarded, somewhat surprisingly, to the Earl of Dorset for his efforts at Harfleur, Holland had nevertheless been granted the earldom of Huntingdon – another of his family titles – after his own, rather more impressive, service during Bedford's sea battle at the mouth of the Seine. It was a decision that would now pay considerable dividends. For on 29 June, the young earl gained an invaluable victory at La Hogue over the Franco-Genoese fleet commanded by the notorious Bastard of Bourbon. Four carracks were captured, along with the Bastard himself who was carrying with him his men's pay for an entire quarter, while the remaining enemy carracks took shelter in the nearest Breton harbours.

It was plainly another glorious triumph, another rich propaganda opportunity, another manifest portent – but this time one achieved by the scion of a family hitherto inextricably linked to the cause of Richard II. And though no further naval threat appeared, it was now none other than the Earl of March, eternally grateful and deeply loyal after his brush with the Southampton conspirators the previous year, who was safely entrusted to guard the seas as the King of England's second coming drew near.

War aims and strategy

Although Henry left London for the south coast on 27 April, it was another three months before his force was ready to sail. Since early March, men had been mustering all over southern Hampshire, while ships gathered in the Solent and just off Portchester Castle. But only after Huntingdon's victory was it wholly safe to proceed, and as always Henry took no chances. Throughout June and July he shuttled between Reading and Salisbury and from Bishop's Waltham to Titchfield, making, in the process, a second will and again appointing his brother John to administer the realm in his absence. Not until 25 July, however, did he board his flagship, and only after another five days had elapsed did he and his armada finally weigh anchor.

Predictably, the army accompanying Henry on 30 July 1417 was both well equipped and primed for victory. His brothers Thomas and Humphrey were once again present and up to 12,000 men-at-arms and archers were also safely stowed, alongside 30,000 others – miners, engineers, armourers, farriers, gunners and so on – who serviced the army's technical needs. Masons, too, were present in large numbers to manufacture the gunstones so crucial to the kind of siege warfare that was to characterise the coming campaign. For Henry was now heading to Normandy with a view to permanent conquest, and this was something that could never be accomplished without the systematic subjugation of key strongholds. Every town or chateau of strategic importance would have to fall, since even a small garrison behind Henry's lines might, with a sufficiently skilled commander, disrupt his communications and supplies.

Just as in 1415, archers continued to outnumber men-at-arms by three to one. But heavy guns rather than longbows were the lynchpin of this new phase of the war, and in this respect the King of England was blessed both by personal expertise and circumstance. Henry was, after all, always first and foremost an artilleryman, who had cut his military teeth in gruelling sieges of mighty Welsh castles, and he was also the beneficiary of what amounted to a technological revolution in heavy gunnery which was gathering pace at precisely this time. More efficient methods of iron production coupled with increased barrel length and greater muzzle velocity gave rise to longer range and more destructive force. For some years, too, the English had been perfecting the art of 'corning' their powder – mixing the constituents while wet – with the result that the explosive did not separate in transport and became up to three times as powerful.

Nevertheless, the task confronting the invading English army remained formidable. Almost every town was heavily fortified and there was also the question of what next? Though Henry might with some considerable stretching of legality lay claim to Normandy as part of his heritage, there was still no denying that it represented only a fraction of French territory. Reaching the capital – his main objective – would be no easy task either, since the Dauphin's forces on the north bank of the Seine at Rouen blocked his way, while the formidable castle of Honfleur controlled the south bank. Besides which, the capture of Paris would give him control of no more than the north of the country. Beyond lay a number of difficult rivers, not to mention the great mountain bastion of the Massif Central.

A lesser leader might well have baulked at the task. Yet boldness, timing, raw ego and a genuine spark of strategic genius pushed Henry inexorably forward. In the first place, his secret choice of Touques as a landing-place had the virtue of surprise, and no available spot could have brought him nearer to Paris. If, furthermore, he was able to spend the autumn and winter subduing lower Normandy, he could then effectively neutralise Brittany and Anjou, widen his base in rich country where foraging would be plentiful, and subsequently turn on Rouen, first cutting it off from Paris. Once lower Normandy and the Norman capital of Rouen were firmly his, the direct road to France's capital would be open, while the eastern approaches could be covered by the Duke of Burgundy and the Holy Roman Empire.

The secret lay in capturing as quickly as possible a line of strongholds facing the direction from which the inevitable French counter-attacks would come. Once this had been achieved, the aim was to overrun the territory behind the line by taking every enemy stronghold contained therein. Since the French would not dare to penetrate his advance positions, he could bombard, mine and blockade his targets at leisure without the need for costly assaults, and when they had been finally subdued, they could be manned by small and comparatively inexpensive English garrisons as the invasion moved forward. The entire scheme was based both on considerations of terrain and on Henry's skilful exploitation of the civil strife currently prevailing in France. By any standards, it was daring, incisive, single-minded and coldly logical. And as such it displayed the King of England's mind to perfection.

The siege of Caen

On 1 August 1417 Henry's invasion fleet followed his lead to the mouth of the little river Touques, and there, a little distance from the local castle, his force disembarked without major incident. Within three days of landing, after the capture of the nearby castles of Bonneville and Auvillers, the Duke of Clarence had advanced with a force of 1,000 horse to overwhelm the town of Lisieux, inspiring such terror that its entire population, with the exception of two aged cripples, had fled by the time of his arrival. And by 14 August, Clarence was in occupation of the suburbs of Caen.

The strategic importance of the second largest town in Normandy was manifest. Not only was Caen an important agricultural market for the produce of the abundant countryside round about, it was also a flourishing centre of both religious and commercial life, boasting more than forty churches and a Europe-wide reputation for its woollen serge. In strategic terms, moreover, Caen was the lynchpin of all lower Normandy. For if it was captured, many of the surrounding towns such as Bayeux and Lisieux, which were less well fortified, would almost automatically surrender, even though other important fortresses like Falaise and Honfleur would need to be besieged in turn.

In the broader scheme of things, using Caen as a centre, a single force could cut off and subdue the various strongpoints of the Cotentin peninsula, thus aiding the naval as well as the military situation, while another could push south to set up a line along the edges of Maine and Anjou. Thereafter, the bulk of the English army could turn northwards to the Seine, in the knowledge that its rear was safe, and set about the isolation and capture of Rouen, the second largest city of France. With all this in mind, Henry therefore led his army westwards towards Caen on 13 August, knowing that everything depended on success here. And having circled the south of the town to cut it off from Paris and Brittany, he began the siege in earnest five days later.

To Henry's advantage, the bitter struggles within France were continuing to rage. On the one hand, John, the new Dauphin, was a feeble and uninspiring youth, and although invested with the grand title of Lieutenant-General of the Realm, he remained entirely under the control of Bernard of Armagnac and Tanneguy du Chastel, the *prévôt* of Paris. In consequence, throughout 1417 the struggle with the Duke of Burgundy steadily intensified as the latter strove to cut all lines of communication to the capital by capturing the surrounding towns of Pontoise, Montlhéry and Chartres. By June the duke had captured Troyes and was advancing in the direction of the capital. Clearly, the value of this conflict to the foreign invader was considerable. Nor was its significance lost upon the Burgundian chronicler Monstrelet who later noted the general astonishment at the 'facility of King Henry's conquests', which, he claimed, was caused by 'the intestine divisions of France'.[14]

Yet Henry still realised to his credit that he must proceed with sufficient care to prevent the contending parties from laying aside their enmity, and it was equally necessary to ensure that his army did not fatally alienate his Norman 'subjects' by pillaging and destroying everything in its path – something that would in any case threaten its ability to survive in the field in the longer term. With this in mind, he issued strict regulations about the treatment of non-combatants, such as clergy, women or common people who surrendered to him. Their goods were not to be seized, nor were they to be personally molested.

It should not be forgotten either that French chroniclers would continue to speak approvingly of English behaviour by comparison with that of their own countrymen. The Bourgeois of Paris, for instance, who wrote so vividly of life in the capital at this time, had no doubt about the relative merits of Henry's soldiers as opposed to Burgundian and Armagnac troops. Those 'honest merchants, reputable men' who had been in the hands of all three, wrote the Bourgeois, 'solemnly affirmed on oath that the English had been kinder to them than the Burgundians and the Burgundians a hundred times kinder than the troops from Paris, as regards food, ransom, physical suffering and imprisonment, which had astonished them, as it must all good Christians'.[15]

For the time being, however, the immediate military task before the English far outweighed considerations of kindness or fair play, since the task itself remained so formidable. In Edward III's day, the immediate perimeter of Caen had been largely unfortified, but now it boasted a wall some seven feet thick with thirty-two towers and deep-water ditches. Within, moreover, stood the great castle begun by William the Conqueror and completed by his son, Henry I, while just outside there still lay two strongly fortified abbeys – St Stephen's on the west where the Conqueror was buried, and the Trinity on the east where his wife Matilda had been laid to rest. Accessible from the sea by the river Orne, Caen was also protected by the heavily fortified church of St Sepulchre, as well as two tributaries, which lapped at its other walls.

Yet Caen, as Henry well knew, was not invulnerable. In the first place, the meanderings of the Orne had created an island, which had not been fortified and which divided the town into two halves. Once captured, this spot could serve as the launching-place for an assault on the town centre. Even more significant was the situation of the adjacent abbeys. Both were formidable strongholds in their own right and were reported to be defended by adequate garrisons. But they were also worryingly close to the town – only some 600 yards away in the case of St Stephen's – and, if taken, would serve as ideal vantage points for continuous bombardment from the English heavy guns, which, as the Monk of Saint-Denys reported, 'threw enormous stones with a noise like thunder amid fearsome clouds of black smoke, so that one might have thought they were being vomited forth by hell'.[16]

In view of this, the capture of the abbeys was a matter of primary importance, and the crucial task was duly achieved by Clarence with typical gusto and panache – not to mention a mighty slice of luck, which came his way when one of the monks guided him to a weak spot in St Stephen's walls, in order to prevent its demolition by his own countrymen. By the time Henry himself crossed the Orne at Eterville on 17 August, therefore, he had already been gifted two excellent fortresses. And from this time forth, his artillery kept up the assault both day and night, wreaking widespread destruction and depriving Caen's populace of much-needed rest. Indeed, so powerful were the heaviest guns that the windows of St Stephen's shattered at the first volley, forcing Henry to pay for the damage later at his own cost.

Yet resistance was stout. And it was not until the morning of 4 September that all was set for one last violent assault which would cruelly exhibit the full savagery of late medieval warfare – so much so, in fact, that the final subjection of Caen, and in particular the 'foul massacre' which followed it, has continued to blacken Henry's name.[17] At first, the English onslaught was successfully repulsed by volleys of crossbow bolts and showers of powdered quicklime, as well as the 'shedding of scalding water and boiling pitch and oil'.[18] But in the process, the young, dashing and distinguished Sir Edmund Springhouse was burned alive by the defenders, who hurled bales of burning straw upon him after he had lost his footing on the ramparts. And it was this act, according to Thomas Walsingham, that encouraged the English to fight with such frenzied ferocity, as Henry ordered a second and third wave of assaults, and the Duke of Clarence began his own attack from the opposite side of the town.[19]

Only now did the defenders at last begin to panic and give ground, whereupon the infamous massacre associated with the siege began to unfold with nightmarish inevitability. Hacking his way towards the centre of the town, Henry, along with the Earl of Warwick, finally met Clarence at the middle to extinguish any remaining resistance, after which, according to some accounts, at least 2,000 people were herded into the market place and slaughtered – allegedly at the king's own instructions. According to the Venetian Antonio Morosini, Henry ordered his soldiers 'to kill and cut to pieces everyone they found, from the age of twelve upwards, without sparing anybody'. 'No one', the Italian added, 'had ever heard of such infamy being committed.'[20] Only, it seems, when Henry discovered the body of a headless woman with a baby in her lap still sucking at her breast did he order the killing to stop.

Yet Morosini's outrage, however understandable, was unlikely to have been as typical as he himself suggested. For even if Henry's French 'subjects' were not actually 'his' at all, he was nevertheless continuing to play the bloody game of conquest entirely by the book. Indeed, the treatment of Caen, in spite of its shocking ferocity, closely conformed to all contemporary military conventions, which were every bit as precise as they were savage. Henry's heralds had, for instance, been despatched, as required, to affirm his claim to the town at the outset of the siege, and an appropriate summons to surrender had also been duly issued before the final assault. If, thereafter, the defenders persisted in their refusal to surrender to their rightful prince, their slaughter was on this basis purely an act of justice. For although churches and clergy were technically exempt from retribution, it was clearly established by long custom that both the lives and property of the general populace should in such circumstances be considered forfeit, as laid down by Deuteronomy XX.[21]

There was, moreover, a further chilling logic behind the ferocity that ended the siege of Caen. In a late medieval context no permanent victory could be won while enemy fortresses remained unconquered. And in Henry's case especially, where the prospect of an endless series of protracted sieges loomed before him as a very distinct and potentially disastrous possibility, the need for terror became, in effect, utterly unavoidable. Only thus could any potential resistor be cowed into early submission during the long weeks and months ahead. So it was no surprise that the Monk of Saint-Denys would later observe how 'by taking the town of Caen, the King of England had inspired such terror in the Normans that they had lost all courage'.[22] By now, in any case, the English army was already irretrievably committed to a war which had little to do with the pious professions of chivalry: one which had much more in common with modern doctrines of total war than is often appreciated, and one in which the line between heroism and barbarity was virtually indistinguishable – even if not for contemporaries themselves.

Caen had, in fact, been plundered by the English even more ferociously in 1345. Nor should it be forgotten that order was swiftly re-established once the bloody lesson had been duly delivered just over seventy years later. And this time Henry was especially anxious to demonstrate his mercy, not only to convince his opponents of his worth as a ruler, but also as an added incentive for any future town or fortress to submit swiftly. When calm was restored, therefore, he issued strict orders to curb further excess, and after the surrender of Caen Castle on 19 September, the terms were not altogether ungenerous. Certainly, Henry saw no need for wanton retribution. On the contrary, all those in the castle were not only granted their lives, but also spared imprisonment. And though the soldiers among them were made to surrender their military equipment, each was nevertheless allowed to take with him his horse, harness and clothes, along with other personal goods to the value of 2,000 crowns. The citizens, meanwhile, were given the choice of taking their clothes and departing, or of staying in Caen under obedience to the king.

Over the following weeks, therefore, Henry was able to exercise the kind of clemency that befitted a conqueror who meant to stay for good. He also had every reason to treat his prize with respect, for its wealth remained considerable, even though the French appear before their departure to have burnt many of the goods meant to be left in the castle. Equally importantly, Henry now had his base for the conquest of lower Normandy, since his ships were able to sail straight up the river Orne to reach it. And now, too, he was at liberty to earmark many of the town's best houses for English settlers, since perhaps as many as 3,000 merchants and tradesmen rapidly left the town rather than accept his rule.

Before long, in fact, the citadel of Caen would become one of Henry's favourite personal residences. With his usual piety, he at once installed a lavishly furnished royal chapel within its walls, and ordered that the famous limestone from the town's nearby quarries was to be used solely for the repair and building of royal fortresses, churches and buildings in both England and Normandy rather than as ammunition for his guns. Having improved the citadel's gardens, it was there that he celebrated the feast of St George a year later. Nor, if the *First English Life* is to be believed, was Henry's personal share of the spoils of victory a large one. After turning over to Clarence the piled-up goods of the town in recognition of his leading role in the assault, the only looted object that the king retained for himself was, it seems, 'a goodlie French booke, of what historie I have not heard'. For this, we are told, was 'a prince from whome all avarice was fair exiled'.[23]

The fall of Falaise

As usual, Henry found little time for self-congratulation after Caen had fallen. Quite apart from reconciling its citizens to foreign rule and reconstituting the town as an administrative base by importing English artisans to repair damage and lifting all customs dues on supplies from home, the king was now faced with an urgent need to press on with the reduction of Normandy's fortresses. The fact that he should choose to begin his invasion in autumn and continue it throughout the winter was, of course, a remarkable testament to his boldness. The traditional model for an English campaign, the so-called *chevauchée*, entailed a summer raid followed by a mutual agreement permitting safe withdrawal. But Henry was not Edward III. Nor was he seeking another Agincourt. He was the skilful and irrepressible general of a triumphant conquering army bent on executing one of the earliest and most successful examples of strategic warfare in medieval Europe.

Even before Caen's surrender, Henry had sent the Duke of Gloucester to attack Bayeux, which capitulated around the same time. Thereafter Henry moved south, taking Argentan, Verneuil and Sées. And though the powerful fortress of Falaise was temporarily bypassed, Alençon, too, had fallen before the end of October – a victory which threatened the borders of Anjou and took the English to within thirty miles of the capital of Maine. In consequence, the Duke of Brittany saw fit to seek a truce for himself as well as Maine and Anjou, which was to last until 30 September 1418. So with peace assured along his southern line of conquest, the King of England was able to focus his attention, first upon Falaise and then north and eastwards.

Still stricken by civil war and stretched to the limit by the growing confidence of the Duke of Burgundy – which Henry, too, viewed with unease – Armagnac opposition to the English was paltry. 'There was no resistance, save for a few poor companions who held out in the woods', wrote Jean Juvénal des Ursins.[24] Nor was the Monk of Saint-Denys in any doubt about the intensity of the invaders' progress. They brought with them, he recorded, 'fire and blood and made everything fall to them, by force of arms, by menace and by terror'.[25] And while many Norman castles were actually induced to surrender by the offer of exemption from taxation, the restoration of privileges, or guarantees of freedom to concentrate upon farming or commerce, the brutality of Henry's advance remained palpable. At best, the claim in the *First English Life* that 'in a short time all the country was brought with goodwill, love and favour under the king's dominion' provided only a very partial glimpse of the conflict's broader realities.[26]

Nevertheless, by December 1417 Henry's army was poised before the grey and mighty walls of Falaise. Built in the twelfth century and situated on a towering crag, the town's citadel was as formidable as its commander, Sire Olivier de Mauny, the King of France's standard-bearer and keeper of the *Oriflamme*. There was also bitter weather to contend with as water froze – 'in such manner that it seemed to be crystal or hard stone than water' – and heavy wind and rainstorms set in. 'Winter', we are told, 'with great cold grieved both man and beast.'[27] And such was the surrounding desolation that provisions had to be brought from as far afield as Holland and Danzig.

Though the defenders offered stalwart resistance, a potent combination of siege engineering and two-foot gunstones had nevertheless rendered the town defenceless by 2 January. By mid-February, moreover, the citadel, too, had surrendered, and this time there was no massacre, though a captured Welshman who had fought to the last was tried and executed before having his quarters fixed to the gates of Caen, Lisieux, Alençon and Verneuil. Meanwhile, the gallant de Mauny was taken prisoner only to be given his liberty six months later. And within a few months all the ancient privileges of the town were duly restored.

Not surprisingly, as towns and castles now began to surrender in anticipation of Henry's coming, his personal reputation began to grow even further – and not merely in terms of military prowess. Though the Monk of Saint-Denys bemoaned the King of England's 'bragging' and 'ruthlessness', he noted, too, that the oppressor of his countrymen was not altogether devoid of grace and charm. According to returning French prisoners, Henry 'behaved in a way worthy of a king', treating 'with the utmost tact those who obeyed him' while 'showing himself pitiless towards rebels'.[28] And while the Monk did not neglect to add that Henry 'knew how many princes have extended their domains by that sort of behaviour', even the celebrated Vincent Ferrer – preacher, reformer and eventual saint – appears have been won over by the king. For after preaching to Henry at Caen in the spring of 1418 and denouncing him with 'marvellous audacity' as a slaughterer of innocent Christians, Ferrer emerged later from a private audience with drastically altered views. Though the nature of their discussion is unknown, the king was not, he admitted, the tyrant he had imagined. Henry was indeed 'the scourge of God', as he himself had said. But his cause was just.[29]

Plate 1 Thomas Hoccleve presenting his book *Regement of Princes* to the Prince of Wales (later Henry V) c. 1411–13, (vellum), English School (fifteenth century) British Library, London UK/© British Library Board. All rights reserved/The Bridgeman Art Library.

Plate 2 Medieval reredos at All Souls College, Oxford, depicting Thomas, Duke of Clarence, Humphrey, Duke of Gloucester, an archer and Thomas Montagu, Earl of Salisbury.

Source: Photograph taken by John Gibbons Studios, Oxford, with kind permission from the Warden and Fellows of All Souls College, Oxford.

Plate 3 Owain Glyn Dŵr's seal.
Source: National Museum Wales.

Plate 4 King Charles VI of France receives the English envoys, from *Froissart's Chronicle*, Bruges, 1470–75, (vellum), Netherlandish School (fifteenth century).

Source: British Library, London, UK/© British Library Board. All rights reserved, The Bridgeman Art Library.

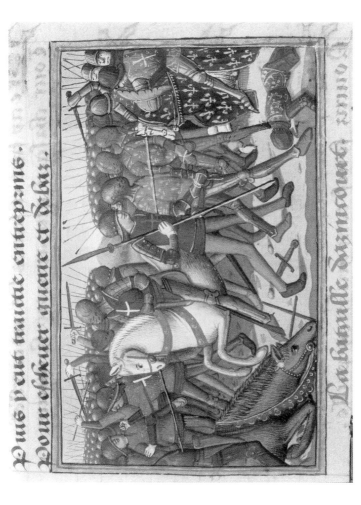

Plate 5 The Battle of Agincourt, 1415, from the *Vigil of Charles VII*, c.1484, (vellum), Martial de Paris (known as Auvergne) fl. fifteenth century.

Source: Bibliotheque Nationale, Paris, France/The Bridgeman Art Library.

Plate 6 Illustration of the siege of Rouen from *Les Vigiles de Charles VII*
Source: Wikipedia: Siege_rouen.jpg.

Plate 7 John the Fearless, Duke of Burgundy since 1404, his assassination on the bridge at Montereau, engraving after miniature, Chronicles of Enguerrand de Monstrelet, mid-fifteenth century.

Source: Bibliotheque de L'Arsenal, Arsenal © Interfoto, Alamy.

Plate 8 Document ratifying the Treaty of Troyes
Source: National Archives, catalogue reference: E30/411.

The government and administration of lower Normandy

By the spring of 1418 nearly all lower Normandy was in English hands. The potent combination of terror and tolerance at Caen had been reinforced by the brilliant tactical victory at Falaise, which now meant that King Henry could organise his second phase of conquest not as a savage and foreign invader but as the rightful Duke of Normandy he proudly claimed to be: the protector of order and justice, the bringer of good government and sound administration.

With this in mind, Henry swiftly opted to organise the territory under his control into four 'baillages'. Each was controlled by an English 'bailiff' – Sir John Radcliffe at Evreux, Sir John Popham at Caen, Sir Roland Lenthall at Alençon and Sir John Ashton in the Cotentin – under whom operated fourteen '*vicomtes*', the great majority of whom were Norman. Central administration, meanwhile, was conducted from Caen under the cleric Philip Morgan as chancellor, and Sir John Tiptoft who acted as president of the Norman *chambre des comptes*. Likewise, a new mint was established, while the local populace were given every opportunity to change their allegiance. For a nominal fee of only ten pennies, all those with an income of less than £60 a year could guarantee their own personal security by swearing an oath of allegiance and purchasing a certificate proving their recognition of the King of England as their rightful overlord.

As might be expected, the response to this offer was often less than enthusiastic. On the one hand, there were many Norman knights who would not take an oath that was also coupled to the King of England's claim to the throne of France, and the upper echelons of the Norman clergy were also decidedly reluctant to comply. As the English approached, the Archbishop of Rouen, along with five other bishops of the province all escaped, while only the Bishop of Sées made an early submission.

Yet the strict discipline imposed upon English troops, not to mention Henry's express commands safeguarding the persons and property of priests, won him many friends among parish clergy in particular. And it was noticeable that within eight weeks of the English landing at Touques some 483 had surrendered to him. The common people, too, were suitably wooed by Henry when he reformed the hated *gabelle* or salt-tax. In place of previous rates of 50 or even 75 per cent, the tax was promptly reduced to a quarter, with the further concession that once it had been paid the salt could be freely sold in the open market. Equally welcome was the news that there would be no further obligation to buy a fixed quantity of salt every three months regardless of whether or not it was wanted.

And though Norman estates were bestowed on English settlers, Henry seems to have avoided wholesale expropriation. Instead, he opted to plant a handful of loyal captains in hostile territory in order to pacify it and, if necessary, to provide the requisite men and arms for further military action. The aim was to establish an army of occupation that could be maintained at no further cost to the Exchequer at home, and if this, like the reform of the *gabelle*, was tinged with opportunism, it nevertheless offered the prospect of significant dividends.

The capture of Rouen

While Henry was consolidating his position in Normandy, the news from England was also good. The Parliament of November 1417 had taken place at Westminster in the presence of the Duke of Bedford, and two tenths and two fifteenths, to be paid on Candlemas 1418 and 1419, were duly granted. For good measure, the same Parliament at last condemned Sir John Oldcastle after his capture on the Welsh border in December during a violent struggle. Roasted alive as he swung in chains from a gibbet at St Giles's Field, Oldcastle is said to have died without a cry. But he died in the knowledge that his former confederate, Owain Glyn Dŵr, was also widely rumoured to be dead. And if the king needed any further glad tidings, there was news, too, from Scotland that the so-called 'Foul Raid', led by the Duke of Albany and Earl of Douglas, had been successfully repulsed by a surprisingly well-equipped English army, which clearly proved that Henry's military resources were still far from exhausted by his exertions across the Channel.

Meanwhile, the state of France in the spring of 1418 was even more chaotic than usual, though this time there were also complications for the English invader. In May 1417, Charles VI's shrewd, ruthless and hopelessly dissolute wife Isabella had been finally banished by her Armagnac enemies – first to Blois and then to Tours. By November, however, she had been rescued by none other than the Duke of Burgundy and conveniently installed as 'regent' in an alternative government based at Troyes. The woman who had shamelessly cuckolded her husband with Louis, Duke of Orléans, thus found herself at the centre of a complex political web, leaving John the Fearless perfectly poised to execute the capture of Paris, which he had been contemplating for some while.

When the attack on the capital came, moreover, it was delivered not on behalf of the duke's English 'ally', but very much in his own interest. Exploiting the power of the notorious Paris mob, Duke John was able to remove Bernard of Armagnac from power on 29 May, and just under a fortnight later the tyrannical count was dragged from his prison cell and brutally murdered. For three days, in fact, his naked and obscenely mutilated body lay in a gutter, while several thousand men, women and children were butchered. In the meantime, Charles, the new Dauphin, who had replaced his dead brother John the previous April, was able to escape and summon a rival Armagnac *parlement* at Poitiers. But by 14 July the Duke of Burgundy was able to enter France's capital in glory. With Queen Isabella at his side, he was graciously received by the deranged King of France, and was duly poised to save his new acquisition from the English.

When Henry set out to conquer upper Normandy in the early summer of 1418, therefore, he knew that there would be Burgundian forces confronting him at his principal objective – the duchy's capital, Rouen. By 8 June, however, he had advanced through Lisieux, Bernay and Le Neuberg to reach the town of Louviers, which held out for almost three weeks. And it was here that a stone ball despatched from the walls ripped through the tent of the Earl of Salisbury, where Henry was in conference at the time. Whether it was this narrow escape that led him to execute eight French gunners upon the town's capture on 20 June is unknown. But the sentence was certainly unusual and the fact that one man was spared on the plea of Cardinal Orsini – albeit with a life sentence of imprisonment – does little to lessen the impression that Henry was both shaken and deeply infuriated by the episode.

Even so, by 20 July the Duke of Clarence's guns had also blasted

Pont de l'Arche into submission, leaving Henry to focus his attention upon 'the most notable place in France save Paris', as he described it to the Mayor and aldermen of London.[30] And Rouen was indeed a special prize. For nearly 300 years, in fact, the 'Master Cittie of all Normandie' had jealously guarded its privileges against archbishops, dukes and kings, and its cloth industry was justly famous.[31] It also received rich revenues from the thriving river trade which linked Paris with the Channel, and apart from its great cathedral, there were thirty-four religious houses and nearly seventy churches within its five miles of wall lying on the north bank of the Seine. With a population of some 70,000, its guildhalls were more splendid than any in England and the work of its goldsmiths was second to none in all France.

It was also well defended. Rouen's five great gates, for instance, bristled with 'many a score' of guns and there were sixty towers along the city walls, which had themselves been recently reinforced by an imposing earth embankment.[32] There were, moreover, 5,000 men-at-arms under the able command of Guy le Bouteiller, as well as a 15,000-strong militia, which included a hand-picked force of crossbowmen under another veteran, Alain Blanchard. To further confound any potential assailant, the ditch on the three sides of the city unprotected by the Seine had been deepened and set with wolf traps, and Rouen's citizens had not hesitated to flatten those flourishing suburbs, which might protect their enemies. Well stocked with food and water supplies, Rouen could not be completely cut off, and its defenders had also been assured by the Duke of Burgundy that they would not be abandoned. They therefore awaited their enemies with considerable confidence.

Nor was their wait a long one, for on the morning of 1 June, Rouen's inhabitants awoke to find themselves almost entirely surrounded by an English force that had arrived by night. Five fortified camps, linked by deep communication trenches to offer protection from the artillery on the city walls, had soon been firmly established, and the city's encirclement was completed by three huge chain booms across the Seine, supported by several warships, which had been hauled overland on wheels for a distance of nearly four miles. Equally impressively, the English built a wooden bridge over the Seine, five miles or so upstream. And from the moment that Henry's ally, the King of Portugal, stationed a fleet at the mouth of the Seine estuary to safeguard supplies from Harfleur once and for all, Rouen's ordeal was assured. For now it could be steadily starved at leisure.

But it was not only in purely martial terms that the English king demonstrated his sharpness. Since it was obvious that the siege would be a long one, he set up a market, protected by armed guards, to encourage traders to increase supplies to his army. Furthermore, when his soldiers wilted under the hot August sun, a letter was swiftly composed to the City of London, which led to the despatch on 8 September of thirty barrels of sweet wine and 1,000 pipes of beer. Even so, he was disturbed by reports of severed heads and dead babies dangling from the horses' necks of Thomas Butler's Irish 'kernes' who had joined his force from Cherbourg.[33] And his concern for everyday discipline amongst his English troops was no less rigorous than ever, as was demonstrated when his orders over the spacing of tents were disobeyed. The orders had been given, it seems, specifically to neutralise the threat from a surprise attack, and disobedience in such a matter was therefore not to be tolerated. As a result, the two offenders were summarily hanged.

Before long, in fact, a siege that had begun with some semblance of respect for the old chivalric codes had degenerated into barbarism, beastliness and tawdry acts of callous bravado. Several gibbets were erected in full view of the city walls, from which the English hanged their captives, while the French responded by suspending their own victims from the city ramparts with dogs tied round their necks. Others were fastened in sacks and flung into the Seine, and when John Blount, the Lieutenant of Harfleur, challenged a Burgundian gate captain to single combat, he was promptly killed and dragged back into Rouen by the victor at his horse's tail.

There was propaganda, too, to fuel the bitterness. From the highest vantage point of the city walls, Robert de Livet, vicar-general of Rouen, publicly excommunicated both Henry and his army – an act that Henry would neither forgive nor forget. Indeed, when Rouen was finally surrendered, Livet was one of five men specifically named to be handed over to the king himself, after which he was bound and chained in prison for the rest of his life and 'miserablie finished his daies'.[34] Whether this was the first clear sign of Henry's increasing sensitivity to any kind of criticism – something which may have grown over time as the impact of prolonged war took its toll – is uncertain. But it was no coincidence, perhaps, that in October 1419 a lowly Southwark haberdasher was swiftly brought before the Council for speaking critically of the king's conduct at the siege.

Certainly, the stubbornness of French resistance can have left Henry with few cheerful memories of Rouen. 'For schoot of goone and quarrelle both / Sawe I nevyr gretter wrothe', wrote John Page.[35] And by this time there was also famine to contend with. As early as mid-October the Burgundian chief of finance in Paris had written to his colleagues in Lille to tell them that 'at Rouen they are eating horseflesh'.[36] By December, however, the better off were paying high prices for dogs and rats, while the poorest survived on dock roots. Young girls sold themselves for a slice of bread made from bran rather than wheat, and even parents and children hid food from each other. As John Page put it, 'hunger passyd kynde and love'.[37] Water supplies, likewise, were seriously reduced when the English were able to cut off one of the tributaries supplying the city.

In these dire circumstances the besieged garrison was driven to desperate action and 12,000 of the non-combatant and unfit refugees who had previously sought shelter in Rouen were now driven from the city so that the remaining provisions could be consumed by the able-bodied. Far from allowing them to pass through the English lines, however, Henry decided to force them back to where they had come from, and when the ragged mass of old and vulnerable people were refused re-entry, they found themselves herded into the great fosse surrounding the city walls, where they were left to the mercy of the pitiless winter cold and unending downpour. Only at Christmas did Henry relent by offering the innocent victims beneath the walls some meagre sustenance. And though the Captain of Rouen rejected the offer, two English priests and a group of servants were nevertheless allowed to venture forth with whatever they could carry.

With typically stone cold resolution, then, the King of England had watched the misery unfold. By now, of course, he knew the hard reality of war all too well. And he would not allow his mercy to be used as a tactical weapon against him by a defiant foe. When asked later by French envoys about the welfare of the refugees, his response was unbending. 'Ye yourselves have sowed the seede of so manie miseries amonge you', he declared, '… ye be the occasion of your famine, and that through your obstinate pride.'[38] Nor would he sacrifice such a golden opportunity at this critical juncture of the whole campaign. For just like his most humble soldier, he too knew that 'hunger brekythe the stone wall'.[39]

So it was that, after the failure of a final mass sortie, Rouen finally agreed to surrender on 19 January if it had not been relieved by noon on that date, and thereafter to pay an indemnity of 300,000 gold crowns. The sum, undoubtedly, was a heavy one, particularly when it is remembered that Henry initially threatened to demand its delivery within a month, before settling for annual collections of 80,000 crowns. There were also reprisals against individuals. Livet, as we have seen, was committed 'unto obscure prison', while Alain Blanchard was condemned to death by hanging.[40] Eighty hostages were taken, too, as security for the indemnity now owing.

Yet if the terms were harsh, they were far from brutal, proving in John Page's opinion that Henry was 'manful when war doth last, and merciful when it is past'.[41] Certainly, there was no repetition of the massacre and looting which had taken place at Caen. Those who swore allegiance to the English king were allowed to keep their property, and the city was left to enjoy all the privileges it had held before the reign of Philip VI. Likewise, the survivors of Rouen's fosse were taken back within the walls, and food and supplies made available to all, while the garrison in its turn was allowed to depart freely – though only after agreeing not to bear arms against Henry for another year.

And if very few of the Norman nobility ever accepted the new status quo happily, there were signs, too, that not all Rouen's citizens reacted adversely to the new circumstances. Some of the richest, it is true, left in order to avoid their liabilities, and there seems to have been much evasion of indemnity payments. Even twelve years later, 40,000 crowns were still unpaid. Yet many minor gentry soon took official appointments under English governance, and some even appear eventually to have worn the red cross of St George as English soldiers. Within only a few weeks of Rouen's surrender, indeed, the city's captain, Guy le Bouteiller, would be swearing the oath of allegiance to Henry – though thereby earning, it must be said, the bitter reproach of a number of French chroniclers.[42]

All in all, then, there was still grudging respect for a king whose justice, though severe, was broadly fair. When, for instance, Henry commissioned Rouen's cathedral architect to build a fortified palace for him in the south-west of the city, he duly arranged that any person losing his property as a result of the new construction should be promptly and justly compensated. There was recognition, too, of Henry's common sense and efficiency, which was demonstrated within a month of the city's capture when a new system of weights and measures was introduced to rectify the existing confusion.

Meanwhile, as the inhabitants of Rouen licked their smarting wounds and settled down once more to business, the Duke of Burgundy was busy blaming Armagnac treachery for the non-fulfilment of his previous pledges and raising the prospect of revenge in time to come. But the threat from the duke was of little immediate significance as the King of England received Rouen's keys on 19 January. The next day, riding sadly, we are told, he passed into the city 'without pride, without pomp or bombast', and made directly for the cathedral, where a thanksgiving mass was sung by the clergy of his chapel.[43] It was the solemn end to half a year of bloodshed and exhausting toil, which had further hardened the King of England in ways that he himself did not, perhaps, fully appreciate. But it was also yet another beginning – one more invitation to further challenges and one more step, too, along the increasingly unavoidable path to further conquest.

Diplomatic efforts: from Alençon to Meulan

During the two months that Henry spent at Rouen, reorganising the capital city of his duchy, his captains were busy completing the conquest of Normandy. Yet throughout this time there would be no let-up in diplomatic activity between Henry and his enemies. As always, the King of England's aim was to manipulate the French civil war to his own advantage, especially after the abortive agreement of St-Maur-des-Fossées in mid-September 1418 had threatened to unite the Dauphin with the Duke of Burgundy against the invader. During October and November, therefore, Henry agreed to negotiate with the Dauphin and his Armagnac associates – who had now become known as 'Dauphinists' – since the Burgundian possession of Paris was a potentially serious stumbling block to both their ambitions. And as soon as these particular talks had foundered, no time was lost either in turning to John the Fearless himself. Such was the flurry of activity, in fact, that the surviving correspondence presents an unusually tangled interpretative maze even by early fifteenth-century Anglo-French standards – not least, because both Burgundian and Dauphinist parties continued to uphold their claim to speak directly for Charles VI.

Nevertheless, the working of the English king's mind, as well as the steady evolution of his aims, remains plain enough to discern in most cases. When, in November, the Earl of Salisbury led an embassy to meet the Dauphinists on the Norman border at Alençon, he was told in no uncertain terms what was expected of him. On the most fundamental issue of all – the Treaty of Brétigny – and, if possible, with regard to the sovereignty of Anjou, Maine, Touraine and the holding of Flanders as a fief, there was to be no compromise. Nor was there to be any flexibility on the issue of England's existing military gains, which the king continued to believe had been granted him by God. Yet any claim to the throne of France was to be used as little more than a bargaining counter. Likewise, the ambassadors were to distinguish carefully between peace and a truce, and to make sure that any compromise, let alone any alliance against Burgundy, would be fully worthwhile.

The result was two weeks of mutual frustration as every inch of land and every claim to sovereignty became subject to interminable squabbling. Henry's projected marriage to Charles VI's daughter Catherine, which was intended to seal the peace and set the scene for a joint attempt to expel the Duke of Burgundy from Paris, was only one of a string of stillborn notions. Even the language in which negotiations should be conducted became a source of heated controversy as the Dauphinists opened proceedings in French only to be met with English assertions that Latin was the long-established language of international diplomacy. Whether, indeed, Henry even intended the talks to succeed is doubtful. Certainly, he had good reason to doubt whether the Dauphinists could actually implement any agreement that might emerge, and by 23 November the Dauphin's ambassadors had withdrawn, saying they could offer no more.

Less than a fortnight later, Henry's representatives were in negotiation with their Burgundian counterparts at Pont de l'Arche, and the resulting proposals, such as they were, also bore no lasting fruit. Though the Burgundians presented Henry with a portrait of the Princess Catherine and 'it pleased him very well', there would be no lessening of his demands.[44] On the contrary, he was soon insisting upon a million gold crowns for her dowry and pressing forward with his claims to Normandy, Aquitaine, Ponthieu and the rest of the lordships cited in the Treaty of Brétigny. His position was, after all, increasingly unassailable as he drove towards Paris, with the dukes of Brittany and Anjou still willing to prolong existing truces, and Gascon lords such as Charles d'Albret and Bernard of Armagnac no longer alive. As Henry grew ever more assertive, therefore, it was perhaps small wonder that negotiations at Pont de l'Arche should peter out after little more than a fortnight.

Yet diplomatic manoeuvres were still not altogether over. The Dauphin's ambassadors were, for example, soon laying plans for a meeting with Henry at Evreux in March 1419, though on the appointed day their master failed to materialise. And while the English railed as usual against the faithlessness of their adversaries, they, too, were continuing to exploit their negotiating options to the limit. Indeed, even before the projected meeting at Evreux had finally died the death, Henry himself was already exploring the possibility of another round of negotiations with Burgundy in late spring or early summer.

John the Fearless had good reason, moreover, to consider further talks. Though Charles VI and Isabella were firmly under Burgundian control in Paris, the Dauphin's forces under Tanneguy du Chastel were still strong enough by May to stage successful raids to the north and east of the capital. Henry's own forces, meanwhile, had now consolidated their control of the approaches to Paris by taking Vernon and Mantes, and were also besieging the redoubtable stronghold of Château Gaillard. Stricken by a morbid fear of assassination, Duke John now slept in a specially built tower containing only a single bedroom, which still stands in the Rue Etienne Marcel today. Leaving his hiding place only in the company of heavily armed guards, the duke openly fuelled rumours that he was a warlock by admitting that the devil himself had persuaded him to kill the Duke of Orléans. But if such talk did little to endear him, John the Fearless remained as canny and formidable as ever – as the King of England would soon discover.

In fact, the conference at Meulan in May, for all its gravity, achieved nothing. Fears that either side might break the truce and seize the opportunity to stage a massacre remained acute, and though the duke and Queen Isabella were reasonably well disposed to English terms, they were well aware that the rest of France was not. When discussion turned to Catherine's dowry, moreover, they offered 800,000 crowns, but argued that three-quarters of this sum be deducted as the amount which should have been returned to France when Richard was deposed and his young Queen Isabella returned home. There was bitter acrimony, too, over the value of the former queen's jewels, which should also have returned to France along with her. Most importantly of all, however, the Duke of Burgundy could not yield on Henry's territorial demands, since to do so would have destroyed any remaining prestige he possessed.

Ultimately, therefore, both sides had opted to overplay their hands, as the King of England brandished his victorious army and Burgundy threatened to come to terms with the Dauphin in a combined attempt to drive the invader from French soil. It was known to Henry that the duke was already in negotiation with the Dauphinist, Tanneguy du Chastel, and as talks ground down to deadlock, tempers became frayed. At their first encounter, the duke had, it seems, 'saluted the king, bending his knee a little and inclining his head'. In return, Henry 'took him by his hand, embraced him and showed him great respect'. Now, however, Henry resorted to threats. 'Fair cousin', he warned his former ally, 'we wish you to know that we will have the daughter or your king or we will drive him and you out of his realm'. 'Sire', answered the duke, 'you may be pleased to say so, but before you can drive my lord and myself out of this realm I make no doubt that you will be heartily tired.'[45]

It was one of Henry's few diplomatic failures. It was one, moreover, which bore a particular significance for him personally. Two days after discussions began he had come face to face for the first time with the Princess Catherine. She was a tall and 'very handsome' girl of 'most engaging manners', eighteen years old and dressed in stunning clothes costing all of 3,000 florins.[46] The result for the still unmarried and celibate king was, perhaps, predictable. As the author of the *First English Life* put it, nothing issued from the meeting at Meulan 'except the flame of Love'.[47]

The renewal of hostilities

True to character, John the Fearless did not take long to change sides. Clement de Fauquembergue, the *greffier* of the *parlement* of Paris, recorded in his journal that the duke met with the Dauphin at Corbeil on 7 July.[48] And four days later a solemn pact committed them to combine against 'the damnable enterprise of our ancient enemies, the English'. By 19 July a royal ordinance had confirmed the treaty and the citizens of Paris and other French towns were said to have 'shouted with joy'.[49]

The news was not slow in reaching the English headquarters at Mantes. A private letter from an unknown member of Henry's staff, written to a correspondent in England on 14 July, recounts how close the talks at Meulan had come to bringing King Henry what he wanted. But the author was now left to reflect once more on the prospect of renewed war. Since the Dauphin and Duke of Burgundy had declared an accord, the letter concluded, 'it is supposed in the King's Host rather war than peace'.[50]

In reality, however, the English had limited grounds for either outrage or unease, since they, too, had been double-dealing and were not bereft of friends and options. King Henry had, after all, been steadily scheming to ring France with an iron curtain of alliances. Attempts had been made, for instance, to have the Duke of Bedford declared heir to the childless Queen of Naples, and to marry him off either to the daughter of the Duke of Lorraine or to the daughter of the Margrave of Brandenburg. And while these efforts may have foundered, Henry was nevertheless still firmly allied with Emperor Sigismund, not to mention the great elector archbishoprics of Cologne, Mainz and Triers, which all received generous English subsidies for their friendship. There was also a trade agreement with Genoa and the further hope that the king's other brother Humphrey, Duke of Gloucester, might be married to the daughter of Charles III of Navarre.

Nevertheless, Henry took the news of his 'betrayal' badly and was quick to act. Indeed, his next move was so sudden and unexpected that his adversaries were actually asleep when he made it. Before sunrise on the morning of 31 July two English divisions made their way to attack Pontoise. Defended by a formidable garrison of 1,200 men-at-arms and 2,000 crossbowmen, the city was the northern gateway to Paris itself. And after scaling the walls around 4.00 a.m., the attackers proceeded, after a bloody struggle, to loot and pillage at will. They did, said Monstrelet, 'innumerable mischiefs'.[51] But they also gained possession, it seems, of stores worth 2,000,000 crowns. It was Henry's first, if not entirely creditable victory, outside his Duchy of Normandy. And he wrote boastfully to the Mayor of London to announce it – fully aware too, no doubt, of the imminent danger mounting before him.[52]

The fragile peace of 1420–21

Murder at Montereau

One week after its fall, Henry had ridden into Pontoise to establish his headquarters less than twenty miles from Paris. Now, from the mighty bluff upon which his newly acquired fortress soared, his gunners and archers could fire down upon the barges bringing supplies to the enemy along the river Oise. And now, too, the whole surrounding area could be subjected to the kind of systematic terror that was intended to sap the enemy's will to fight. 'In those days', wrote the Bourgeois of Paris, 'the only news one heard concerned the ravages of the English.' 'Pillaging, killing and robbing' as they went, Henry's troops were able, it seems, to spread ruin and devastation at will, 'sending everything, loot and prisoners, back to England'. 'No Saracen', the Bourgeois concluded, 'ever harmed Christians so sorely.'[1]

But as Henry began the task of relocating his court, and his men set about the time-honoured practice of plundering booty from helpless civilians, there was also the need for keen vigilance. The lines of communication with Caen and Rouen were dangerously stretched, and there were mutinies and anti-English conspiracies at Rouen and Dieppe to contend with. Brigandage, too, was reported to be growing within Normandy as a whole. And to make matters worse, the French had also enlisted foreign aid. Indeed, by September 1419 a Castilian fleet had brought 6,000 Scots to the Dauphin's court at Bourges – ready, so the Mayor of Bayonne told Henry, 'to do mortal war with you'.[2] All hinged, therefore, upon the firmness of the anti-English pact fashioned at Corbeil between the contending French parties, and here, yet again, fortune favoured the King of England – on a scale that even he could never have hoped for.

When the time came for the July treaty between the Dauphin and Duke of Burgundy to be implemented, it was agreed that a meeting should be held on 10 September upon the bridge at Montereau, some forty miles south-east of the capital. Such was the mutual distrust between the two sides that barricades were built at either end, with a special wooden enclosure in the middle where discussions were to occur. Under conditions of the strictest security, the Dauphin and duke were each to be accompanied by ten retainers to prevent a surprise attack by one side or other. And though proceedings appear to have begun cordially enough, within minutes they had indeed descended into the kind of bloody slaughter that both sides feared so badly.

The precise train of events is unknown, but John the Fearless soon lay dead from a sword thrust to the belly and a blow to the head from a battle axe that had also severed his chin. Whether the deed was premeditated is unknown, though the sixteen-year-old Dauphin is perhaps unlikely to have been directly involved in what appears to have been a spontaneous act of rage and hatred. More probably, the culprit was Tanneguy du Chastel. Nevertheless, the news of the murder sent shock waves throughout France and set the scene for new depths of disunity and bitter reprisal. Duke John's son, Philip – the twenty-three-year-old Count of Charolais who was to become known as Philip the Good – was now duty bound to avenge his father's murder. And with the King of England firmly in control of Normandy and looming at the gates of Paris, there was little choice for the new Duke of Burgundy but to make common cause with him.

Henry in his turn was, of course, acutely aware of this. Upon hearing of the murder, he is said at first to have expressed regret. John the Fearless was, he declared with no apparent sense of irony, 'a good and loyal knight and prince of honour'. But Henry was also quick to acknowledge that 'by his death, and the help of God and St George, we are at the achievement of our desire'.[3] Significantly, there was mention, too, of the fair Princess Catherine, though now her charms had broadened as she emerged in stark relief as the key to the kingdom of France itself. Ten days after the murder, Queen

Isabella exhorted the King of England to avenge Duke John, and at the same time sought Philip's protection from her son. Within the month, at a meeting held at Arras, the entire Burgundian faction had urged Philip to ally with Henry. Nor was honour the only spur to action, for while knights and noblemen talked at length of justice, Flemish merchants were hungrily eyeing the restoration of commercial links with their business friends in England.

As if by madness, then, the Dauphinists had wrecked their most promising opportunity to drive the invader from their lands. If defeat had not exactly been snatched from the jaws of victory by their action, they had nevertheless cruelly miscalculated and in doing so they had propagated a new and altogether more lethal ambition in their enemy's mind. Indeed, by smashing any hope of an offensive alliance to thwart him, they had opened the way for him to achieve it. Fittingly, perhaps, it was left to a Carthusian prior in Dijon to reflect a century later how the English had ultimately entered France through the hole in the Duke of Burgundy's skull.[4]

Normandy and England: consolidation and concerns

While Henry was keenly surveying new horizons, there remained a number of wearisome sieges to complete, as well as the practical application of English rule in Normandy for him to consider. According to the *First English Life*, the king 'gave not himself to rest and sloth but with marvellous solicitude and diligence laboured continually'.[5] But by January 1420 the Duke of Bedford had nevertheless been called from his post in England and replaced by Humphrey, Duke of Gloucester, in order to assist with the civil administration of his eldest brother's new duchy. Having already distinguished himself as regent in the king's absence, he would now demonstrate similar skills across the Channel by encouraging the sensible policy of gradual reconciliation that Henry himself had already initiated.

Though major administrative offices were kept in English hands, minor posts were freely offered to native Normans, and as good sense and pragmatism overcame the violence of conquest, modest efforts were also made to encourage economic recovery. Breton, Flemish and Parisian merchants were, for instance, encouraged to renew their Norman contracts, while at Harfleur, Caen, Cherbourg and Rouen, English traders and craftsmen were on the whole 'planted' with minimal friction. Certainly, the Calendar of the Norman Rolls suggests that comparatively good order and prosperity returned surprisingly quickly to the war-torn area.[6] Henry and Bedford's efforts were even successful enough to allow the effective levying of some taxation, which would facilitate the process of reconstruction and go some way, perhaps, to paying for the war.

Yet while Normandy rose achingly to its feet, there were stirrings of a less encouraging kind back home. In August, the king had written to the City of London thanking them for the offer of a voluntary loan.[7] However, it is clear from the unusual intensity of Henry's gratitude that the strain of maintaining a large army was taking an increasing toll on royal finance. The process of extracting funds from Normandy was still, after all, in its early stages, and the Commons would soon prove increasingly grudging. While the Parliament of October 1419 granted a fifteenth and a tenth, payable in February, and a tenth for the following November, the sums were nevertheless smaller than before. The coinage, too, was a cause of concern, since so much money was being shipped out of the country to France.

The king's financial straits even help to explain the extraordinary imprisonment of his stepmother, Queen Joan, which occurred around this time. On 25 September 1419 the Archbishop of Canterbury informed his bishops that Henry desired their prayers for protection against necromancers. The king's long-standing concerns about supernatural activity were, in fact, widely known. Nevertheless, the arrest of the queen dowager only four days later came as a bolt from the blue. According to evidence presented to Parliament, she had been accused by a Franciscan friar from Shrewsbury 'of compassing the death and destruction of our lord the king in the most treasonable and horrible manner that could be devised'.[8] And though the friar had been swiftly despatched to the Tower that summer after interrogation by the king at Mantes, his accusations were now heeded.

The implications were clear enough and what followed is often treated, far from implausibly, as a striking demonstration of the king's ruthlessness and proof of his growing anxiety about the state of the royal treasury. To her cost, Joan was indeed in possession of a dowry, which at 10,000 marks amounted to more than 10 per cent of the Crown's regular annual income. Furthermore, Henry's decision to deprive his stepmother of all her possessions and to hold her – albeit in comparative comfort – at Leeds Castle for three years was made without any due process of law. Joan's father, the aptly named King Charles the Bad of Navarre, had, it is true, established his own unfortunate reputation for sorcery before his death, and one of her sons by her first marriage, Artus de Richemont, would also be rumoured later to dabble in the black arts. Nor, for that matter, had the piratical sailors of another of her sons, Duke John of Brittany, done anything to endear Joan to her English subjects.

Yet Henry's actions remain perplexing. When religious panic allied the persecution of heretics with witch-hunting and hatred of foreigners in 1419, the whole unsavoury mix coincided all too neatly with his growing financial predicament, and he seems to have weakened accordingly. Certainly, he did nothing to save his stepmother. But he was also, to his discredit, prepared to exploit an apparently baseless accusation for his own ends. In truth, Joan had no obvious motive for killing her stepson and though she was eventually restored to favour, there remains no trace of honour for Henry in the incident. On the contrary, it was a serious, if comparatively rare, blot on his moral copybook and he seems ultimately to have accepted his guilt. For on his deathbed he ordered not only Queen Joan's release but also the restoration of her goods and income 'lest it should be a charge unto our conscience'.[9]

Alliance with Burgundy

On hearing the news of his father's murder, Philip the Good had taken to his bed, where he writhed, rolled his eyes and gnashed his teeth in a mixture of rage and grief. But the French queen and *parlement* of Paris did not even wait for the new duke to declare his intentions. From the royal court at Troyes, negotiations were immediately opened with Henry in an effort to conclude the alliance that had been abandoned earlier at Meulan. Indeed, by the time that John the Fearless's body had been fished from the Seine, where it had been flung by his assassins, and hastily buried in the parish church of Montereau, the usually measured pace of diplomacy was already becoming increasingly frenetic.

From the end of September, in fact, the process of negotiation was almost non-stop, as safe-conducts, commissions and appointments for ambassadors poured forth from both headquarters. Under the strain, Henry's health may even have suffered, for the Exchequer records reveal that Master Peter Henewer, a physician, was specially despatched to Normandy around this time. But the Christmas festivities at Rouen were sweetened by the appearance of the Duke of Burgundy's ambassadors, led by the Bishop of Arras, who agreed a general truce and accepted the principle of full-scale alliance on the most generous terms possible. Receiving them in his haughtiest manner, Henry had told his visitors that if they did not act quickly, he would march on Paris without delay. The price of his friendship, moreover, was to be the hand of Princess Catherine and the crown of France for him and his heirs as soon as Charles VI died. In the interim, he would act as France's regent, restoring good order to the realm and helping to avenge the murder of John the Fearless.[10]

It was, quite literally, an irresistible package, which once again confirmed not only the king's toughness, but also the shrewdness of his approach. Henceforth, the struggle for the French throne would be presented more and more as a contest between rival personalities. And in this respect Henry's strategy could not have been more 'modern'. On the one hand, he offered himself as an experienced and proven leader – an invincible soldier who loved peace, and a gifted administrator whose reputation for justice was as renowned as his religious zeal. The Dauphin, by contrast, could be dismissed as an object of derision – callow and unproven, the willing tool of a vicious and self-interested political faction and, perhaps worst of all, a murderer rejected by his parents.

Henry's ability to turn tactical advantage into concrete political gain was therefore no less impressive ultimately than his ability to dominate a battlefield or raze a stronghold. It was based primarily upon a masterful and single-minded appreciation of the logic of events. Once committed, he would not relent. Once ascendant, he would push on ever more remorselessly to his desired goals. But his success was founded, too, upon the keenest possible understanding of the whole political process, with all its subtleties as well as its baser elements. As he celebrated the great Christmas truce on the day following its signature, Henry could therefore survey the scene with no little satisfaction. For if the past year had presented him with considerable challenges, he was now poised for what would long be celebrated, rightly or wrongly, as his crowning achievement.

Joint military action and further diplomatic manoeuvres

Although England and Burgundy were now allied, there was still no formal treaty between Henry and Charles VI. In consequence, the spring of 1420 witnessed a further spate of diplomacy, as well as a series of joint enterprises between English and Burgundian forces against Dauphinist strongholds. But the military co-operation was neither very cordial nor very successful. The engagements at Roye and Compiègne, for instance, demonstrated that the Dauphinists were by no means defeated and that the new alliance was far from wholehearted. At Roye there had been outright dissension, and in January the Dauphin's Castilian allies were able to win a demoralising naval victory over the English off La Rochelle.

In the meantime, Duke Philip had marched south from Arras and joined the French king and his wife in Troyes on 23 March 1420. With Dauphinist forces harrying the surrounding countryside, the town was actually far from secure. But this did not prevent the progress of negotiations. Nor did it affect the outcome. For by 29 April the outlines of a formal treaty had been agreed, and letters describing the proposal were duly sent to a special gathering at Paris, which included representatives of the university, the bishop and the capital's citizenry. The letters declared that the Duke of Burgundy had been moved by the desire for peace rather than vengeance, and they acknowledged, too, that the King of England was 'prudent and wise, loving God, peace and justice'.[11]

But the proposed treaty was far from lenient. Indeed, it was a bitter pill, which the French had no other choice than to swallow. According to its terms, the King of England was to marry Princess Catherine, as he desired, and her dowry was to be set at 40,000 crowns per year. Meanwhile, Charles VI was to remain King of France until his death, after which the French crown would belong forever to Henry and his heirs. For the time being, Charles's illness was used to justify Henry's immediate appointment as regent, aided by a council of French nobles. But the Dauphin was to be disinherited and crushed militarily, and all English conquests made so far were to be subject to the French crown once Henry finally became king, though the current status of Normandy was left unspecified. Finally, from the time of his succession, Henry was to rule his new kingdom according to its ancient laws and customs, confirming the *parlement* in its ancient authority and recognising the established privileges of all churches and universities.

To all appearances, it was a truly remarkable triumph for English arms and Henry's unrivalled expertise in the practice of *realpolitik*. At the same time, it was the most ringing indictment possible of French impotence. Though nothing had yet been signed, Henry therefore left Rouen for Troyes on 8 May, justifiably confident that the climax to his military exertions of the past four years was now in sight. Destiny, or so he believed, had called him to his task, and now the king and queen of France, along with the Duke of Burgundy, were about to acknowledge that destiny, too.

The Treaty of Troyes

It was, perhaps, yet another example of Henry's supreme confidence that the great market city of Troyes in Champagne was chosen for the official signing of the treaty. Situated about a hundred miles to the south-east of Paris, the surrounding countryside was, in effect, a no-man's-land where Dauphinist forces staged frequent raids from their numerous strongholds. But this did not deter him. On the contrary, his journey resembled at times a triumphant progress, as Parisians greeted him with surprising cordiality, and in spite of famine and general distress, sent him four cartloads of their best wine. With typical self-assurance he had marched his men in a semi-circle around the north of the capital to worship at the abbey of Saint-Denys before proudly parading his troops past the city's battlements in full military array without deigning to enter. For as usual Henry was determined that the reality of military and political control should be wholly borne out by the symbols and display of that ascendancy.

The King of England's arrival at the court of Charles VI's was, however, entirely cordial. The French king was, it seems, once more 'in his malady', and when the Duke of Burgundy escorted Henry into his presence, Charles appeared bewildered. But the French queen who was now fat, agoraphobic and prone to vicious bouts of gout-induced fury, which even her gigolos and menagerie of leopards, monkeys and turtle doves could not assuage, was wholly prepared to marry her daughter to him. And when Henry greeted Catherine, he is said to have bowed low and kissed her 'with great joy'.[12] In truth, she was a largely passive figure whose chief impact upon history may ultimately have been the transmission of her father's schizophrenia to the future Henry VI, but the accounts of her husband-to-be's passion for her are too numerous to be discounted lightly, and his delight in her company was now palpable.

Likewise, on 21 May when the treaty was finally ratified in Troyes Cathedral in the presence of King Henry, the Duke of Burgundy and Queen Isabella – though without Charles VI – all was rapture and delight. The agreement was signed in strict accordance with the terms already agreed, along with a special reaffirmation of Henry's commitment to ensure that after his succession as King of France each realm would retain its own laws 'neither being subject to the other'. 'All hatreds that may have existed between England and France', it was declared, 'shall be ended, and mutual love and friendship take their place.' Henry, meanwhile, promised to regard Charles and Isabella as 'Our Father and Mother', honouring them 'especially before all other temporal princes of this world'.[13]

But were the ensuing celebrations merited? On 2 June, Henry would make his way through the crooked streets of Troyes 'as if he were at that moment king of all the world'.[14] Yet many of the fair prospects engendered by Henry's day of triumph were not to last indefinitely. On the one hand, the future Henry VI was prone to the same mental illness as his French grandfather, and would later lose the throne he had inherited in 1422 when only nine months old. Nor was there any overwhelming enthusiasm for the treaty in France, even from the earliest days. In truth, both the queen and Duke of Burgundy viewed it merely as the lesser evil, while the Dauphin's supporters would continue to maintain French national aspirations south of the Loire until the catalyst provided by Joan of Arc breathed new life into their cause. Yet the so-called 'perpetual peace' would still require more than a decade to founder once and for all under a string of chance events and miscalculations. And for the time being the only Burgundian nobles who did not uphold the alliance tended to derive their opposition from specific local conditions.

Meanwhile, if Frenchmen in general may have resented the new status quo they, too, knew that the alternatives were hardly appetising. Even the Monk of Saint-Denys, who was no friend to the English, was aware of their king's potential to heal France's wounds. For he held out the promise of peace and 'good governance', and this in itself might well be worth the inconvenience of being ruled by him. 'If he is the strongest, then so be it!', declared the monk. 'Let him be our master, just so long as we can live in the lap of peace, safety and plenty.'[15]

But the indignity entailed by English control would clearly be hard to endure at times – not least of all because English manners were not French manners. The Earl of Huntingdon, for example, was soon refusing at the siege of Sens to deal with the town's ambassador, since the man was bearded. The king himself angrily rebuked the Marshal of France, l'Isle-Adam, for daring to look him in the face when speaking to him, and when the Marshal replied that it was the French custom to do so, he was told icily that the English way was different. According to the Bourgeois of Paris, the one exception to the norm was John, Duke of Bedford, 'for he never wanted to make war on anybody, whereas the English, essentially, are always wanting to make war on their neighbours without a cause'.[16]

More importantly still, there were a number of ominous structural tensions within the treaty. It was, after all, a triangular agreement between three uneasy bedfellows, carried out at the expense of the Dauphin who remained, in spite of everything, a key political player in his own right. Likewise, the careful legalisms upon which the treaty had been founded were far from fireproof. More worrying still, in its need for continued conquests by Henry, the treaty was premised, at least in the medium-term, upon ongoing civil strife in France and continued pressure upon England's far from infinite financial resources.

Much, perhaps everything, would therefore ultimately depend upon the King of England himself – his strong hand, his nimble brain, his tireless energy, his charisma and, of course, his longevity, since any real chance of success required the potential for the long haul. And herein lay the crux of the matter. At thirty-three, Henry was still a comparatively young man, and even his father, plagued with long-term illness, had nevertheless survived to the age of forty-seven. With God's grace, which had so far been in such plentiful supply, a long life and healthy heir were hardly unlikely prospects. Certainly, there was nothing to suggest at this stage that Henry's ambitious plans were bound to falter. Whether, therefore, the treaty would stand the test of time, only time would tell.

From Troyes to Paris

Henry V had never been one to linger over formalities, and after a two-day stint of marital bliss with his new bride, he deemed it fit to renew the business of war. The feasting and celebrations were abruptly halted and when some of his knights bemoaned the early end of their tourneying, they were curtly reminded of the more serious business still in hand. The town of Sens, some thirty-eight miles away, remained in Dauphinist hands and must be brought to heel. 'There', said Henry, 'we may all tilt and joust and prove our daring and courage, for there is no finer act of courage in the world than to punish evildoers so that poor people can live.'[17]

On Wednesday 4 June, therefore, an English and Burgundian army left Troyes and headed for the first of its remaining conquests on the road to Paris. Henry, Charles VI and the Duke of Burgundy rode side-by-side with the queens of France and England in tow, and after a week's resistance, Sens duly capitulated. By 24 June, moreover, the well-fortified castle at Montereau, which was now of special significance to all Burgundians, had also been carried by assault. It was here that John the Fearless had been unceremoniously buried in the aftermath of his murder, and his body was now exhumed and solemnly transferred to the Burgundian Charterhouse at Dijon.

The capture of Montereau also served to illustrate all too graphically the darker aspects of contemporary justice. Before the castle itself was captured, eleven French gentlemen were taken prisoner in the assault on the town. Thereafter, Henry swore that they would be hanged unless the garrison surrendered. And when Montereau's captain, the Lord of Guitry, refused their pleas to him, which were delivered on bended knees in full view of their families, they were duly executed before the castle walls. For good measure, Henry also hanged one of his favourite grooms at Montereau for losing his temper and killing – albeit accidentally – an English knight.

But what might now be seen as callous disregard for human life was once more nothing of the kind. In contemporary terms, the lower social status of Henry's groom, not to mention his personal association with the king, rendered his action inexcusable. Nor is it insignificant that the execution of Henry's prisoners went wholly uncondemned by the French chroniclers who described it.[18] The fact that the Lord of Guitry decided to surrender in any case, only eight days after the executions, rendered his action both sinful and contumacious. And in warfare of this kind such naked brutality was merely the flip side of clean-cut justice and ice-cold logic.

The next obstacle on the journey to Paris was the formidable stronghold of Melun. The town's core was an island in the Seine, which had expanded to both the right and left banks since Gallo-Roman times, and all three sections now had their own imposing walls, linked together by a long bridge from bank to bank. The town's commander, moreover, was Arnaud Guillaume, Lord of Barbasan, who was widely praised, even by English chroniclers, as the 'most excellent of deeds of armes of all the knights in those daies that were knowne in Fraunce'.[19] Though faced with an enemy force of perhaps 20,000 and supported by as few as 700 men, Barbasan was nevertheless experienced and resourceful. He was also determined. When Henry had King Charles's herald demand the town's surrender, its commander responded by announcing that Charles could not be obeyed until he had been freed from English control.

Clearly, a siege that began with such defiance was unlikely to be quickly resolved, and even the presence of King James of Scotland, who was specially transported from England to prevail upon the Scottish contingent assisting the defenders, was of little value. In the event, mining and counter-mining led to epic scenes of underground fighting in which Henry and the Duke of Burgundy both participated. At one point, the King of England even clashed by torchlight with Barbasan himself until both men discovered the other's identity. Above ground, on the other hand, the largest-calibre English guns wrought their usual havoc. And though the besiegers were stricken by disease, and the Burgundian Count of Conversen deserted, hunger finally began to tell upon the defenders. After four months therefore, on 18 November 1420, the heroic defenders of Melun gave up the struggle.

As Thomas Walsingham commented, it was a 'glorious but costly victory' and the severity of the surrender terms reflected the bitterness of the struggle.[20] The lives of all those not implicated in the murder of John the Fearless, whether soldiers or civilians, were duly spared, but they were to be disarmed and held as prisoners until their ransoms were paid. Four hundred others were sent to various castles, mainly in Paris, and twenty Scottish mercenaries were swiftly hanged on grounds of disobedience to King James, their liege-lord. Barbasan, in his turn, was imprisoned at Château Gaillard where he would remain until 1430 when it was recaptured by the French. His life had been spared according to the laws of chivalry, which laid down that since he had fought against Henry in person in the tunnels of Melun, he could not be condemned by his 'brother-in-arms'.

One of Henry's favourite captains, however, was not so fortunate. Bertrand de Chaumont, who had fought on the English side at Agincourt and was a member of the king's household, was accused of succumbing to bribery and allowing some of those implicated in the Montereau murder to escape. And though the Duke of Burgundy and the king's own brother, Thomas, Duke of Clarence, appealed for mercy, they were met with intransigence. 'By St George, fair brother', Henry declared to Clarence, 'had it been yourself we should have done the same.'[21] Clearly, the firmness of a royal order was not any more negotiable now than it had ever been in Henry's eyes.

Yet any claim that Henry may have been descending by degrees into wanton brutality – perhaps as a result of constant pressure or gradual physical deterioration – remains largely unconvincing. If Jean Juvénal des Ursins is to be believed, the French prisoners taken at Melun were subject to abominable mistreatment. After they had been brought back to Paris, several, he tells us, were cast into deep ditches. 'And when they asked for food and screamed from hunger, people threw straw down to them and called them dogs. Which was a great disgrace to the King of England.'[22] There is, however, no evidence directly linking Henry to such barbarity, which was in any case blatantly detrimental to his broader interests. Doubtless, he would neither have denied nor regretted the claim of Jean de Waurin that he was 'much feared and dreaded by his princes, knights and captains, and by people of every degree, because all those who disobeyed his orders or infringed his edicts he would put to death without mercy'.[23] For Henry, however, human suffering seems to have remained a means to an end, and if the line between cruelty and justice sometimes became blurred in the white heat of war, it was rarely entirely lost.

In any event, the way to Paris was now open at last, and on 1 December 1420 Henry and Charles, accompanied by the Duke of Burgundy, entered the capital by the Grande Rue Saint-Denys, amid colourful decorations and carols of rejoicing. Free wine, running in conduits, was drunk with gusto, for Parisians, if not pro-English, were solidly pro-Burgundian in their sympathies. And though their optimism would soon be dashed, for the moment at least there was hope of better things to come. If, after all, an end to war was truly imminent, then France's other ills might soon be in retreat. And if the problems facing the new regent were indeed numerous, might not his own prodigious talents still prevail against the odds? By now, of course, Charles was fifty-two and could not be expected to live indefinitely. If so, what altogether brighter prospects might then unfold under his gifted successor?

Regent of France and ruler of Normandy

Henry V was the first and last of his kind – the only English king to be welcomed in Paris as victorious conqueror, Regent of France, de facto ruler of Normandy and heir to the French throne. But when Henry sat alongside Charles VI on 6 December at the Hôtel de Saint Pol to meet the States-General, the men before him represented only a fraction of the whole country. No Dauphinists were present, of course, which meant that most of France south of the Loire, with the exception of Gascony, was uninvolved. Indeed, there were still numerous centres of Dauphinist resistance in Picardy and even in the Île de France. Nor, for that matter, were any Normans on hand, since their duchy was at this stage entirely under English control and therefore excluded from proceedings.

The main business of the States-General was to ratify the Treaty of Troyes, and this was achieved without difficulty. But members were reminded, too, that good governance depended upon an efficient system of taxation and a revalued and standardised coinage. A uniform standard of weights and measures was quickly established, and the *gabelle* or salt tax reimposed, along with taxes on wines. There was also to be a sales tax on all merchandise except food. And in order to ensure that a new coinage could be introduced effectively, arrangements were made for a general levy on silver, assessed according to wealth and excepting the poorest sections of the populace.

It was in the area of currency reform, however, that Henry's very first action had already backfired. The failure of his predecessors to provide centralised control had resulted in a bewildering variety of coins over and beyond the official French currency, the *livre tournois*. The *livre bordelaise* and the *livre parisis*, for example, both circulated independently in the regions where they were favoured and both fluctuated significantly in value. To make matters worse, no uniform system of exchange existed, and as the supply of gold and silver continued to decline, the weight of coins had also been altered unevenly. As Henry well knew, the prospects for economic recovery – and, for that matter, political centralisation – were seriously limited while this situation obtained. But his decision to devalue the *parisis* in the capital had already caused food prices to more than double within a week of his arrival, and by Christmas prices had spiralled hopelessly out of control, forcing Parisians to eat pigswill and cabbage roots, as wolves swam the Seine to gnaw at unburied corpses.[24]

In much the same way that Parisians lamented their own condition, they were equally distressed, it seems, by the treatment of their king. For while Henry established his court in splendour at the Louvre, Charles languished shabbily at the Hôtel de Saint Pol, attended only by his old servants and persons of low degree. The palace itself was splendid enough, but the King of France was 'poorly and meanly' served by a threadbare staff, according to Monstrelet, which was 'disgusting for all true and loyal Frenchmen'.[25] Though his queen was left with no choice but to remain by his side, every noble of real significance was with Henry or paying court to either the Duke of Burgundy or the Dauphin. As the Flemish noble Georges Chastellain observed, there was little to encourage French pride. 'Every road', he wrote, 'led to sadness.'[26]

Resistance, however, remained an unappealing option. For if Henry's own position was far from totally secure, that of his Dauphinist opponents was significantly worse. On 23 December, a *lit de justice* held jointly by both kings had condemned the Dauphin in his absence and solemnly declared him incapable of succeeding his father as king because of his crimes. Others implicated in the murder of John the Fearless, including Tanneguy du Chastel and Guillaume le Bouteiller, were also formally sentenced. In fact, the trial made no pretence at offering evidence, but nevertheless laid down clear guidelines concerning the nature of punishment. Those captured in battle were to be put to death, while the rest were to suffer public humiliation.

The Dauphin himself remained a far from inspiring figure. Born in 1403, the future Charles VII had a fearful nature, which mirrored his puny physique, and as well as being a physical weakling, he was a moral one to boot. Bookish and solitary, a patron of the occult, he was by nature both ruthless and lethargic, and unlike his two deceased brothers, he had never been intended for a throne. Moreover, in spite of his undoubted shrewdness and the loyalty that his status generated among those around him, the Dauphin also laboured under grave disadvantages of a less personal kind. Not least of all, he possessed neither a standing army nor the money to pay for one, even though the revenue from the territories under his control – which remained undevastated, of course – was potentially very considerable. As often as not, his funds were either embezzled or improperly collected. And in the meantime, he faced the daunting task of surviving the sinister intrigues of his court at Bourges. If, therefore, the King of England faced his coming labours with any misgivings – and there is no evidence that he did – his main rival is bound have considered his own position with outright fear and near despair.

Such, indeed, was Henry's comparative confidence that by 27 December he had left Paris for Rouen in the company of his new wife. Four days later his journey was complete, and for the next three weeks he busied himself with the internal affairs of Normandy and the additional area extending outward from the duchy to within fifteen miles of Paris that now lay under his control. There was no denying that Henry's hereditary pretensions to the duchy had been wholly ignored at Troyes. But this was largely because the facts were clear enough and because Henry did not appear to require further affirmation of a principle that he plainly considered self-evident. He did not hesitate, therefore, to call together the three 'estates' of Normandy – nobles, clergy and bourgeois – upon his arrival at the duchy's capital. Nor did he dally in exercising his right by conquest to take decisive action regarding Normandy's administration.

Naturally enough, the devastation in the Norman capital remained all too apparent after the recent siege, as it would continue to be for years to come. Nor had other towns and the surrounding countryside escaped the impact of the siege, as general impoverishment, fear and demoralisation led to depopulation on a scale that further impeded the speed of any economic recovery. Emigration by the thousand had, for instance, put paid to Caen's already declining cloth trade, as many exiled weavers set up their looms in Brittany and competed with those who had stayed behind. In the meantime, a further 1,700 left Argentan, along with 1,500 from Sées and Exmes, and 2,500 from Alençon. Indeed, there were soon exiled Norman craftsmen all over France, while some of duchy's ironworkers even fled as far as Germany.

Fear rather than loyalty to the French crown was probably the main reason for the exodus, and Henry's offers of amnesty to all returning Norman refugees, combined with threats of reprisal, were beginning by 1420 to have the desired effect.[27] But as the disruption to commerce continued, the collection of revenues still had to be enforced with the help of troops. For around Rouen particularly, the roads were being rendered unsafe by brigands of mainly peasant origin. Indeed, the duchy as a whole would eventually become so troubled that between May 1421 and September 1422 a total of 386 brigands were either captured or hanged. Even nature itself seemed to be increasingly unforgiving as desperate weather conditions underlined the general misery and the number of *louvetiers*, or wolf-catchers, was increased. A matter-of-fact order to the effect that executed criminals should be cut down and buried rather than left hanging was actually inspired by the need to discourage hungry wolves from entering inhabited places.[28]

As if these problems were not serious enough in their own right, sections of the nobility remained sullenly unsupportive. Although most of the more prudent families with extensive lands arranged to have members on each of the opposing sides, as useful insurance against the fortunes of war, Henry continued to find it difficult to guarantee the allegiance of the people he needed most. And he was sufficiently worried to tell the Council of his concern 'that in substance there is no man of estate come into the king's obedience and … right few gentlemen, the which is a thing that causeth the people to be full unstable and is no wonder'.[29] Some, it seems, merely voted with their feet, and by the beginning of 1421 their absence was being deemed an act of rebellion. It was also providing a convenient pretext for expropriation of their lands, although by the end of the year a full pardon was being offered to men of all classes as long they took the oath of allegiance before Candlemas 1422 in the presence of the nearest *bailli* or garrison commander.

In general, the redistribution of confiscated lands was slow and carefully planned, and did not, as might be expected, take the form of a rush to share out the spoils of victory. On the contrary, Henry remained determined to safeguard the future health of the duchy by taking a measured and meticulous approach. Of 358 grants recorded between September 1417 and June 1422, almost exactly two-thirds were not made until 1419, the year of consolidation after the siege of Rouen. At the heart of the land settlement, too, was the notion that beneficiaries should provide the manpower for their own defence. Failure to perform the required military services could therefore result in confiscation, as James Linde and Walter Hasclat discovered when they failed to answer the summons to 'several campaigns, sieges and armies against our enemies'.[30]

Predictably, there was resistance to the overall land settlement and even Rouen itself was sometimes at risk. In July 1419 the Earl of Warwick was sent by Henry to investigate what is likely to have been a plot to hand the city over to the Dauphinists. Some French noblemen, meanwhile, were inclined to opt for more overt forms of action. The counts of Aumale and Harcourt, for instance, who had both been deprived of their lands and titles, now used their respective bases in Picardy and Anjou to lead private armies against the English. And the *bocage*, or hilly wooded country, would eventually become so dangerous that rent collectors like the Duke of Exeter's were too fearful to venture there. Such was Henry's concern about these and other activities, in fact, that he issued instructions for all castles that could not be garrisoned properly to be demolished, lest they become rallying points for 'brigands'.

If, then, the problem of imposing order upon France as a whole was potentially massive, even the somewhat smaller-scale challenges posed by the king's 'own' duchy were truly daunting. Yet most of Henry's early moves continued to be firmly founded upon common sense and gradualism, and once again demonstrated his willingness to apply political as well as military solutions to complex problems. They demonstrated, too, his tendency to think in terms of psychology as well as structures. Not least of all, Henry deliberately pandered to Norman separatism by reiterating that Normandy was his by right of inheritance. In a meeting with his English nobles in 1414, he had affirmed his claim to Normandy by 'true title of conquest and right heritage'.[31] And the author of the *Gesta* reiterated the point by writing of Normandy as a duchy 'which belongs to him entirely by a right dating from the time of William the first, the Conqueror'.[32] It was no coincidence, therefore, that when the Norman nobility were summoned before him in the spring of 1419, he was apparently robed as their duke rather than as the King of England.

And it was Henry's decision to apply this same approach more generally that demonstrates his continuing wish to mix firmness and resolution with subtlety. At all times, in fact, he made it abundantly clear to the broader population that he had no intention of ruling Normandy as an English colony. Though the 'planting' of English trading families shows that he planned bridgeheads on the coast which might one day have converted Harfleur, Honfleur, Caen and Cherbourg into towns resembling Calais, it was never his intention to expel the indigenous population as a whole. Aside from other considerations, Henry knew only too well that England did not have the population to support emigration to Normandy on such a scale. His real concern, if anything, was actually to prevent English settlers leaving once they had arrived rather than to initiate a flood of further immigration. It was this, for instance, that explains his order of 1421 instructing the captains of major Norman ports not to allow repatriation without special licence.

Most important of all, Henry wished to gain acceptance by the Normans as a visible demonstration of the legitimacy of his claims. From the very outset he had offered his protection to those who swore the oath of allegiance to him, confirming their right to keep the lands, homes and offices they had held on 1 August 1417, the date of the English invasion. And with just the same approach he had already adopted at Paris, he wisely avoided any disturbance to local laws and practices – preferring instead merely to superimpose his military rule upon existing native institutions. So while Englishmen such as William Alyngton and Hugh Luttrell were carefully installed in key positions, Norman officials were allowed to continue in office below them. The *baillis*, for example, who directed the seven main territories of civil administration, were all English by 1421, but their assistants – the thirty or so *vicomtes* who were responsible for collecting and paying out the regular revenues from royal lands and vassals – were, without exception, natives. The same was true of the receivers to whom parish officials paid the proceeds of a hearth tax granted by the estates general, and the *grenetiers* who were responsible for the salt tax.

Central government, on the other hand, was left in the hands of the 'Great Council' at Rouen under its president, the Chancellor of Normandy, who at this time was Bishop John Kemp of Rochester, while financial affairs were administered from Caen. There an English treasurer-general was answerable to the *chambre des comptes* whose head was the Norman knight, Louis Burgeys – one of the very few who had defected outright to the English side. Judicial affairs, in their turn, were supervised by a *cour du conseil*, which from very early on in the next reign would be challenging the sovereign claims of France's highest court, the *parlement* of Paris. And in almost all other respects, too, the machinery of Norman government was left very largely intact. Only one significant innovation was implemented when Henry revived the authority of the Norman seneschal, who had been the duchy's senior official during the time of Henry II's Angevin empire. Although he had no control of finance, his primary role now was to act as overseer of all officials, civil and military, and specifically to direct the activities of the *baillis* within their '*bailliages*'.

On the military side, moreover, there were certain grounds for concern. In particular, soldiers' complaints about their pay appear to have been numerous – with all this entailed for lawlessness and mistreatment of the local populace. 'I am here without wages', wrote Sir John Pelham from Caen in January 1418, while in summer of the same year a soldier at the siege of Cherbourg complained of the 'long time we have been here, and of the expenses that we have had at every siege we have come to, and have had no wages since that we came out of England, so that we have spent all that ever we had, wherefore I beseech you heartily to send me £20'. Nor does the problem seem to have been solved almost two years later. At the end of 1419, for instance, Sir Gilbert Halsale, Captain of Evreux, complained that he had received neither pay nor provisions since Michaelmas and warned that his men were going to desert – a warning that he repeated in 1420 before payment finally arrived that summer.[33]

To his credit, however, Henry made every effort to rectify the situation. With his usual energy, he personally issued instructions for the payment of each garrison – first from the Exchequer at home and later, in theory, from the Norman treasury. In December 1418, moreover, all those who had suffered as a result of soldiers' misdemeanours were allowed to seek justice from the courts of the local *vicomtes*. Likewise, in August a strict code of discipline was implemented for English soldiers, followed by a further ordinance forbidding unofficial tolls and requisitioning, which was drawn up during one of Henry's visits to his wife at Rouen in January 1421. Yet in April and December of the same year, further edicts and threats of fines, imprisonment and even hanging were still necessary. And in August 1422, Henry would commission the Captain of Pont-de-l'Arche to arrest 'certain vagabond English who wander from place to place robbing and inciting the soldiers to desert'.[34] It was not only common soldiers either who oppressed the local population. In 1420, for instance, the inhabitants of Mantes complained to the king about the extortions of the Earl of March.

Ultimately, therefore, neither administrative solutions nor vigorous punishment were any substitute for regular pay, and it was here that Henry's central Norman dilemma lay. Predictably, finance was the primary focus of his deliberations with the estates of Normandy in January 1421, and now there were signs of strain. Initially, of course, Henry had been keen to appease his new 'subjects', knowing full well that the battle for hearts and minds could only be won in the longer term by a lighter fiscal touch. But his reduction of the *gabelle* at Caen in 1419 was already proving a false dawn, as two tenths were now requested from the clergy, and a hearth tax was imposed upon Norman towns, which added an equivalent sum of 400,000 *livres tournois*. Furthermore, while Henry chose to condemn the unofficial exaction of tolls by his men, this did not prevent him from relying heavily upon unpopular levies of his own in the months ahead. The *patis*, *courses*, *sauvegardes*, *billets* and *congés*, which were raised in his name, all became important sources of revenue. Yet even the sums raised by these or any other means would never fully succeed in enabling him to achieve his two main fiscal aims: first to make Normandy largely self-financing, and second, to make it carry some share of the financial burden entailed by his military efforts.

So when Henry received an urgent summons to return to England during the Christmas festival of 1420, he was clearly leaving what was, at the very least, a work in progress. With mounting financial commitments, serious trade depression and the hostility of significant sections of the Norman nobility to contend with, a lesser ruler's resolve might well have wilted. It was, after all, always easy for a conqueror to promise peace and prosperity, but not so easy for these things to be delivered – especially when the conquered have to suffer not only an army of occupation but also continual raids and lawlessness from their new ruler's enemies. Yet far from buckling or even backing down, the victor of Agincourt, Caen, Rouen and countless other encounters was now set once more to meet his latest challenges head-on in a characteristic effort to turn adversity to advantage.

7   Unfinished war, 1421–22

Homecoming

When Henry V left the French capital in late December 1420 to return to England, he was still, it seems, without misgivings. He had appointed Thomas, Duke of Clarence, as Lieutenant of France in his absence and given the guardianship of King Charles to the Duke of Exeter. And for the time being at least, there seemed little imminent danger. On the contrary, the provincial parliament of Normandy's officials and nobles that convened that month seemed to confirm the King of England's growing authority. Not only did Arthur of Brittany pay homage for his Norman lands, but the Count of Armagnac, whose father had formerly headed the Dauphinist cause, also sent deputies to offer his submission. Depressed by heavy losses and with the former heir to the French throne reduced to outlaw status, there seemed little other choice.

Indeed, by the time that Henry set out for Calais on 19 January, he had firm grounds for believing that the problems he left behind him were not only manageable in the short term but soluble in the longer run. Order, justice and the prospect of peace were, of course, powerful incentives to conform, especially among the burghers and mercantile elites of many urban centres who were already sensing that the King of England was a man with whom they might do business. And at various points along his journey Henry was met with gifts and loyal greetings, while at Amiens, which had previously been a centre of stubborn hostility, he was now accorded an outright royal welcome.

Though chroniclers' accounts are briefer than before, there was no outward sign either that Henry was any less popular in England than upon his return five years earlier. This, after all, was by far the most widely acclaimed monarch in Europe, as well as the most firmly established upon his throne. So it was no real surprise, perhaps, that he was welcomed 'as if he had been an angel from God'.[1] Certainly, the royal entry into London was as magnificent as ever, as the full weight of Lancastrian pageantry and symbolism were brought to bear. Once more the king wore purple, the colour of Christ's passion, but the scene around him remained triumphal. And when the time of rejoicing was duly concluded by the coronation of the queen at Westminster on 24 February, the splendid banquet that followed maintained the familiar theme. For at the climax of the feasting, the king's pastry cooks produced their masterpiece – a breathtaking creation of a chained tiger led by St George.[2]

During the next two months, Henry and his wife travelled extensively throughout the kingdom. By this time he had been absent for some three-and-a-half years and was, it seems, no longer the smooth-faced figure with the pudding-basin crop, depicted in his most famous portrait. Instead, the crowned effigy of him on a stone screen at York Minister, begun about 1425, sports thickly curled hair and a forked beard, just like the figure represented on the obverse of his Great Seal around this time. Long campaigns abroad had clearly had their effect in more ways than one, but in spite of his preoccupation with the crown of France, Henry remained above all else King of England. And it was imperative, therefore, that he showed himself to his people, gauged their sentiments and made every effort to tap their purses for the struggles to come.

In a breakneck schedule that confirmed his undiminished energy, the king visited St Albans, Bristol and his beloved Kenilworth, along with the midland towns of Coventry, Leicester and Nottingham, as well as Shrewsbury, where he investigated reports of disturbances on the Welsh border. From there he turned north to Pontefract and York, paying a brief visit also to the shrine of St John of Beverley, to whom he attributed his victory at Agincourt. But the main purpose of his journey was never far beneath the surface. For wherever Henry went, his commissioners were invariably close behind, receiving loans from laymen and clergy alike. Nor were the activities of these commissioners confined to places visited in person by the king. Instead, they covered the whole country. According to Monstrelet, Henry everywhere 'explained with great elegance what great deeds he had performed through his prowess in France, and what yet remained to be done for the complete conquest of that kingdom'. He underlined, it seems, his need for men and money, and, the chronicler added, he received both in abundance.[3]

The Battle of Baugé

It was during Henry's swing to the north, just after he had left Beverley, that a messenger brought him news of his first major setback in France – the death of his brother, the Duke of Clarence, in the disastrous Battle of Baugé. Clarence had evidently been provoked by Dauphinist aggression northeast of Paris, and impulsively chose to thrust deep into the heart of his opponents' territory to the west and south, in the hope of winning a pitched battle that might rival his brother's success at Agincourt. He had not, however, accounted for the arrival of substantial Scottish support for the enemy under the earls of Buchan and Douglas, and he paid the price accordingly.

Though the details of the ensuing battle are unclear, the outcome was not. Wearing a splendid jewelled coronet around his helmet, Clarence was among the first to fall, and he was swiftly followed by Gilbert Umfraville, Lord Roos and John Grey, the 'Count of Tancarville'. The earls of Huntingdon and Somerset, meanwhile, were taken prisoner, along with Lord Fitzwalter and Sir Edmund Beaufort. And further disaster was only forestalled by the decisive action of the Earl of Salisbury, who brought up a contingent of archers to rescue what remained of the English force with considerable difficulty. If the Scottish scouts had performed more effectively, not a single Englishman is likely to have escaped, and the fact that Salisbury's men were ultimately able to regain Clarence's body to ship it back to England for burial in Canterbury Cathedral was scant consolation.

In fact, the Battle of Baugé was a rout in which the enemy had lost not a single man of note. 'Verily', observed Martin V upon hearing the news, 'the Scots are the antidote of the English', and under the circumstances, the Pope's claim seemed far from implausible.[4] Though the engagement had been fought by comparatively small forces, the myths of English invincibility and divine approval for the English cause had been struck a withering blow. Besides eliminating a clutch of Henry's best commanders, the French had also killed the current heir to the throne of England, who happened to be acting as leader of the English government in France at that very time.

Such, then, was the news that greeted Henry around 10 April. But with characteristic composure, he kept his own counsel until the following day, when his advisers readily agreed with his decision to return to France before the feast of St John the Baptist on 24 June. In fact, the move was neither forced nor impulsive, since Henry had already declared his intention to cross the Channel 'in the immediate future', even before learning of his brother's death.[5] Indeed, in a document issued from York on 7 April, he had instructed the earls of Northumberland and Westmorland to raise loans for his imminent campaign in France, and to pay over the money at the royal treasury before the beginning of May. With his response duly determined, it merely remained for Henry to resume his tour by way of Walsingham, where he took time to pray at the shrine of the Virgin, before arriving in London for the opening of Parliament.

The condition of England

The last Parliament that Henry ever attended was opened in the Painted Chamber of Westminster palace on 2 May 1421. It was not an extraordinary session occasioned by the defeat at Baugé, for the writs of summons had been issued as early as 27 February. Instead, its ostensible task was 'to remedy any wrongs and excesses that had been committed in the realm since the last passage of the king'.[6] And the session was duly completed without any visible sign of acrimony. There was, it is true, one ominous petition which suggested that, as a result of pestilence and war, there was now a shortage of suitable candidates for the offices of sheriff and escheator.[7] But Thomas Walsingham informs us that all business was 'successfully finished within a month'.[8] No special taxes were imposed for the forthcoming expedition, and the clergy in their turn readily granted a 'tenth', which was to be used to reimburse Henry Beaufort for the £14,000 he had already lent to the crown.

Likewise, the Treaty of Troyes was ratified without demur, even though it had already been the source of some concern at the previous session when the king had felt it necessary to guarantee that England would never be absorbed into France. At that time, firm assurances were given that the two realms were always to remain separate, each ruled according to its own laws and customs under the same ruler. And on this occasion, after Henry's Chancellor, Bishop Langley, had further explained the terms, Parliament readily 'agreed, approved, praised and authorised the peace'.[9] All, then, was apparently harmony, light and mutual satisfaction.

From many perspectives this was hardly surprising. For during the king's absence his regime had held up extremely well under the able guidance of the Duke of Bedford. Sir John Oldcastle was now dead, and even if characters like Sir John Mortimer were continuing to seethe behind the scenes, previous supporters of Richard II had all but given up the ghost. The Welsh, too, were locked in sullen acceptance of their fate, while north of the border, the Duke of Albany and Earl of Douglas had been crushed almost casually at the time of the 'Foul Raid'. For good measure, the French pirates who had once been such a menace were now subdued, along with their Castilian counterparts, who had been deprived of their French bases by Henry's occupation of Normandy and his alliances with Burgundy and Brittany.

Yet while there is no evidence in the official records that the king's wars were resented, there were, it seems, stirrings in some quarters. Adam Usk, for instance, wrote of 'our lord the king rending every man throughout the realm who had money, be he rich or poor' and of the 'grievous taxation of the people to this end being unbearable, accompanied with murmurs and with smothered curses among them from hatred of the burden'.[10] As early as 8 May 1417, moreover, Archbishop Chichele had urged both clergy and laity to greater participation in processions, litanies and prayers for victory, as such devotions were still being practised only 'tepidly', in spite of earlier exhortations.[11] And it should be remembered that even Parliament had not been entirely compliant. The session of 1419 had, of course, resulted in smaller sums than before, while in 1420, as we have seen, there were complaints about petitions having to be sent abroad, even though the king had been meticulous in responding, no matter how demanding the military objective consuming his time.

By now, in fact, the financial pressure upon Henry was considerable, since his subjects expected him to carry on a great foreign war without additional taxation, and the government's budget took no real account of the king's other extraordinary expenses. In a financial statement submitted to the king by his Council on 6 May 1421, the predicament was apparent. The anticipated revenue for the Exchequer year ending in Michaelmas 1421 was recorded at just over £55,743, out of which had to be paid the regular expenses of the central government, including provision for Ireland, the Scottish Marches and Calais. From the small remaining balance of just over £3,507, moreover, funds had to be found for the chamber, the household and the privy wardrobe, for public works, such as a new tower at Portsmouth, for officials, such as the clerk of the king's ships and the Constable of the Tower, and for a host of other items, including custody of the king's lions. No provision either had been made for sums owed by the wardrobe and household, not to mention the unpaid bills of Henry IV – which amounted to almost £40,000 – and 'the debts of the king while he was prince'.[12]

But was such a 'pitiless catalogue' of debts and commitments indicative of financial meltdown?[13] And was the perpetrator being steadily driven to desperation by an obsession with conquest on the basis of resources which existed only in his head? Certainly, the financial documents of Henry's reign, though incomplete and difficult to interpret, indicate the very narrow financial base from which he was operating. To his credit, however, he had the good sense to appreciate that any appeal to Parliament for money would only have damaged his cause at a time when the Treaty of Troyes required all possible support. And the loans that he raised instead had unquestionably produced a considerable yield. On 13 May, in fact, £34,131 was raised from both individuals and towns in a single day by a judicious mixture of threats and personal persuasion, while the lion's share, £17,666 in all, was donated by Bishop Beaufort as heavy recompense for his frustrated attempt in 1417 to accept a cardinal's hat without royal permission.

It was true, of course, that even sums like these were far from adequate, and by the time of Henry's death the Exchequer had accumulated a deficit of some £30,000 for the years 1416–22, as well as expenses left over from the Agincourt campaign and further debts of over £25,000. Yet the success of a late medieval ruler's fiscal policy was determined by a triangle of considerations. At the apex was the amount of money borrowed, the acceptance of which depended upon the purpose for which the sum was raised and the success or otherwise with which that purpose was achieved. Crucial, too, was the question of whether any gap between royal income and expenditure was likely to be temporary or long-term. From this perspective, Henry was so far delivering an unprecedented return on any outlay. He was doing so, moreover, at a pace and on a scale, which seemed to place a clear limit to the current burden. And comparatively few of the king's subjects were, in any case, currently being asked to empty their pockets, while those that were could hardly protest in light of the cause concerned.

Plainly, the king's financial problems were pressing, but he was nevertheless continuing to meet them with imagination and on the strength of a well-founded reputation for good credit. Among his first acts as ruler had been provision for repayment of all his father's household debts, along with his own debts as prince. And if the cost of war had temporarily overtaken him, there was still none of the rampant household expenditure or careless frittering of recent reigns. Set beside the debt mountain of £200,000 accumulated by Edward III in ten years of campaigning, or the £300,000 that was owed overseas in 1340, Henry V's demands were hardly profligate. At no stage either did his indebtedness produce a collapse in royal credit to prevent him from prosecuting his plans effectively. On the contrary, his personal reputation for economical government bore the strain of his spending, so that there was never any serious prospect of financial or political crisis. By the time of his death, therefore, he had stretched his realm's resources to the limit, but never to breaking point.

Religious and diplomatic initiatives

Preoccupied as he was, Henry still found time during his three-month stay in England to insist upon wholesale reform of the Benedictine Order. The so-called 'Black Monks' had included some stalwart supporters of Richard II, while those at Shrewsbury and Wenlock were also said to have connived at Sir John Oldcastle's escape. And at a special assembly of 400 monks held on 5 May, the king reminded his audience of his ancestors' generosity before presenting them with a document which pilloried their laxity in thirteen hard-hitting articles. Yet far from satisfying a grudge, Henry's intervention seems to have been prompted mainly by a shrewd acceptance that heresy could never be quashed by repression alone. If, moreover, religious reform could best be achieved by the assertion of the royal will in ecclesiastical affairs, then so much the better.

Diplomacy, too, was high on Henry's agenda during his brief stay in England. The Scots, whose king was still an English captive, were continually assisting their Dauphinist allies, and their intervention at Melun and Baugé had increased the need for urgency. Using his royal prisoner as a bargaining chip, therefore, Henry engineered a two-year truce by which the Earl of Douglas promised 200 Scottish knights and 200 mounted archers to serve on the English side in the forthcoming campaign across the Channel. In return, James would be restored to his kingdom within three months of Henry's return, on condition that he furnished hostages for his loyalty and agreed to marry Joan Beaufort, niece of the Bishop of Winchester.

Fittingly enough, this pragmatic solution to a particularly thorny problem followed another skilful piece of bargaining. In Rouen during March, a short time after Henry's departure for England, an agreement was finally reached concerning the Duke of Bourbon, one of the most important French prisoners taken at Agincourt. By accepting the Treaty of Troyes and promising to pay a ransom of 100,000 crowns the captive nobleman was to be released. In addition, he was to leave his younger son and ten other notables as hostages, along with six major castles as surety for his ransom. As it transpired, the duke was eventually unable to raise the necessary money and was finally forced to return to England, where he died a sick and broken man. But the significance of the episode should not be underestimated. For now at last a Frenchman of the highest rank, other than the Duke of Burgundy, had actually acknowledged the principle of Henry's ultimate right to the French throne. Furthermore, he had even been persuaded to agree that the treaty was 'good, reasonable and just'.[14]

Final return to France

By the time that Henry embarked once more for Calais on 10 June, he faced another typically daunting task. The Battle of Baugé had been only one of a series of setbacks, and by now the Dauphinists were making progress on numerous fronts, especially in the south-west, where only the Duke of Exeter's tiny force at Chartres blocked the way to Paris. It was true that the Duchy of Normandy represented a formidable block of territory that pierced almost to the capital, but in the broader scheme of things Henry was faced with growing hostility in Brittany, not to mention a series of enemy strongholds on his left flank, where the unreliable Burgundians were his mainstay. Beyond the Loire, meanwhile, stretched more than half of France, hostile and unbowed.

Yet Henry V's great strength continued to lie in his ability to maximise his own advantages, while carefully exploiting the deficiencies of his enemies. And once more he would also have that crucial ingredient – luck – on his side. For by the time he set sail from Dover there was already heartening news to balance the bad. During the three months that had elapsed since Baugé, the Dauphin had proved much less decisive than some of his lieutenants, and the Earl of Salisbury had considerably improved English morale by a series of raids through Maine and Anjou, penetrating as far as Angers and Alençon. Moreover, although a Dauphinist raid from Dreux at the start of the month had reached Bec in Normandy, it was so effectively quashed that Salisbury was able to inform Henry upon his landing that his duchy 'stood in good plight and never so well as now'.[15]

Nor, arguably, was Henry's strategic acumen ever demonstrated more effectively than at this time. Predictably, his plan for the new campaign was on a sweeping scale. Using his Norman garrisons as a platform, he planned to plough his way down to the Loire, well to the west of Paris, reducing every Dauphinist castle as he passed. Thereafter, he intended to proceed up the Loire before striking northeastwards again, reducing his enemies' strongholds on the borders of Champagne, and arriving ultimately to the east of Paris. In doing so, Henry's army would follow a wide arc, which would take in those towns threatening the capital and interfering with his control of the upper Loire. A great wedge would thereby be driven into Dauphinist spheres of influence, and the way prepared for a further broad advance in the south.

The army of 4,000 men that crossed with Henry from England was smaller than any he had hitherto mustered, but Salisbury's force in Normandy was sizeable and, as Salisbury himself professed, already well rested. Furthermore, Henry's decision to land in Calais, though sometimes criticised, made good sense under the circumstances. True, the main threat was from the Loire south-west of Paris, a long and dangerous march away. But Jacques d'Harcourt's raids in Picardy made it necessary, in Henry's words, to put the area 'in better governance'.[16] It should not be forgotten either that the Calais route took Henry close to the Duke of Burgundy's Flemish headquarters, thereby affording some opportunity to refurbish his relations with his ally after the damage done by his unwise and largely inexplicable decision to harbour the duke's cousin Jacqueline of Hainault, after she had deserted her husband John IV, Duke of Brabant.

Wasting no time, therefore, Henry marched out of Calais early in June 1421, having learned upon his arrival that a force of up to 20,000 Dauphinists was now besieging Chartres and threatening both Normandy and Paris. However, as Henry approached the beleaguered city after a brief stay in Paris, it was confirmed that the English army's reputation – and, above all, his own – was still by no means lost. For even before his arrival, the Dauphin chose to withdraw southwards into Touraine. The excuse was shortage of food, inclement weather, plague and the steady desertion of his men. But the truth was much simpler and altogether obvious to all concerned. In brief, he feared battle against a hitherto invincible opponent who was now further inflamed by the defeat at Baugé. And as the Dauphin's will to press his advantage rapidly drained, so the commanders of his numerous strongholds likewise lost the will to resist.

Dreux, for example, was a strongly fortified town, situated some fifty miles from Paris, which was the only major Dauphinist stronghold between Normandy and the western side of the capital. The Dauphin's retreat to the Loire, however, had made all hope of the garrison's relief futile. And though it offered largely token resistance from 18 July onwards, its soldiers had marched out freely on 12 August and given over possession to the English. By the time of Henry's return to Dreux on 20 August, moreover, a string of other castles threatening the security of Paris had also fallen. Crocy, Tillières, Nogent, Parman and Galardon were now all in English hands, enabling Henry to strike down the Loire towards the substantial army gathering on the river's north bank near Beaugency. Rather than await attack, he intended, 'as was his manner', to bring the Dauphin to battle, but as the *First English Life* tells us, 'against him came no man, nor no enemie aboade his comminge'.[17] Once more, then, the Dauphin had chosen to avoid his supplanter, and after a blockade of fifteen days, Beaugency submitted, though not before the Dauphin's retreating army had stripped the surrounding countryside of supplies.

As a result, the spread of famine and subsequent outbreak of what des Ursins termed 'a marvellous pestilence of stomach flux' was soon making itself felt in the English camp, leaving numerous soldiers lying dead along the roadsides as the army proceeded on its way.[18] Once again, however, there was still no question of lessening the pace, even though Henry's army may soon have numbered as few as 3,000 men. Indeed, in spite of hunger and disease, the English force forged its way onward in a north-easterly direction towards Joigny and Villeneueve-le-roi, which had been intercepting provisions sent from Dijon to Paris, while avoiding, for the moment, the great metropolis of Orléans. By now, in fact, soldiers and horses alike were breaking down in ever greater numbers, and many more men might have died, it seems, had Henry not ordered 'in his pity' that carts should be used for transporting them.[19]

Some relief, thankfully, was obtained from the audacious capture of the castle of Rougemont, which was well supplied with provisions. However, there was savagery as well as ferocity on display, for Rougemont had become the refuge for raiding Dauphinists. In return for the loss of one English soldier in its capture, Henry saw fit to burn the place, before hanging its garrison and drowning in the river Yonne every enemy fugitive he could recapture. Some sixty men in all met their death in one way or another. And though he had once again acted according to the letter of the contemporary military code, which laid down that the lives of any defenders of a stronghold taken by storm were deemed forfeit, the usual misgivings about his actions have persisted.

Whether Henry's brutality at Rougemont was suggestive of

failing health, chronic fatigue or even growing disillusionment remains once again a matter of speculation. Certainly, Thomas Walsingham suggested that the illness which finally killed him was of long standing, and there is no denying either that with the kind of sustained campaigning that Henry had been conducting, nervous exhaustion was always a possibility. But he had been responsible for similar actions before, and his reputation as a rigorous and at times cruel dispenser of justice was long established. More significantly, Henry's powers do not seem to have been failing in other areas. On the contrary, his preparations for this campaign had been as meticulous as ever, and his dynamism remained undiminished once it was underway. The usual stream of edicts and ordinances continued to be issued, while letters, including answers to petitions from England, still flowed with typical frequency. After Baugé, as we have seen, there had been neither hesitation nor misgivings, and he had already carried all before him on his current campaign, striking no less fear and awe into his enemies than he had always done. As such, the slaughter at Rougemont still seems more indicative of a king in a hurry than a man in the early stages of physical or mental decline. Besides which, his final military masterpiece was still to come.

The siege of Meaux

Following the capture of Nemours on 18 September and the surrender of Villeneuve-le-roi four days later, no great fortress threatened Paris from the north for around twenty-five miles until the large and well-fortified town of Meaux, which commanded the valley of the river Marne. Unlike Orléans, however, it was too near Paris to be left untaken, and by 6 October it was being invested. Just like Henry's second campaign, there would be no let-up for winter, even though his own army was both small and depleted. Nor would the strength of the town's defences, its ideal strategic location, or the formidable reputation of its commander and garrison be allowed to serve as any kind of deterrent.

Situated on a great bend of the Marne, which divided it into two sections – the old town and the market – Meaux was protected on three sides by the river and on the fourth by a canal. Its commander, meanwhile, was the brave and resourceful Guichard de Chissay, who had at his disposal not only a ferocious garrison, comprised it was said mainly of brigands, but also the so-called 'Bastard of Vaurus'. Little more than a brigand chief himself, Vaurus had systematically terrorised the surrounding countryside in the lead-up to the siege. Indeed, well before the English arrival, there was an elm-tree outside the town, which had come to be known as the 'Tree of Vaurus'. There the Bastard had hung his victims, eighty of whose corpses greeted Henry upon his arrival. According to the Bourgeois of Paris, even a pregnant girl had been tied there one night, after which she had given birth to her child before wolves arrived to consume both.[20]

But while the king made real efforts to alleviate the suffering, in the long and arduous siege that now ensued he could prevent neither the full horrors of war nor the disease that invariably accompanied them. Since the road from Paris was far from secure, Henry had food distributed amongst the soldiers at his own expense and turned his own household into a feeding station for as many as 1,000 people a day. He also took special pains for markets to be established, where the local inhabitants were at liberty to sell their produce in safety to the English soldiers – a marked contrast to their treatment at the hands of the Bastard of Vaurus. Yet even the redoubtable Sir John Cornwaille had to be sent home from the siege, swearing that he would never again fight Christians, after his seventeen-year-old son was decapitated by French cannon fire. And the king himself was a temporary casualty of an unknown malady before recovering after the despatch of a physician from England.

There were early signs as well that Henry's subjects were beginning to harbour misgivings of their own. According to des Ursins and the Monk of Saint-Denys, for instance, the English people had agreed to the conquest of Normandy, but never contemplated the subjection of the whole country.[21] If, after all, every fair-sized town in France was to resist like this, the task of subduing all France would be unimaginable. For the conflict was now more than ever a war to the limit – with all the beastliness that involved. In consequence, there were also numerous desertions to contend with, and by December Henry was actually contemplating the use of German mercenaries.

But if sheer will power was going to be decisive, the English still had grounds for faith in their leader. And as the attackers kept

Christmas and Epiphany entrenched before the walls of Meaux, their gloom was lightened when news arrived on 6 December that a son and heir had been born to the king at Windsor. When the birth was proclaimed in Paris on 22 December, the bells of the city pealed, as citizens staged processions of thanksgiving and lit great bonfires in celebration. Throughout England, too, according to Jean de Waurin, 'there was perfect joy displayed' – 'more', he added, 'than there had been for a long time about any other royal infant'.[22]

Already, then, there was an heir to the dual monarchy of England and France – confirming once more the belief that God's favour lay firmly with the English cause. But throughout spring, the defenders of Meaux continued to offer desperate resistance. By that time Henry was employing more cannon than ever before, and as extra guns of all shapes and sizes arrived each day from Paris, their effects became increasingly harrowing. At every stage, too, Henry was prepared to innovate, so that Jean le Fèvre observed how it was 'a pretty thing' to see the siege unfold.[23] Just before the end, the king was experimenting, for instance, with a high tower which was to be floated downstream and attached to the town's walls, providing the besiegers with a further point of attack. Thereafter, he bombarded the town's fortified mill-towers so that the Earl of Worcester's men-at-arms could charge over the improvised drawbridge and storm the towers. And though the earl himself was killed by a heavy stone dropped from the battlements, the assault itself was successful, ensuring that the garrison was left without flour.

Towards the end of April, therefore, the defenders offered to negotiate their surrender and by 2 May agreement had been reached. All stores and equipment in the market, as well a library of over a hundred books of canon law and theology, which were reserved for the king's personal use, were to be handed over to the victors, and the whole of the garrison was to be left at Henry's mercy. However, with twelve exceptions the defenders would all escape execution. Among the unlucky was the Bastard of Vaurus whose death was readily accepted by both English and French chroniclers alike. Dragged on a hurdle through what was left of the streets of Meaux, the Frenchman's right hand was severed before he was beheaded and hung from the tree that he himself had employed for his own victims. Brutally executed, too, was a trumpeter called Orace who paid the price, it seems, for someone's decision to deride Henry by displaying an ass on the town's ramparts, beating it till it brayed and then calling upon the English to come and rescue their king. And while Meaux was not sacked, some 800 other prisoners were sent 'like pigs' either to Paris or various other prisons in Normandy and England.[24]

Baugé, then, had been avenged and Henry's reputation restored, albeit at considerable material and human cost. Indeed, the siege of Meaux had absorbed valuable time and resources over seven long months, and it had also cost the lives of both the Earl of Worcester and Lord Clifford. But the town's capture did not merely help secure Paris, for numerous other strongholds that threatened communications between Paris and Burgundian Flanders also swiftly capitulated. Crépy-en-Valois and Offremont were only two of these trophies, and in each and every case Henry traversed the French countryside receiving the surrender of his prize in person.

There was no denying, of course, that the situation, even in northern France, was far from settled. Although it had been recovered after ten days, Meulan, for instance, had been briefly captured by the Dauphin's forces while the siege of Meaux was still in process. And in the region of Picardy, both Amiens and Abbeville were requesting Henry's help. Similarly, though Compiègne had surrendered to the Duke of Burgundy, he received news at Senlis soon afterwards that Cosne-sur-Loire – fifteen miles upstream from Orléans and on the direct route to Dijon, Burgundy's capital – was under threat. Yet the summer of 1422 was undeniably another high point for the King of England. Though his enemies were continuing to fight, the military initiative was anything but theirs. And if a mighty swathe of France remained unconquered, the portion he most desired was now most decidedly his.

Illness and death

With Meaux secure, the King of England and Regent of France felt free to return to Paris to rest from his labours and greet his wife, who had returned to the land of her birth with their infant son. On Saturday 30 May the couple feasted in great splendour at the palace of the Louvre and three days later, the glittering royal retinue crossed the Seine to the Hôtel de Nesle, where they witnessed a mystery play on the life of St George, performed by a group of Parisians who hoped to flatter the heir to the French throne by this portrayal of his favourite saint.[25] Meanwhile, the contrast between Henry's lavish treatment and the squalid surroundings of Charles VI at the Hôtel de Saint Pol remained as striking as ever.

As always, there was business to attend to. Henry was keenly aware, for instance, that the December Parliament, which had granted him a fifteenth, had nevertheless allowed the first half to be paid in lightweight old coins. At the same time, there had been the usual grumbling about the further drain of men and supplies to France. The brewers of London, for their part, were complaining to the Mayor about the high price of malt and bemoaning the fact that the absence abroad of so many men made it difficult for them to make a living.[26]

The pace of diplomatic activity also showed no sign of slackening. In early April, Henry was informed that the Holy Roman Emperor was too involved with the Hussite uprising in Bohemia to lend his support in France, and it now became increasingly urgent to maintain imperial interest in English plans. Certain Gascon nobles, on the other hand, were continuing to hedge their bets by suggesting modifications to the Treaty of Troyes, while the Duke of Brittany remained reluctant to swear the oath of acceptance. Last but not least, the valley of the Oise, north-east of Paris, was yet another area in need of attention, so that Burgundy's routes to the capital could be kept clear.

Clearly, the lull in Henry's campaign could never be more than brief, and by 11 June he was on the move once more – first to Senlis and thence to the newly surrendered fortress of Compiègne. But it was bad news from the south that swiftly altered his plans. Notified by Burgundian messengers that enemy forces were besieging the town of Cosne, he also discovered the full scale of the threat posed by the main Dauphinist army operating from Sancerre on the Loire some fifty miles away from Orléans. If Cosne were to fall, the Dauphin could stage a major thrust towards Dijon, the Burgundian capital, leaving Henry with no choice other than to assist his ally with all urgency. Not only would the king help, he would come in person.

By the time of his return to Senlis from Compiègne, however, it was already clear that Henry was gravely ill. According to the

Bourgeois of Paris, the excessively hot weather had led to an outbreak of smallpox, which had been prevalent within the English army, and it was this, in the chronicler's view, that had now stricken the king himself.[27] There was a rumour, too, of leprosy and further reports of erysipelas, or what contemporaries termed 'St Anthony's fire'. 'I have since been reliably informed', wrote Jean de Waurin, '... that it was an inflammation, which seized him in the fundament, which is called the disease of St Anthony.'[28] Thomas Basin, on the other hand, suggested that Henry had been laid low by 'St Fiacre's evil' – a raging dysentery complicated by various intestinal growths – 'because he had ordered, or had allowed, his troops to sack the oratory of St Fiacre and its glebe near Meaux'.[29] And though Basin's invocation of divine wrath may be somewhat colourful, the balance of probability does indeed suggest that dysentery of some kind was the cause of the king's rapid decline.

With remarkable fortitude, however, Henry insisted upon joining his army on the march to Corbeil – first on horseback and then, as weakness overcame him, in a horse-drawn litter. By 7 July the University of Paris was already offering prayers for his recovery. But it would take several more days for him to arrive at Corbeil – the farthest south he ever reached. There he remained for more than a fortnight before learning that his enemies had beaten a hasty retreat from Cosne. Deciding to return to Paris, he was then taken by barge to Charenton, where he made one final effort to mount his horse in a manner fitting for a king, only to collapse not far from his final destination at Vincennes. Thereafter, he was carried back to his barge and made his way down the Seine once more, arriving around 10 August.

The royal apartments at Vincennes were situated in the massive donjon tower erected by Philip VI, and there, on the second floor, above the great hall, Henry lingered for a further three weeks in the splendid regal chamber, with its decorated chimney and high vaulted ceiling rising from a central pillar. But far from succumbing to the agonies of his illness in his 'bed of pain', he seems to have planned – albeit belatedly – the future of the dual monarchy that awaited his successor, informing his advisers 'with marvellous prudence' of the just and right ways which they should follow and the political regimen they should observe after his death.[30] While Queen Catherine remained in Paris with her mother and father and did not feature in any of Henry's last words, the dukes of Bedford and Exeter, along with the Earl of Warwick and other councillors, remained close by throughout.

Bedford was to be Regent of France, Governor of Normandy and guardian of Henry VI, while Humphrey, Duke of Gloucester, was to remain subordinate to his elder brother as Regent of England. Henry Beaufort, in his turn, was to join Bedford, Exeter and Warwick as governor and tutor to the new king. In the interests of his infant son, the most important French leaders, such as Orléans, the Count of Eu and Gaucourt, were to be held in England until the boy achieved majority, but the other prisoners were to be given their freedom. Above all, however, Henry urged his Council to maintain the alliance with Burgundy. Although he must never give up Normandy whatever the cost, Bedford was told to offer the government of France to Duke Philip first, and only if he refused was the king's eldest surviving brother to take up the office of regent himself. Henry warned his brother, too, not to argue with Philip and especially to discourage Duke Humphrey from doing so. Sir Hugh de Lannoy, the Burgundian representative at Henry's deathbed, was to convey a special message to Burgundy, recommending the nine-month old heir as the one who 'most in the world could bring advancement or grief'.[31]

Until the very end, therefore, Henry remained acutely aware of how his achievements might eventually unravel, if all due skill and subtlety were not exercised by those who came after him. He admitted, too, on his deathbed that he had occasionally done wrong and sought forgiveness for his treatment of the heirs of Lord Scrope and in particular the injustice done to his stepmother, who was to be restored to her former freedoms and dignities. But at the very point of death, Henry reiterated that he had fought his wars purely to obtain his rights and promote the cause of peace. And he reaffirmed too, we are told, his unfulfilled wish to 're-edify' the walls of Jerusalem by crusade.[32] Nor were these hollow words, for only a year earlier an envoy had been despatched to explore the possibilities for war in the eastern Mediterranean. Finally, the king's will gave clear notice that all outstanding debts, both his own and his father's, should be duly paid, along with appropriate sums to his faithful servants.

Only at one point during those last hours did Henry display any hint of self-doubt when he let out a cry, as if, says the author of 'Pseudo-Elmham', he had been addressed by an evil spirit. 'Thou liest, thou liest', the king affirmed, 'My portion is with the Lord Jesus Christ!'[33] Not long afterwards, at between two and three in the morning of 31 August, the thirty-five-year-old monarch breathed his last, clutching a crucifix, so we are told, and uttering a final invocation to God: 'In thy hands, O Lord, thou hast redeemed my end' – while those around him, the *Brut* declared, 'would rather have felt that he fell asleep than died.'[34]

Two weeks later the king's wasted corpse began its final journey from Vincennes to Westminster. Most accounts suggest that his entrails were removed in advance, as standard practice demanded, and the flesh separated from the bones, so that his remains might withstand the long trip home. If so, the relevant organs appear to have been buried at the church of St-Maur-des-Fossées, not far from where he breathed his last. According to 'Pseudo-Elmham', however, which is particularly detailed on all aspects of Henry's death, his body was so ravaged by disease that there had been no need for dismemberment. Instead, it was merely embalmed, wrapped and encased in a leaden coffin.[35]

In the meantime, the Duke of Burgundy had arrived at Vincennes, and Bedford, in accordance with his brother's wishes, had duly offered him the regency of France. As Henry had almost certainly foreseen, however, such an offer could only be refused, for the duke's ambitions were bound to be best served by detaching himself from responsibility for the enforcement of the Treaty of Troyes. Just like Henry before him, the balance of power was the key to his ambition and this was best maintained by remaining a comparatively free agent. Significantly, too, Duke Philip played no further part in the dead king's obsequies – a potentially ominous sign, perhaps, and an indication that the affair of Jacqueline of Hainault had bitten deep.

Notwithstanding the duke's absence, however, the full force of Lancastrian display would now be brought to bear, in one last effort to fuel the mythic status of the deceased king. It took more than two months, in fact, before the magnificent funeral procession finally culminated at Westminster in a ceremony of interment that exceeded all precedent, at a time when the propaganda of public ritual was a major art in its own right. The first stop was Saint-

Denys – the traditional burial place of French kings – where Henry lay in state in the choir of the great church, and from there the procession made its way slowly through Rouen, Abbeville, Hesdin and Calais. At Rouen, the burghers of Henry's Norman capital greeted his body in ceremonial mourning, escorting it to the castle, where Queen Catherine eventually arrived to join the mourners. At every other important town, too, the local dignitaries carried a rich canopy to shelter the carriage, while day and night the attendant clergy sang masses, held vigils and attended to all the other religious observances over which the king himself had always been so meticulous.

Not all Frenchmen, of course, regarded the final departure of their conqueror so sentimentally. It was the view of the Bourgeois of Paris, for instance, that 'the people murmured very much' at the adulation accorded to this foreign prince, 'but had to endure it for the time being'.³⁶ And according to Monstrelet, an elderly Picard knight by the name of Sarrassin d'Arly could not believe that he had finally seen the last of his country's bane. Disabled by gout, he had been unable to witness events himself and proceeded to ask one of his household who had been present as the coffin passed through Abbeville whether the king was still wearing his boots. When told he was not, d'Arly's response captured the mood of many of his countrymen all too aptly, as he quipped that Henry might yet be returning for them at some later date.³⁷

In England, meanwhile, Henry's passing evoked altogether deeper and more widespread sympathy, though even here the authorities left nothing to chance. A revealing extract from the book of the brewers' guild gives clear instructions on how Londoners were to behave upon the funeral party's arrival in the capital. Every householder of every craft was to wear a black or russet gown with a black hood, and to be present at the burial. Each craft was also to pay for its share of the torches in the procession. And at the door of every house along the route from London Bridge, a servant was to hold a burning torch to light the coffin on its way.³⁸

Yet what ensued was no cynical outpouring of empty, state-sponsored grief. On the contrary, the meticulous organisation behind the spectacle at grass-roots level merely reflected the depth of grief at the king's passing. Though Monstrelet, writing some years after the event, would observe that 'greater pomp and expense were made than had been done for two hundred years', he conceded, too, that 'even now as much honour and reverence is daily paid to his tomb, as if it were certain he was a saint in Paradise'.[39] Plainly, Henry had vanquished his enemies. But he had also restored good governance at home. Where there had once been rebellion, lawlessness and impotence, now there was order, justice and a residing sense of glory restored. And in reviving both the Crown's credibility and the nation's pride, the king had also created a reputation that would, for good reason, endure long beyond his own lifetime – one which duly encapsulated his own era and, for both better and worse, profoundly affected those that came after.

Conclusion

If a man's final resting-place is any measure of his stature in life, then Henry V's chantry chapel at Westminster Abbey could not proclaim his memory more eloquently. Completed around 1441 in close accordance with the specifications laid down in his will, it dwarfs the shrine of Edward the Confessor and towers above the Plantagenet graves beneath, so that future congregations might witness, from far along the nave, the endless masses offered up for the king's immortal soul. It was surely no coincidence that Henry was the first English monarch to be laid to rest in his own separate chantry, and there was nothing accidental either about its ornamentation. For many centuries, the saddle, helm and shield which were part of his funeral 'achievements' were hung on high from a wooden beam clearly visible from the choir, while on the north side a sculpture still depicts the king galloping pell-mell into battle astride a mighty warhorse. Elsewhere, figures of St George and St Denis bear glorious testimony to the two kingdoms nominally united under his son. 'Henry V, hammer of the Gauls, lies here', we are told, and the point is neatly reinforced by a somewhat less prominent row of prisoners hanging from the battlements of a captured French castle. Nor is the rest of the inscription above the ledge on the tomb platform any less evocative of the man, his deeds and his aspirations. 'Virtue conquers all', we are reminded. 'Flee idleness.'

Even as Prince of Wales, Henry had bristled with purposeful energy, and by the time of his accession, there were already five years of active involvement in government and more than a decade of front-line military experience to his name. In consequence, he was better prepared for kingship than any previous monarch since Edward I. From early 1410 to November 1411, the prince and his associates had dominated the Council, and his experience in Wales not only taught him invaluable lessons about command, military finance and siege warfare, but also placed him in intimate contact with those men who were later to become the leading lights of his royal household and army. His record, it is true, was not unblemished. But he nevertheless ascended the throne of England a known quantity, with a strong reputation for the right intentions and the added benefit of a realm that had become weary of his father. If, moreover, Henry IV had been shadowed by rebellion at home, impotence abroad and the nagging burden of insolvency, he had at least survived, and, in doing so, he had also unconsciously created the preconditions for what amounted to a wholesale national resurgence under the controlled intensity of his heir.

The first two years of the new reign witnessed considerable strides towards the kind of good governance that the Parliament of May 1413 had craved at the very outset. Noble families previously opposed to the Lancastrian dynasty were swiftly and effectively reconciled. Royal creditworthiness was also restored by a potent combination of strict controls on expenditure and more effective exploitation of existing sources of revenue. In effect, the new king thereby created what amounted to a 'virtuous circle' of solvency, founded upon his own good housekeeping and Parliament's consequent willingness to grant taxation. Just as incisive was the concerted attack upon public disorder, as thousands of offenders – including many powerful Lancastrian supporters whose misdeeds Henry IV had conveniently chosen to ignore – were brought to heel before the Court of King's Bench. And when Lollards conspired in corners and the Southampton plotters made their feeble play, both were decisively crushed.

It cannot be denied that Henry V was lucky. By the end of the previous reign, some long-standing problems were already subsiding, and he was to inherit several of his father's most trusted retainers, such as Sir John Tiptoft and Sir Thomas Erpingham, who provided an important thread of continuity in government. More importantly still, he was backed not only by the talent and tenacious loyalty of his Beaufort uncles, but by a noble class that was both keen for war and largely pliant. The Holland, Mowbray, Montagu and Percy families who had opposed Henry's father were now led by young men of about his own age, untainted by personal involvement in rebellion and anxious to make good the disinheritance of their families in the previous reign. So with England recovering, France divided and prostrate, and a wealth of exceptional commanders, including his own brothers, at the king's disposal, the path to future glory was firmly laid. With the further backing of the Church guaranteed by his own unwavering orthodoxy, the opportunities were, in fact, unprecedented.

But if Henry V was fortunate enough to be in the right place at the right time, he was not, like us, the beneficiary of hindsight, and it is this which makes his vision, vigour, fortitude and unremitting self-confidence so distinctive and impressive. For he alone, perhaps, fully appreciated the possibilities before him, both at the outset of his reign and throughout what followed. To his credit, he had the wisdom to make the most of his advantages, as well as the initiative, where necessary, to turn misfortune into opportunity. He was also passionately, perhaps obsessively, protective of his 'rights', as even the Pope would find out when Bishop Beaufort was refused his cardinal's hat in 1417, on suspicion that he was to be used as a means of reasserting papal control in England. Yet Henry remained starkly logical, and it was logic, religious conviction and an implacable sense of justice rather than ego that drove him to conquest and underpinned his success. Ultimately, of course, he was only able to defer the full consequences of the intractable financial problems that dogged all Lancastrian kings. But even in this area, his efforts in relation to the scale of his conquests, not to mention the woeful failures of some of his predecessors, remain notable. Nor should it be forgotten that while Henry was hotly pursuing his programme of domestic 'good governance', he was also invariably immersed in extensive diplomatic negotiations and military preparations.

This, then, was no mere warrior-king. On the contrary, Henry's very success as a military commander has often obscured the broader elements of his kingship, and sometimes blinded us to the fact that domestic peace, skilful diplomacy and martial prowess were all, from his point of view, part of an integrated whole. Henry went to great lengths to make his wars a genuinely 'national' effort, and his military campaigns were closely co-ordinated with complex diplomatic initiatives, involving offers of compromise and alliance when occasion demanded. Neither was he a warmonger. In 1413, he inherited what amounted to, at best, a half-peace, so that to hesitate in a position of advantage was merely to invite the inevitable onslaught of one's enemies as soon as events turned to their favour. And when it is remembered that France was, in any case, not only 'rebelliously' resisting English claims under the Treaty of Brétigny, but also riven by faction and civil war and committed to the support of a schismatic Pope, the much wider thrust of Henry's approach falls into altogether sharper relief. For in his eyes this was a just and noble dispute conducted for the salvation of a stricken kingdom and the good of Christendom itself.

But if Henry never forgot that success in war is predicated upon politics, and saw war itself as a desperate last resort to ensure ultimate peace both between and within England and France, it is military command for which he is almost inevitably remembered – and not without some considerable justification. In 1415, after all, he was the mastermind behind all aspects of his campaign, taking full command at the siege of Harfleur as well as Agincourt, where he exhibited outstanding tactical skill, particularly in the choice of his army's position. Nor was this the only occasion or respect in which he led from the front. Logistics and military discipline remained under his direct control, and it was he who planned the invasion of Normandy from 1417 onwards and organised the most formidable sieges. In practical terms, it is no exaggeration to say that he transformed the objectives and methods of English warfare in France. No major French town had been taken by his predecessors since the capture of Calais in 1347. But the *chevauchée* now gave way to prolonged campaigns, uninterrupted by winter, which were designed to achieve co-ordinated long-term goals. Whereas Henry's predecessors thought tactically, he thought strategically. And when Normandy was finally his, the task of reconstruction received the same intensely personal attention that he had previously devoted to crushing his foes.

In the meantime, as Henry transformed the nature of warfare, so military success played upon his own nature, amplifying his self-confidence still further, reinforcing his sense of mission and compelling him to even more irresistible challenges. After Agincourt, the potential strategic blunder that might have placed his army in grave danger was utterly ignored, and, although he had hitherto fought only one other pitched engagement, he was established overnight as a superb commander in the field. He had conclusively demonstrated his ability to inspire common soldiers, he had excelled in hand-to-hand combat and he had confirmed beyond all shadow of doubt the deepest of all his convictions: God's approval of his cause. From then onwards, therefore, Henry became the centrepiece of an elaborate myth to which he himself fully subscribed. In brief, Agincourt not only altered men's perception of their king, it also changed him irrevocably.

Yet the object of this mounting glorification continued to perceive himself as instrument rather than agent, and retained a caution and humility that befitted his role as God's chosen warrior. As such, the notion that he was marred by some kind of personal craving for power or similar dark defect remains unconvincing. True, his demands hardened as his opponents continued to collapse from within – especially after the catastrophic assassination of John the Fearless at Montereau in September 1419. But there were clear indications beforehand of his preparedness to sacrifice his claim to the French throne in return for a suitable territorial settlement. And even after Montereau, he remained comparatively magnanimous. Not least of all, he spurned the very definite strategic option of attempting to topple Charles VI by force, and, more importantly still, displayed a striking willingness to preserve French rights in the subsequent Treaty of Troyes. In almost all its clauses, in fact, the treaty bears testament not so much to Henry's overweening ambition as to his genuine desire for justice and reconciliation. If, moreover, the treaty was unrealistic in terms of its expectations – and this is by no means certain – it was nevertheless founded upon a thoroughly pragmatic appreciation that lasting peace was far more likely to be achieved by compromise than coercion.

Not altogether surprisingly, however, it is common for books on Henry V to conclude with baleful accounts of what came after, accompanied in some cases by withering criticisms of the king's tunnel vision and the long-term damage that this caused. Already, in 1420 and 1421, he had experienced difficulties in England over the voting of parliamentary taxation for the war and was forced to increase his reliance on loans. 1421 also witnessed Henry's first defeat at Baugé and the gruelling siege of Meaux. There were growing reservations, in turn, about the prospect of a dual monarchy, which would be likely to prolong the king's absences abroad and might even lead ultimately to England becoming the junior partner in an uneasy relationship with her ancient enemy. Most important of all, the war was effectively transformed after Troyes into an internal French conflict between that country's king-elect and his rebellious subjects. Under such circumstances, how long would Parliament be willing to assist with funding?

But France, of course, was not without problems of its own. With the possible exception of Bernard of Armagnac, it had consistently lacked the leaders to cope with Henry and even the formidable count proved unable to control a government and an army without money. For though the French monarchy had benefited from a fiscal revolution in the 1360s, which had greatly enhanced its income over that of its English rival, much of this financial imbalance had been steadily eroded by conquest, defection and downright mismanagement. By early 1418 French men-at-arms were refusing to take to the field, because their king 'could no longer worthily reward military success', and later in the same year, while increasingly arbitrary demands were being made on submissive towns, such as Noyon, the coinage rights in Paris were sold to the Duke of Burgundy in a desperate effort to raise cash.[1] In reality, then, the French monarchy was by no means the effective organ of national power that its English counterpart had already become. Nor, for that matter, was French national consciousness far advanced. Ironically, it would take more than three decades of English occupation to alter this, and in 1429 it was the townsfolk of Paris who defended their city against Joan of Arc. So with Charles VI the effective puppet of his kingdom's conquerors from 1420 onwards, and the Dauphin's regime at Bourges stricken by discord and crippling financial needs of its own, few contemporaries were likely to have shared the opinion that French resurgence was only a matter of time.

Nevertheless by 1453 the only French territories remaining in English hands were Calais and the Channel Islands, and in the intervening period, while the Crown's debts soared, Lancastrian England lurched painfully to the brink of civil war. Perhaps the main cause of the financial problems after Henry's death was his decision to divide authority between the dukes of Bedford and Gloucester, which left the former, as Regent of France, without any official connection to the London treasury. As a result, the problem was not so much that England was too heavily exploited, but that it could not be exploited heavily enough. Yet to look at Henry V's legacy from the vantage point of the mid-century is at least partially misleading. On becoming regent in 1422, the Duke of Bedford inherited an experienced and confident army of some 12,000 English troops, which retained the loyalty of every one of France's *'bonnes villes'*. Equally importantly, Henry VI's government in both England and Normandy remained surprisingly solvent during the first six years of his minority. Plainly, the Lancastrian monarchy evoked no deep loyalty in France, but it remained, nevertheless, a not altogether unattractive alternative to the rigours of Dauphinist domination on the one hand and the anarchy of civil war on the other. Lacking real legitimacy, much would depend upon the quality of Lancastrian rule. But in this particular area Henry V had already proven himself eminently well equipped. And if his ideal of a dual monarchy eventually came to grief because it failed to engender a sense of common purpose between old enemies, this, too, was something that the king's own skill, charisma and tenacity of purpose might well have done much to encourage over time.

Ultimately, it would take the French twenty-seven years to recover what Henry had taken in barely more than a quarter of that time, and it should not be forgotten that the early years of his son's minority also continued to witness significant military victories. The initial dilemma for Henry's successors was how to press forward against the isolated hostile castles north and east of Paris and in Picardy without exposing the broader Norman frontier. But the spectacular triumph at Verneuil in 1424 confirmed the ability of the English to hold their own, and represented a victory of far greater strategic importance than Agincourt. In its wake, the Dauphin's army was profoundly weakened, and thereafter the English were able to stage a powerful surge into Maine and Anjou. By the end of 1425, indeed, the conquest had been pushed as far as the Loir, leaving little doubt that Henry had left the structures, the means and the personnel in place to maintain the initiative.

At this stage, the scale of the English occupation was without parallel in northern Europe since 1066, and if the final requirement was a decisive peace founded upon a definitive victory, then by 1429 such an outcome was tantalisingly close. Everything hinged, in fact, upon the siege of Orléans, for if France was not broken here, a war of attrition would follow which English manpower could not sustain in the long term. Initially, Bedford and the Earl of Salisbury had disagreed whether the siege should be attempted at all, and the latter's death from a cannon ball robbed the English of the one man – other than Henry V himself – who might have prosecuted the attack successfully. Yet by this time Normandy had been held for ten years, Paris for eight, and the victory that never came might well have proved the *coup de grâce* to the Dauphinist cause. The counter-factual possibilities are, to say to the least, intriguing.

In the six years that followed, moreover, there was still no really decisive French success, and the Franco-Burgundian alliance, which resulted from the Treaty of Arras in 1435, remained fragile. As events would demonstrate, Philip the Good was no breaker of kings and kingdoms in his own right, and only a year later the Duke of Gloucester was able to rout a besieging Burgundian force outside Calais. In effect, the war now became a direct and evenly matched struggle between England and France, which explains why it continued to grind on for so much longer. Indeed, rather more significant than the Treaty of Arras, was the death in September of the same year of the Duke of Bedford who had pursued the aims of his brother with such ability and tenacity.

So why, then, did Henry V's grand enterprise founder so emphatically in the long term? Ironically, perhaps, it is not so much his own premature demise as the death of Charles VI soon afterwards that may well hold the key. If Bedford's regency in Paris had enjoyed the umbrella of the French king's 'approval' for longer, while the Dauphin mouldered on the political fringes – outcast, inept and increasingly penurious – the task of consolidation was likely to have been prosecuted steadily and effectively. Much depended, too, upon the Dauphin's own continued survival, which, in light of his elder brothers' short lives, could not perhaps be taken for granted. Once again, the possibilities offer tantalising, yet barren, ground for speculation. Might Henry's successors, with better fortune, have realised his ambitions – assuming, that is, that those ambitions can ever be known? Who is to say? Where, for that matter, might the king's policies have led had he lived? Who can possibly decide? For even if dead rulers are to be judged on the likely consequences of their actions, it seems hard to apply this principle when the continued life of the individual concerned was so intrinsic to both the direction and success of his plans.

Suffice it to say that what Henry V achieved while living remains of immense significance for the kingdom he ruled, though his most significant legacy is rather less tangible than is often appreciated. There was undeniably something unique about the grandeur of his vision, not to mention the energy and skill with which he pursued it. As military commander, conqueror, guardian of religious unity, protector of law and order, administrator, diplomat and promoter of national consciousness, his contribution was truly exceptional. Yet in all but the last case, perhaps, there were limitations and imperfections. And while Henry's apparent obsessiveness was driven in part by the logic of events, there is no denying the strain that it imposed upon his realm. Ultimately, therefore, Henry should be remembered not only for what he did – or failed to do – but also for what he came to epitomise, since he left behind an ideal as well as a testing situation. And it is this ideal – of good and wise governance, heroism and nationhood – that rightly left his subjects and subsequent generations in no doubt about his stature.

Suggestions for further reading

C. T. Allmand's major biography, *Henry V* (London, 1997), gives full and extremely authoritative coverage of all aspects of the reign, while K. Dockray, *Warrior King: The Life of Henry V* (Tempus, 2005), provides a very valuable overview, with separate sections covering modern debates and perspectives, and historical evidence. For those interested in discovering more about late medieval historiography, there is also Antonia Gransden's *Historical Writing in England, Vol. II, c. 1307 to the Early Sixteenth Century* (Routledge and Kegan Paul, 1972). Malcolm Mercer's *Henry V: The Rebirth of Chivalry* (National Archives, 2004) provides a useful survey of the reign, as well as a sample of documentary material. But perhaps the best introduction of all is to be found in Chapters 14 and 15 of G. L. Harriss, *Shaping the Nation: England 1360–1461* (Oxford, 2005) and Chapter 15 of M. H. Keen, *England in the Later Middle Ages* (Routledge, 2003).

More specialised discussion occurs in G. L. Harriss (ed.), *Henry V: The Practice of Kingship* (Oxford, 1985), which deals with a range of issues, including finance, religion, the management of Parliament, diplomacy, the conduct of the war with France, and the king's relations with his magnates. In the same volume is an excellent essay on law and order by E. Powell, who has explored this subject at greater length in his monograph, *Kingship, Law and Society: Criminal Justice in the Reign of Henry V* (Oxford, 1989). Other works to be consulted by any serious student are T. B. Pugh, *Henry V and the Southampton Plot* (Southampton Record Series, 1988), and G. L. Harriss, *Cardinal Beaufort* (Oxford, 1988).

On the military side, Anne Curry has been associated with much important research in recent years, some of which is encapsulated in *Agincourt: A New History* (Tempus, 2005). She has also produced *The Battle of Agincourt: Sources and Interpretations* (Woodbridge, 2000), a comprehensive collection of original sources, supported by detailed commentary. Another work well worth consulting is M. K. Jones, *Agincourt 1415* (Pen and Sword Books, 2005), which provides a novel and convincing account of the battle. For more general perspectives on the contemporary military ethos, there is M. H. Keen, *The Laws of War in the Late Middle Ages* (Routledge and Kegan Paul, 1965), along with T. Meron, *Henry's Wars and Shakespeare's Laws: Perspectives on the Law of War in the Later Middle Ages* (Oxford, 1993). A number of other relevant themes are explored in A. Curry and M. Hughes (eds), *Arms, Armies and Fortifications in the Hundred Years War* (Woodbridge, 1994).

Henry V's management of French affairs is dealt with in C. T. Allmand, *Lancastrian Normandy, 1415–1450: The History of a Medieval Occupation* (Oxford, 1983), as well as R. A. Newhall, *The English Conquest of Normandy, 1416–1424: A Study in Fifteenth Century Warfare* (Yale, 1924), which in spite of its age retains considerable value. For a discussion of the more general French context assisting Henry's conquest of France, readers might begin by consulting R. C. Famiglietti, *Royal Intrigue: Crisis at the Court of Charles VI, 1392–1420* (New York, 1986), or R. Vaughan, *John the Fearless: The Growth of Burgundian Power* (London, 1966). B. Guenée, *Un meurtre, une société. L'assassinat du duc d'Orléans, 23 novembre, 1407* (Paris, 1992) is of considerable value, as is B. Schnerb, *Armagnacs et Bourguignons, la maudite guerre* (Paris, 1988). See also Anne Curry on the Treaty of Troyes in G. Richardson (ed.), *The Contending Kingdoms: France and England, 1420–1700* (Ashgate, 2008), pp. 23–42.

Two other authors merit particular attention, since both have been widely acclaimed and gone on to achieve considerable popularity with general readers. Ian Mortimer's innovative *1415: Henry V's Year of Glory* (Bodley Head, 2009) has provided a number of fresh and provocative perspectives on the king by intensively examining what is arguably the single most significant year in his rule, while Juliet Barker's *Agincourt: The King, Campaign, the Battle* (Little, Brown, 2005) provides a gripping account of the reign's most famous episode. The follow-up to this volume, entitled

Conquest: The English Kingdom of France, 1417–1450 (Little, Brown, 2009), focuses mainly on the next reign but also deals briefly with Henry's later military expeditions.

Some mention must be made finally of J. H. Wylie and W. T. Waugh, *The Reign of Henry V* (3 volumes, Cambridge University Press, 1914–29). Though the work tends to present its combination of observations and historical evidence in a frustratingly random manner, it represents nonetheless a testament to the authors' compendious knowledge and remains a mine of information for those prepared to tackle it.

Chronology

Date	Personal	Political	General
1386	16 September: Probable date of Henry's birth.		
1394	Death of mother, Mary de Bohun.		
1398	Father exiled to France.		
1399	John of Gaunt dies at Leicester.		
	Henry accompanies Richard II to Ireland.		
		Bolingbroke deposes Richard II and ascends the throne as Henry IV.	
	Becomes heir to the throne and is created Prince of Wales.		
1400	Campaigns with father in Scotland.	Murder of Richard II.	
	Beginning of Owain Glyn Dŵr's revolt.	Failure of the Epiphany Rising.	
1401			Scots routed by the Percies at the Battle of Homildon Hill.

Date	Personal	Political	General
1403	Appointed King's Lieutenant of Wales.	Hotspur defeated and killed.	
1405	Wounded at the Battle of Shrewsbury.	Failure of the 'Tripartite Indenture'.	
		Revolt of the Earl of Northumberland defeated.	
		Archbishop Scrope executed.	
1406	Henry reappointed Lieutenant of Wales and now assumes outright command.	Parliament reduces Henry IV's control.	
	Besieges Aberystwyth.		
	Becomes nominal head of the Council.		
1407			Louis of Orléans assassinated by Duke John the Fearless of Burgundy.
1408		Earl of Northumberland defeated and killed at the Battle of Bramham Moor.	
		Aberystwyth surrenders.	
		Collapse of Glyn Dŵr's rebellion.	
1409			Charles of Orléans, son of the murdered Duke Louis, marries the daughter of Bernard VII, Count of Armagnac.

Date	Personal	Political	General
1410	Prince of Wales becomes dominant force on the Council.		League of Gien formed by opponents of Burgundy. Opposition to the Duke of Burgundy crystallises into a powerful 'Armagnac' party.
1411	Presides at the trial of John Badby. Dismissed from Council after Henry IV's recovery.	Earl of Arundel's expedition in support of Burgundians.	
1412	Rumoured to be plotting to depose his father.	Duke of Clarence's expedition to France in support of Armagnacs.	Treaty of Bourges.
1413	20 March: Becomes king after death of Henry IV		
1414		Sir John Oldcastle's Lollard rebellion crushed.	Council of Constance commences.
1415		July: Southampton Plot defeated. August: invasion of France begins. September: Harfleur surrenders. October: French defeated at Agincourt.	Execution of Jan Hus. Election of Pope Martin V. Council of Constance concludes.
1416		Emperor Sigismund visits England. Franco-Genoese fleet defeated by English in the Seine.	
1417	August: Henry invades Normandy. September: Caen captured and sacked.		May: Queen Isabella banished by her Armagnac enemies. November: Isabella installed as 'regent' by John the Fearless in an alternative government based at Troyes.

Date	Personal	Political	General
1418		February: Falaise captured.	December: Sir John Oldcastle executed.
1419		July: siege of Rouen commences. January: Rouen surrenders. Conquest of Normandy completed. June: negotiations with Duke of Burgundy and French queen begin.	September: murder of John the Fearless at Montereau.
1420		December: Anglo-Burgundian alliance. May: Treaty of Troyes between Henry V, Charles VI and Philip of Burgundy. June: marriage to Catherine of Valois. December: arrival in Paris.	
1421		July to September: siege of Melun. March: Thomas, Duke of Clarence, defeated and killed at the Battle of Baugé. October: siege of Meaux begins. December: birth of Henry VI.	
1422.		May: Meaux surrenders. June: onset of illness. August: death at Vincennes.	

Notes

Introduction

1. *Gesta Henrici Quinti: The Deeds of Henry the Fifth*, trans. and ed. F. Taylor and J. S. Roskell (Oxford, 1975), 81, 67, 85, 87, 93.
2. Ibid., 181.
3. Ibid., 13
4. Ibid., 7.
5. Ibid., 17.
6. *Memorials of Henry V*, ed. C. A. Cole (Rolls Series (RS)), London, 80.
7. T. Rymer, *Foedera, conventiones et litterae et cujuscunque generis acta publica* (London, 1709), X, 661–2.
8. T. Livius de Frulovisiis, *Vita Henrici Quinti*, ed. T. Hearne (London, 1716), 2–3.
9. Ibid., 1–2.
10. *Vita et Gesta Henrici Quinti,* ed. T. Hearne (London, 1727).
11. *First English Life of king Henry V*, ed. C. L. Kingsford (Oxford 1911), 4.
12. Strecche, *The Chronicle of John Strecche for the reign of Henry V (1414–1422),* ed. F. Taylor (Manchester, 1932), 187.
13. John Capgrave, *Liber de Illustribus Henricis*, F. C. Hingeston (RS, 1858).
14. The two standard editions for many years have been *The St Albans Chronicle, 1406–1420*, ed. V. H. Galbraith (Oxford, 1937) and *Historia Anglicana*, ed. H. T. Riley (RS), London, 1864. The version usually referred to here, however, is *The Chronica Maiora of Thomas Walsingham,* trans. D. Preest (Woodbridge, 2005).
15. *Chronica Maiora*, op. cit., 445; *Ypodigma Neustriae a Thoma Walsingham*, ed. H. T. Riley (RS), London, 1876.
16. *The St Albans Chronicle*, op. cit., 97, 99, 113.
17. Adam of Usk, *The Chronicle of Adam of Usk, A.D. 1377–1421*, ed. S‑ E. M. Thompson (Llanerch, 1990).
18. Thomas Otterbourne, *Chronica Regum Angliae*, ed. T. Hearne (Oxfo *Memorials of Henry V*, ed. C. A. Cole (RS), London, 1858.

19. Bodleian Library, MS Arch, Selden B. 26; John Hardyng, *Chronicle*, ed. H. Ellis (London, 1812).

20. *The Brut or the Chronicles of England*, ed. F. W. D. Brie (Early English Text Society, Original Series 136), II, London, 1908.

21. Georges de Chastellain, *Chroniques, 1419–1422*, ed. Kervyn de Lettenhove (Brussels, 1863), I, 221–2; Robert Blondel, 'De Reductione Normanniae' in *Letters and Papers Illustrative of the Wars of the English in France*, ed. J. Stevenson (London, 1861–81), 179.

22. Alain Chartrier, *Le Quadrilogus Invectif*, ed. E. Droz (Paris, 1923), 4.

23. *Chronique du Religieux de Saint-Denys*, ed. F. Bellaguet (Paris, 1839–54), VI, 165.

24. Ibid., 481.

25. *Parisian Journal: A Parisian Journal 1405–99*, trans. from the anon. *Journal d'un bourgeois de Paris* by J. Shirley (Oxford, 1968), 126–7.

26. Enguerrand de Monstrelet, *Chroniques*, trans. T. Johnes (London 1853), 485.

27. Jean Juvénal des Ursins, *Histoire de Charles VI*, ed. Michand et Poujoulet in *Mémoires relative á l'histoire de France* (Paris, 1850).

28. H. Dénifle, *La desolation des églises, monasteries et hôpitaux en France pendant la Guerre de Cent Ans* (Paris, 1897–99), I, xvi.

29. P. S. Lewis, 'War-propaganda and historiography in fifteenth-century France and England', in *Trans. Roy. Hist. Soc. Ser.* 5 xv (1965), 10 n. 6.

30. F. Bérier, 'Remarques sur l'évolution des idées politiques de Nicolas de Clamangues' in *Pratiques de la culture ecrite en France au XVe siècle*, ed. M. Ornato and N. Pons (Louvain-la-Neuve, 1990), 45–79.

31. Chastellain, op. cit., I, 312.

32. C. L. Kingsford, *Henry V: The Typical Medieval Hero* (New York, 1901), 401.

33. Ibid., 10, 402; I. Mortimer, *1415: Henry V's Year of Glory* (Bodley Head, 2009), 2–5.

34. I. Mortimer, op. cit., 4–5.

35. K. B. McFarlane, *Lancastrian Kings and Lollard Knights* (OUP, 1972), 124–33.

36. M. H. Keen, *England in the Later Middle Ages*, 2nd edn (Routledge, 2003), 298–300.

37. G. L. Harris, *Shaping the Nation: England 1360–1461* (Clarendon Press, 2005), 589.

38. Ibid., 552.

39. Ibid., 587.

40. A. Curry, 'Henry V: a life and reign' in A. Curry (ed.), *Agincourt 1415* (Tempus, 2000), 9–20.

41. E. Powell, *Kingship, Law and Society: Criminal Justice in the Reign of Henry V* (Clarendon Press, Oxford, 1989), 270–5.

42. M. Lannoy, *The Hundred Years War*, trans. W. B. Wells (London, 1951), 235.

43. Ibid., 251.

44. F. Autrand, *Charles VI: La folie du roi* (Fayard, 1986), 506, 528.

45. Ibid., 526–7.

46. Ibid., 589.

47. P. Contamine, *La Guerre de Cent Ans* (PUF, 2002), 86–7.

48. R. Vaughan, *John the Fearless: The Growth of Burgundian Power* (London, 1973), 205, 214; D. C. Douglas in M. Lannoy, op. cit., xviii–xix.

49. D. Seward, *Henry V as Warlord* (London, 1987), 215.

50. E. F. Jacob, *The Fifteenth Century, 1399–1485* (OUP, 1963), 202.

51. T. B. Pugh, *Henry V and the Southampton Plot of 1415* (Alan Sutton, 1998), 145.

52. Ibid., 138–40.

53. Ibid., 143.

54. Ibid., 49.

55. P. Strohm, *England's Empty Throne: Usurpation and the Language of Legitimation, 1399–1422* (Yale University Press, 1998), 85.

56. Ibid., 91.

57. Ibid., 89; xiii.

58. C. T. Allmand, *Henry V* (London, 1997), 426–43.

59. Ibid.

60. Mortimer, op. cit., 543–50.

61. G. L. Harriss, 'Introduction: the exemplar of kingship', in G. L. Harriss (ed.), *Henry V: The Practice of Kingship* (OUP, 1985), 27–9.

62. 'O deus immense', lines 83–6, in *The Complete Works,* ed. G. C. Macaulay, 4 vols (Oxford, 1899–1902).

63. C. L. Kingsford, *Henry V: The Typical Medieval Hero* (New York, 1901).

1 The making of a Lancastrian prince

1. In the fifteenth century, one pound sterling (£1) was divided not only into twenty shillings (20s) and 240 pence (240d), but also into six parts: one sixth (3s 4d) was known as a crown, a third (6s 8d) as a noble and two-thirds (13s 4d) as a mark.

2. J. Nichols (ed.), *A Collection of All the Wills Now Known to be Extant of the Kings and Queens of England* ... (1780, repr. New York, 1969), p. 203.

3. *Chronicles of the Revolution, 1397–1400*, ed. C. Given-Wilson (Manchester, 1993), 177–8.

4. T. Walsingham, *Historia Anglicana,* ed. H. T. Riley (RS), II (London, 1864), 148.

5. *Historia Vitae et Regni Ricardi Secundi,* ed. G. B. Stow (Philadelphia, 1977), 81.

6. *Rotuli parliamentorum*, (London, 1767–77), III, 5.

7. T. Rymer, *Foedera, conventiones et litterae et cujuscunque generis acta publica* (London, 1709), IX. 291.

8. J. H. Wylie, *History of England under Henry the Fourth* (4 vols., London, 1884–98), III, pp. 326 and iv, app. A.

9. DL 28/1/5, fo. 32.

10. *Issues of the Exchequer from King Henry III to King Henry VI inclusive*, extracted and trans. Frederick Devon, Record Commission Publication, London 1837.

11. *Memorials of Henry V,* ed. C. A. Cole (RS), London, 1858, pp. 64–5.

12. DL 28/1/6 fo. 39.
13. Thomas Johnes (ed.), *Chronicles of England, France, Spain and the adjoining countries ... by Sir John Froissart* (2 vols, 1848), pp. 667–8.
14. *First English Life of King Henry V,* op. cit., 8.
15. *Memorials of Henry V,* op. cit., p.65.
16. Thomas Otterbourne, *Chronica Regum Angliae,* ed. T. Hearne, Oxford 1732, p.205.
17. *The Brut or the Chronicles of England,* op. cit., II. p. 545.

2 Military and political apprenticeship, 1399–1413

1. *Proceedings and Ordinances of the Privy Council,* ed. H. Nicholas (London, 1834–7), I, 107–8.
2. K. B. McFarlane, *Lancastrian Kings and Lollard Knights* (Oxford, 1972), 99.
3. M. D. Legge (ed.), *Anglo-Norman Letters* (Oxford, 1941), no. 331.
4. *Proceedings and Ordinances of the Privy Council,* op. cit., I, 277.
5. *Rotuli parliamentorum,* III, 573.
6. Creton, *French Metrical History of the Deposition of Richard II,* ed. and trans. J. Webb, in *Archaologia, XX,* London 1819, 204 and 394–5.
7. H. D. Ellis (ed.), *Original Letters,* 2nd series, I, 4–6 (London, 1824–46).
8. Usk, op. cit., 107.
9. Thomas Walsingham, *The Chronica Maiora of Thomas Walsingham,* trans. D. Preest (Woodbridge, 2005), 322.
10. Usk, op. cit., 107.
11. H. D. Ellis (ed.), *Original Letters,* op. cit., I, 10–13.
12. J. D. Griffiths Davies (ed.), *An English Chronicle of the Reigns of Richard II, Henry IV, Henry V and Henry VI,* Camden Society, Old Series 64, 9 (1856), 27.
13. Usk, op. cit., 123.
14. Legge, op. cit., 312–13.
15. Ibid., 290.
16. Ibid., 296.
17. *Proceedings and Ordinances of the Privy Council,* op. cit., II, 61–3.
18. Walsingham, op. cit., 328.
19. T. Livius de Frulovisiis, *Vita Henrici Quinti,* ed. T. Hearne (London, 1716), 3.
20. R. Theodore Beck, *The Cutting Edge: Early History of the Surgeons of London* (Lund Humphries, 1974), 75–6, 117.
21. H. D. Ellis (ed.), *Original Letters,* op. cit., I, 359–60.
22. *Welsh Records in Paris,* ed. T. Matthews (Carmarthen, 1910), 25–31.
23. Usk, op. cit., 243.
24. John Stowe, *Survey of London,* ed. C. L. Kingsford (Oxford, 1908), I, 236.
25. J. A. Giles (ed.), op. cit., 62–3; *First English Life of King Henry V,* op. cit., 11.
26. Monstrelet, op. cit., I, 43.
27. *First English Life of King Henry V,* op. cit., 13.
28. *Gesta Henrici Quinti: The Deeds of Henry the Fifth,* op. cit., 13.
29. Monstrelet, op. cit., 240.

3 Unity and honour, 1413–15

1. Walsingham, op. cit., p.389.
2. *First English Life of King Henry V*, op. cit., 17.
3. *Thomae de Elmham Vita et Gesta Henrici Quinti,* ed. T. Hearne (1727) (Pseudo-Elmham).
4. L. Mirot, 'Le proces de Maitre Jean de Fusoris, chanoine de Notre Dame de Paris (1415–1416)', *Memoires de la Société de l'histoire de Paris et de l'Ile de France,* 27 (1901), 175.
5. *Thomae de Elmham Vita et Gesta Henrici Quinti,* op. cit., 12–13.
6. *First English Life of King Henry V,* op. cit., 16–17.
7. *Gesta Henrici Quinti: The Deeds of Henry the Fifth,* op. cit., 3.
8. J. H. Wylie and W. T. Waugh, op. cit., I, 195.
9. R. Holinshed, *Chronicles* (1586), III, 583.
10. *Chronique du Religieux de Saint-Denys,* op. cit., V, 380.
11. *First English Life of King Henry V,* op. cit., 5. See I. Mortimer, *1415: Henry V's Year of Glory* (Bodley Head, 2009), 34–5.
12. J. H. Wylie and W. T. Waugh, op. cit., I, 191.
13. T. Rymer, op. cit., X, 317.
14. *First English Life of King Henry V,* op. cit., 17.
15. *Brut: The Brut or the Chronicles of England,* op. cit., II, 494-5; Walsingham, op. cit., 394.
16. *Chronique du Religieux de Saint-Denys,* op. cit., IV, 770.
17. D. Seward, *Henry V as Warlord* (London, 1987), 36–7.
18. *Chronique du Religieux de Saint-Denys,* op. cit., IV, 770.
19. Walsingham, op. cit., p.389.
20. D. Seward, op. cit., 41.
21. *Rotuli parliamentorum,* III, 623–4.
22. Ibid., IV, 3–165.
23. R. L. Storey, *Thomas Langley and the Bishopric of Durham, 1406–1437* (Church Historical Society, 1961), 111.
24. J. H. Wylie and W. T. Waugh, op. cit., 134–5.
25. *Rotuli parliamentorum,* IV, 15.
26. E. Powell in G. L. Harriss (ed.), op. cit., 66.
27. *Brut: The Brut or the Chronicles of England,* op. cit., II, 595–6.
28. Quoted in E. Powell, op. cit., 275.
29. N. P. Tanner (ed.), *Heresy Trials in the Diocese of Norwich, 1428–31* (Camden Fourth Series, 20, London, 1977), 142.
30. *A Confession of William Ayleward, Register of Bishop Chedworth of Lincoln,* Archive Office, REG 20, fol. 61 r.
31. *Calendar of Close Rolls, 1413–19,* Public Record Office Publications, 86.
32. *Gesta Henrici Quinti: The Deeds of Henry the Fifth,* op. cit., 3.
33. J. Loserth, 'Uber die Beziehungen zwischen englischen und bohmischen Wiclifiten', *Mitteilungen des Osterreichen Instituts fur Geschichtsforschung,* 12 (1891), 266–9.
34. Walsingham, op. cit., 390.

35. P. Strohm, *England's Empty Throne: Usurpation and the Language of Legitimation, 1399–1422* (Yale University Press, 1998), 63–86.

36. Ibid., 87.

37. Walsingham, op. cit., 405.

38. *Gesta Henrici Quinti: The Deeds of Henry the Fifth*, op. cit., 9.

39. *Rotuli parliamentorum*, IV, 15, 26.

40. Owen Ruffhead (ed.), *Statutes at Large, From Magna Carta to the End of the Last Parliament in Eight Volumes* (1763), I, 493.

41. J. Catto, 'Religious Change under Henry V' in G. L. Harris (ed.), op. cit., 106–7.

42. J. H. Wylie and W. T. Waugh, op. cit, I, 280–1.

43. Ibid., I, 477.

44. Ibid., I, 163.

45. Thomas Johnes (ed.), *Chronicles of England, France, Spain and the adjoining countries … by Sir John Froissart*, op. cit, 295.

46. Sir John Fortescue, quoted in A. L. Brown, *The Governance of Late Medieval England* (1989), 18; *Rotuli parliamentorum,* IV, 22.

47. *Rotuli parliamentorum,* IV, 4.

48. *Gesta Henrici Quinti: The Deeds of Henry the Fifth,* op. cit., 2–3.

49. T. Rymer, op. cit., IV, II, 77.

50. *Journal d'un bourgeois de Paris, 1405–99*, op. cit., 53.

51. *Rotuli parliamentorum*, IV, 34.

52. *Proceedings and Ordinances of the Privy Council*, op. cit., 150–1.

53. *Chronique du Religieux de Saint-Denys*, op. cit., V, 513–25.

54. *Gesta Henrici Quinti: The Deeds of Henry the Fifth*, op. cit., 17–19.

55. *Chronique du Religieux de Saint-Denys*, op. cit., V, 526–8.

4 God's chosen warrior, 1415

1. J. H. Wylie and W. T. Waugh, op. cit., I, 511.

2. T. Rymer, op. cit., IX, 288–9.

3. *Proceedings and Ordinances of the Privy Council*, op. cit., II, 148.

4. A. Morosini, *Chronique d'Antonio Morosini: Extraits relatives á l'histoire de France, 1414–28,* II, 20–3.

5. Monstrelet, op. cit., 329.

6. E403/621 m. 2.

7. E30/1695.

8. *Gesta Henrici Quinti: The Deeds of Henry the Fifth*, op. cit., 16–17.

9. *Rotuli parliamentorum*, IV, 62.

10. Mowbray, MS, fos 14–16, Microfiche MF 1480, Gloucestershire Record Office.

11. A. Curry, *Agincourt: A New History,* op. cit., 62–71.

12. J. H. Wylie and W. T. Waugh, op. cit., I, 483.

13. Christine de Pizan, *The Book of Deeds of Arms and of Chivalry,* ed. and trans. Charity Cannon Willard and Sumner Willard (Pennsylvania State University Press, 1999), 18.

14. T. Rymer, op.cit., IX, 289–92.
15. *First English Life of King Henry V*, op. cit., 14.
16. *Gesta Henrici Quinti: The Deeds of Henry the Fifth*, op. cit., 19.
17. Ibid.
18. T. B. Pugh, op. cit., 167–77.
19. Walsingham, op. cit., 403; *Gesta Henrici Quinti: The Deeds of Henry the Fifth,* op. cit., 19.
20. *Brut: The Brut or the Chronicles of England,* op. cit., II, 375–6.
21. *Gesta Henrici Quinti: The Deeds of Henry the Fifth*, op. cit., 19.
22. K. B. McFarlane, *The Nobility of Later Medieval England* (Oxford University Press, 1980), 246.
23. *Gesta Henrici Quinti: The Deeds of Henry the Fifth*, op. cit., 18–19.
24. P. Strohm, op. cit., xii.
25. I. Mortimer, *1415: Henry V's Year of Glory*, op. cit., 318–9.
26. See S. Relzneck, 'Constructive treason by words in the fifteenth century', *American History Review*, xxxii (1927–28), 544–52.
27. *Gesta Henrici Quinti: The Deeds of Henry the Fifth*, op. cit., 21.
28. Ibid., 23.
29. *First English Life of King Henry V,* op. cit., 36.
30. Ibid., 35.
31. *Gesta Henrici Quinti: The Deeds of Henry the Fifth,* op. cit., 35.
32. T. Rymer, op. cit., X, 107.
33. *Memorials of Henry V*, op. cit., 109; *First English Life of King Henry V*, op. cit., 38; *Thomae de Elmham Vita et Gesta Henrici Quinti,* op. cit., 46.
34. *Gesta Henrici Quinti: The Deeds of Henry the Fifth*, op. cit., 39.
35. John Capgrave, *The Chronicle of England*, ed. F. C. Hingeston (1858), 311.
36. See A. Curry, *Agincourt: A New History*, op. cit., 131; I. Mortimer, *1415: Henry V's Year of Glory*, op. cit., 380.
37. M. K. Jones, *Agincourt 1415* (Pen & Sword Books, 2005), 63.
38. Capgrave, *The Chronicle of England,* op. cit., 313.
39. *First English Life of King Henry V*, op. cit., 40.
40. N. H. Nicolas, *History of the Battle of Agincourt,* 3rd edn (London, 1833), Appendix, 24–8.
41. *Gesta Henrici Quinti: The Deeds of Henry the Fifth*, op. cit., 55.
42. *Brut: The Brut or the Chronicles of England*, op. cit., II, 337.
43. T. Rymer, op. cit., IX, 313.
44. *Memorials of Henry the Fifth*, op. cit., 114.
45. *Gesta Henrici Quinti: The Deeds of Henry the Fifth*, op. cit., 61.
46. *First English Life of King Henry V*, op. cit., 42.
47. J. H. Wylie and W. T. Waugh, op. cit., II, 76.
48. A. Curry, *Agincourt: A New History*, op. cit., 131.
49. *Chronique (1408–35) de Jean le Fèvre, seigneur de Saint-Rémy,* ed. F. Morand (Paris, 1876), I, 231; Jehan de Waurin, *Recueil des croniques et anchiennes istories de la Grant Bretaigne a present nomme Engleterre,* ed. W. Hardy and E. L. C. P. Hardy (RS), London 1864, op. cit., II, 158.
50. *Journal d'un bourgeois de Paris, 1405–99*, op. cit., 94.
51. *Gesta Henrici Quinti: The Deeds of Henry the Fifth*, op. cit., 75.

52. T. Livius de Frulovisiis, op. cit., 19-20.

53. *Gesta Henrici Quinti: The Deeds of Henry the Fifth*, op. cit., 77.

54. Ibid., 77.

55. *Chronique du Religieux de Saint-Denys*, op. cit., V, 554; Jean Juvénal des Ursins, op. cit., 518.

56. Flavius Vegetius Renatus, *On Roman Military Matters*, trans. Lt. J. Clarke (St Petersburg, 2008), 67, 73.

57. Monstrelet, op. cit., 339.

58. Walsingham, op. cit., 410.

59. H. D. Ellis (ed.), *Original Letters*, op. cit., I, 95.

60. Waurin, op. cit., II, 201.

61. *Chronique du Religieux de Saint-Denys*, op. cit., V, 548.

62. See A. Curry, *Agincourt: A New History*, op. cit., 178.

63. *Gesta Henrici Quinti: The Deeds of Henry the Fifth*, op. cit., 83.

64. See A. Curry, *Agincourt: A New History,* op. cit., 182–7, for full discussion.

65. Ibid., 187.

66. P. Contamine, *Guerre, état et société á la fin du Moyen Age: Études sur les armées des rois de France, 1337–1494* (Paris/The Hague, 1972), 223.

67. R. Vaughan, op. cit., 139.

68. I. Mortimer, *1415: Henry V's Year of Glory,* op. cit., 421–3.

69. *Gesta Henrici Quinti: The Deeds of Henry the Fifth*, op. cit., 77; *First English Life of King Henry V*, op. cit., 50.

70. *Gesta Henrici Quinti: The Deeds of Henry the Fifth,* op. cit., 81.

71. Waurin, op. cit., II, 208.

72. Pierre Cochon, *Chronique normande de Pierre Cochon*, ed. C de Robillard de Beaurepaire (Société de l'Histoire de Normandie, 1870), 273.

73. *Chronique du Religieux de Saint-Denys*, op. cit., V, 556.

74. *Brut: The Brut or the Chronicles of England*, op. cit., II, 378.

75. Walsingham, op. cit., 410.

76. Jean Juvénal des Ursins, op. cit., 519.

77. Monstrelet, op. cit., 340.

78. *Brut: The Brut or the Chronicles of England,* op. cit., II, 378.

79. *Gesta Henrici Quinti: The Deeds of Henry the Fifth*, op. cit., 89.

80. 'Chronique anonyme du régne de Charles VI', trans. from text printed in *La Chronique d'Enguerran de Monstrelet*, ed. L. Douet-D'Arcq (Société de l'Histoire de France, 6 vols., Paris, 1857–62), VI (1862), 228.

81. Hardyng, op. cit., 375.

82. *Gesta Henrici Quinti: The Deeds of Henry the Fifth,* op. cit., 89.

83. T. Livius de Frulovisiis, *Vita Henrici Quinti*, op. cit., 67.

84. *Gesta Henrici Quinti: The Deeds of Henry the Fifth*, op. cit., 89.

85. *First English Life of King Henry V*, op. cit., 60.

86. Ibid.

87. Waurin, op. cit., II, 216.

88. Hardyng, op. cit., 375; E. Halle, *The Union of the Two Noble and Illustre Families of Lancaster and Yorke* (London, 1809), 70.

89. Ghillebert de Lannoy, *Oeuvres*, ed. C. Potvin (Louvain, 1878), 49–50.

90. Waurin, op. cit., II, 216.
91. Monstrelet, op. cit., 89; *Brut: The Brut or the Chronicles of England*, op. cit., II, 596.
92. *Chronique du Religieux de Saint-Denys,* op. cit., V, 567; Cochon, *Chronique normande de Pierre Cochon*, op.cit., 276.
93. *Chronique (1408–35) de Jean le Fèvre, seigneur de Saint-Rémy*, op. cit., I, 260.

5 Consolidation and conquest, 1415–19

1. *Chronique (1408–35) de Jean le Fèvre, seigneur de Saint-Rémy*, op. cit., I, 261.
2. *First English Life of King Henry V*, op. cit., 64.
3. *Memorials of London Life in the xiiith, xivth and xvth centuries*, ed. H. T. Riley (London, 1868), 620–2.
4. *Rotuli parliamentorum,* op. cit., IV, 69.
5. Printed in Taylor and Roskell (eds), op. cit., APP. IV, 191.
6. Bodleian Library, MS Arch, Selden B. 26.
7. N. de Baye, *Journal*, ed. A. Tuetey (Paris, 1885–8), II, 224.
8. Strecche, op. cit., 13.
9. Walsingham, *Historia Anglicana*, op. cit., 344; 'Versus Rhythmici' in C. A. Cole, *Memorials of Henry V*, op. cit., 70.
10. T. Rymer, op. cit., IX, 558.
11. G. R. Owst, *Literature and Pulpit in Medieval England*, 2nd edn (Oxford, 1966), 72.
12. *Rotuli parliamentorum*, op. cit., IV, 70.
13. *Brut: The Brut or the Chronicles of England*, op. cit., II, 381.
14. Monstrelet, op. cit., 394.
15. *Journal d'un bourgeois de Paris, 1405–99*, op. cit., 107.
16. *Chronique du Religieux de Saint-Denys*, op. cit., V, 104.
17. J. H. Wylie and W. T. Waugh, op. cit., III, 61.
18. *First English Life of King Henry V*, op. cit., 89.
19. Walsingham, op. cit., 425.
20. Morosini, op. cit., II, 146–9.
21. M. H. Keen, *The Laws of War in the late Middle Ages* (London/Toronto, 1965), 119–23.
22. *Chronique du Religieux de Saint-Denys*, op. cit., VI, 134.
23. *First English Life of King Henry V*, op. cit., 92.
24. Jean Juvénal des Ursins, op. cit., 539.
25. *Chronique du Religieux de Saint-Denys*, op. cit., VI, 161.
26. *First English Life of King Henry V*, op. cit., 96.
27. Ibid., 102.
28. *Chronique du Religieux de Saint-Denys*, op. cit., VI, 165.
29. *First English Life of King Henry V*, op. cit., 131; Otterbourne, op. cit., 280.
30. R. W. Chambers and M. Daunt, *A Book of London English 1384–1425* (Oxford, 1931), 71–2.
31. *First English Life of King Henry V*, op. cit., 114.
32. John Page, 'The siege of Rouen', in *The Historical Collections of a Citizen of*

London in the Fifteenth Century, ed. J. Gairdner, Camden Society, New Series, 17 (London, 1876), 1–46.

33. Page, op. cit., 12; Monstrelet, op. cit., 404.
34. *First English Life of King Henry V*, op. cit., 135.
35. Page, op. cit., 15.
36. T. Rymer, op. cit., IV, 128, 131.
37. Page, op. cit., 19.
38. *First English Life of King Henry V*, op. cit., 134.
39. Page, op. cit., 22.
40. *First English Life of King Henry V*, op. cit., 135–6.
41. Page, op. cit., 22.
42. Monstrelet, op. cit., 411; Waurin, op. cit., II, 256, 264.
43. Page, op. cit., 44–5.
44. *Chronique (1408–35) de Jean le Fèvre, seigneur de Saint-Rémy*, op. cit., I, 348.
45. Monstrelet, op. cit., 415–16.
46. Ibid.
47. *First English Life of King Henry V*, op. cit., 145.
48. C. de Fauquembergue, *Journal, 1417–35*, ed. A. Tuetey (Société de l'Histoire de France, 1903–6), I, 306.
49. T. Rymer, op. cit., IX, 775 ff.
50. Ibid., IV, 125.
51. Monstrelet, op. cit., 419.
52. Walsingham, op. cit., 433.

6 The fragile peace of 1420–21

1. *Journal d'un bourgeois de Paris, 1405–99*, op. cit., 126–7.
2. T. Rymer, op. cit., IV, 128.
3. Waurin, op. cit., II, 286.
4. R. Vaughan. op. cit., 274–86.
5. *First English Life of King Henry V*, op. cit., 153.
6. *Rotuli Normanniae*, ed. T. D. Hardy (London, 1835), II, 332–71.
7. R. W. Chambers and M. Daunt, op. cit., 82–3.
8. *Brut: The Brut or the Chronicles of England*, op. cit., II, 422 and 424.
9. Monstrelet, op. cit., 483; Waurin, op. cit., II, 386 ff.; *Thomae de Elmham Vita et Gesta Henrici Quinti*, op. cit., 332 ff.
10. *Thomae de Elmham Vita et Gesta Henrici Quinti*, op. cit., 238; T. Rymer, op. cit., IX, 821 ff.
11. C. de Fauquembergue, *Journal, 1417–35*, op. cit., I, 361.
12. Georges de Chastellain, *Chroniques,1419–1422*, ed. Kervyn de Lettenhove (Brussels, 1863), I, 131–3.
13. T. Rymer, op. cit., IX, 895–904.
14. Monstrelet, op. cit., 439.
15. *Chronique du Religieux de Saint-Denys*, op. cit., VI, 163.
16. *Journal d'un bourgeois de Paris, 1405–99*, op. cit., 307.
17. Ibid., 151

18. Waurin, op. cit., II, 321–2; *Chronique (1408–35) de Jean le Fèvre, seigneur de Saint-Rémy*, op. cit., II, 11–12.
19. *First English Life of King Henry V*, op. cit., 167.
20. Walsingham, op. cit., 438.
21. Monstrelet, op. cit., 450; Waurin, op. cit., II, 343; *Chronique (1408–35) de Jean le Fèvre, seigneur de Saint-Rémy*, op. cit., II, 24.
22. Jean Juvenal des Ursins, op. cit., 561.
23. Waurin, op. cit., II, 429.
24. *Journal d'un bourgeois de Paris, 1405–99*, op. cit., 146, 156.
25. Monstrelet, op. cit., 452.
26. Chastellain, op. cit., 198-200.
27. R. A. Newhall, 'Henry V's policy of conciliation in Normandy, 1417–22', in *Anniversary Essays in Medieval History of Students of C. H. Hoskins*, ed. C. H. Taylor (Boston, 1929), 208–9. See also L. Puiseux, *L'Emigration Normande et la colonisation anglaise en Normandie au XVe Siécle* (Caen, 1866), 17–18, 38–40.
28. *Rotuli Normanniae*, op. cit., II, 356.
29. *Proceedings and Ordinances of the Privy Council*, op. cit., II, 351.
30. C. T. Allmand, *Lancastrian Normandy, 1415–1450: The History of a Medieval Occupation* (Oxford, 1983), 55, n.14.
31. *Brut: The Brut or the Chronicles of England*, op. cit., II, 374.
32. *Gesta Henrici Quinti: The Deeds of Henry the Fifth*, op. cit., 17.
33. R. A. Newhall, *The English Conquest of Normandy* (New Haven, 1924), 240–2.
34. Ibid., 236.

7 Unfinished war, 1421–22

1. Monstrelet, op. cit., 453.
2. *Brut: The Brut or the Chronicles of England*, op. cit., II, 447.
3. Monstrelet, op. cit., 453.
4. *Scotichronicron*, ed. T. Hearne (Oxford, 1722), IV, 216.
5. T. Rymer, op. cit., X, 96.
6. *Rotuli parliamentorum,* IV, 129.
7. Ibid., 148.
8. Walsingham, op. cit., 440.
9. Ibid., 135.
10. Usk, op. cit., 190.
11. *The Register of Henry Chichele, 1414–43*, ed. E. F. Jacob (Oxford, 1938–47), IV, 167–8.
12. *Proceedings and Ordinances of the Privy Council*, op. cit., II, 312–15.
13. E. F. Jacob, *The Fifteenth Century, 1399–1485* (Oxford, 1961), 195.
14. T. Rymer, op. cit., X, 127–8.
15. Ibid, X, 131.
16. J. Delpit, *Collection générale des documents français qui se trouvent en Angleterre*, (Paris, 1847), 231.
17. *First English Life of King Henry V*, op. cit., 174.
18. Jean Juvénal des Ursins, op. cit., 139.

19. *Thomae de Elmham Vita et Gesta Henrici Quinti,* op. cit., 314.
20. *Journal d'un bourgeois de Paris, 1405–99,* op. cit., 171 ff.
21. Jean Juvénal des Ursins, op. cit., 562; *Chronique du Religieux de Saint-Denys,* op. cit., VI, 448.
22. Waurin, op. cit., II, 361.
23. *Chronique (1408–35) de Jean le Fèvre, seigneur de Saint-Rémy,* op. cit., II, 45.
24. *Journal d'un bourgeois de Paris, 1405–99,* op. cit., 178.
25. C. de Fauquembergue, *Journal, 1417–35,* op. cit., II, 50–1.
26. R. W. Chambers and M. Daunt, op. cit., 144.
27. *Journal d'un bourgeois de Paris, 1405–99,* op. cit., 173.
28. Waurin, op. cit., 426.
29. Thomas Basin, *Histoire de Charles VII,* trans. C. Samaran (Paris, 1964–65), I, 79.
30. *Thomae de Elmham Vitae et Gesta Henrici Quinti,* op. cit., 331–3.
31. Chastellain, op. cit., I, 259.
32. *First English Life of King Henry V,* op. cit., 182.
33. *Thomae de Elmham Vitae et Gesta Henrici Quinti,* op. cit., 334.
34. R. W. Chambers and M. Daunt, op. cit., 144–6.
35. *Thomae de Elmham Vitae et Gesta Henrici Quinti,* op. cit., 336.
36. *Journal d'un bourgeois de Paris, 1405–99,* op. cit., 183.
37. Monstrelet, op. cit., 485.
38. R. W. Chambers and M. Daunt, op. cit., 144–46.
39. Monstrelet, op. cit., 484.

Conclusion

1. *Chronique du Religieux de Saint-Denys,* op. cit., VI, 148.

Index